Acclaim for *How D*

G000124703

Often textbooks are dry. They offer bits to chew on before they offer stude cise, remixed. *How Dare We! Write: a discourse* offers a much needed corrective to creative writing pedagogy. The collection asks us to consider the following questions:

- What does it mean for an indigenous, or Black, or Latinx, or Asian, or Middle Eastern, or LGBTQIA+ (or a combination of these identities) American to become a fiction writer?

- How does a poet who might be considered marginalized push themselves to the center of the page in spite of a racist, sexist, heterosexist, and classist culture?

- How does a memoirist begin to tell their story, to write from and about their experiences in an academic climate that is increasingly insular, and often reflects the narrow-minded vision of the culture-at-large?

- What does it mean to work through resistance from supposed mentors, to face rejection from publishers and classmates, to stand against traditions that silence you, to stand in your truth about your identity so that you can claim, fearlessly, your history, your trauma, your joy?

- How can writers and teachers even begin to make diversity matter in meaningful ways on the page, in the classroom, and on our bookshelves?

- How can we begin to value the sacred nature of creativity, particularly when spirituality drives the imagination of so many poets and writers of color?

How Dare We! Write: a multicultural creative writing discourse is an inspiring collection of intellectually rigorous lyric essays and innovative writing exercises; it opens up a path for inquiry, reflection, understanding, and creativity that is ultimately healing. The testimonies provide a hard won context for their innovative paired writing experiments that are, by their very nature, generative.

—Cherise A. Pollard, PhD, Professor of English,
West Chester University of Pennsylvania

So-called "creative writing" classes are highly politicized spaces, but no one says so; to acknowledge this obvious fact would be to up-end the aesthetics, cultural politics (ideology) and economics on which most educational institutions are founded. *How Dare We! Write*, a brilliant interventive anthology of essays, breaks this silence. This so-necessary book takes "finding your voice" to a whole new level, redeeming the privileged individualism of that cliché by documenting the powerful experiential writing of those writers of color who dare to acknowledge that, in the words of contributor Wesley Brown, "the most valuable stories are those which we would prefer not to hear." To paraphrase another contributor, here is marvelous, energetic proof of "writing [as] a form of social justice."

—Maria Damon, Pratt Institute of Art,
co-editor of *Poetry and Cultural Studies: A Reader*

How Dare We! Write is a collection of brave voices calling out to writers of color everywhere: no matter how lonely, you are not alone; you are one in a sea of change, swimming against the currents.

—Kao Kalia Yang, author of *The Latehomecomer: A Hmong Family Memoir*, and *The Song Poet*–Winner, 2017 Minnesota Book Award in Creative Nonfiction/Memoir

How Dare We! Write is a much needed collection of essays from writers of color that reminds us that our stories need to be told, from addressing academic gatekeepers, embracing our identities, the effects of the oppressor's tongue on our psyche and to the personal narratives that help us understand who we are. I found myself in many of the shared experiences in this anthology and I hope it fuels the reader to keep on writing, as it has fueled me to write more loudly and freely about the stories inside me.

—Rodrigo Sanchez-Chavarria, writer, spoken word poet/performer, contributor to *A Good Time for the Truth: Race in Minnesota*

This collection of essays about writing and navigating the literary world by writers of color—including Sherrie Fernandez Williams, Marline Gonzalez, Ching-In Chen, Sagirah Shahid, Wesley Brown, and Hei Kyong Kim—offers wisdom, insight, support, and advice on how to carve out a more expansive space for diverse voices. The essays are paired with inspiring and generative writing exercises, and the book is divided into sections focusing on themes such as literary gatekeeping, the tyranny of grammar, identities, personal narratives, rejection, and healing.   —*Poets & Writers*, Best Books for Writers list

Like most of America, the higher up you go in Academia the whiter it gets. With that comes the white privilege of criticism and writing, whether intentional or not. The vast majority of writing anthologies and handbooks are written by white authors, which reemphasizes certain styles, modes, and approaches. Editor Sherry Quan Lee's *How Dare We! Write: A Multicultural Creative Discourse* is a new creative writing anthology by writers of color. Through what are essentially literacy narrative essays, the writers share how they struggled to write in an environment where they "are to listen, be silent, and be awed by the 'right way' to tell a story as defined by those in the ruling class going back to Aristotle" (Stark 51). These writers are doing what writers in the past have done: teaching us how to read literature. They educate us, though this education is not on an artistic aesthetic, like Imagism or Vorticism, but for cultural aesthetics. As a white, hetero-normative, cis-male who tries to check his privilege, I was often surprised at certain privileges I had that I was not even aware of, such as how "italicizing non-English language contributes to otherizing our tongues" (Gómez R. 87), and more of which I'll point out below. This book is eye-opening, critical, and personal.

—Tom Holmes, *Redactions: Poetry & Poetics*

As intended by the editor of the book, this book will help writers of color and of the LGBTQI+ community feel less alone in the world where they constantly have to prove their existence to publishers, colleagues, and professors who see them through the White standards of excellence, creativity, and diversity. It may give writers who are struggling to tell their stories the motivation to write narratives which can represent them in a new light.

As a foreign-born woman of color who was raised in East Asia and has spent the entirety of adulthood in the United States, I have had difficulty finding stories to which I can relate. Before I opened the first page of this book, I hoped to read some stories with which I could resonate. To my surprise, the writers' stories hit close to home for me as a writer and an academician of color, as well as an Asian woman who has tried very hard to make her existence known to the world. I hope that my experience with this book is also helpful for readers and writers of color who are waiting to tell their stories...

—Wonbin Jung, *The Qualitative Report*

I very much appreciated each essayist's very personal (and well written) sharing of experiences in childhood and adulthood related to finding their writing voice. Each was a painful journey, with racism and no place for a voice of color to be accepted at the core of the struggle. A theme of hope runs through the book. Each essayist reveals how they made their way through the challenges, still struggle but have been successful in varying degrees. Defining success by their own experiences and accomplishments rather than by the critical judgment of the predominant "white" voice of academia. They provide, in my opinion, encouragement and guidance for others struggling with same or similar issues. This book deserves a spot in every MFA, English, or related writing program across the US and beyond. I highly recommend *How Dare We! Write* for writers of color, professors, editors, publishers, and writers not "of color." I am so glad this book found its way to my nightstand stack!

—Bonnie A. McKeegan, LCSW

HOW DARE WE! WRITE

A Multicultural Creative Writing Discourse

Edited by

SHERRY QUAN LEE

Second Edition

Modern History Press

Ann Arbor, Michigan

ISBN 978-1-61599-683-4
ISBN 978-1-61599-684-1
ISBN 978-1-61599-685-8

Published by
Modern History Press, an imprint of
Loving Healing Press Inc.   Tollfree 888-761-6268
5145 Pontiac Trail   Fax 734-663-6861
Ann Arbor, MI 48105   info@ModernHistoryPress.com

Library of Congress Cataloging-in-Publication Data

Names: Lee, Sherry Quan, 1948- editor.
Title: How dare we! write : a multicultural creative writing discourse / edited by Sherry Quan Lee.
Description: 2nd Edition. | Ann Arbor, Michigan : Modern History Press, 2022. | Includes bibliographical references and index. | Summary: "Collects the personal experiences of 30 writers and their struggles to fit in with the white, heteronormative academic culture in the USA . These writers display a variety of ethnicities, racial mixtures, native languages, and LGBTQIA+ orientations or gender identities"-- Provided by publisher.
Identifiers: LCCN 2022033236 (print) | LCCN 2022033237 (ebook) | ISBN
  9781615996834 (paperback) | ISBN 9781615996841 (hardcover) | ISBN
  9781615996858 (epub)
Classification: LCC PS508.M54 H69 2022 (print) | LCC PS508.M54 (ebook) |
  DDC 810.8/0920693--dc23
LC record available at https://lccn.loc.gov/2022033236
LC ebook record available at https://lccn.loc.gov/2022033237

Contents

Introduction

As a poet and memoirist and a creative writing teacher in academia and for community organizations, I have asked for years: Where are the textbooks by writers of color about the craft of writing? A text that would address the experiences and needs of writers of color whose work has been/is being silenced, ignored, and recklessly criticized; writers who have been vocally undermined, or on the other hand, patronized.

I arrived here, as editor of *How Dare We! Write,* at the end of a very long journey that began in the late 1970s. A journey in search of myself, and a journey to make myself, a woman of color, a mixed-race woman, a woman "of the mix," visible.

How did you get here? I ask my students. Not just, *I skipped dinner, got hung up in traffic, but how did you get to this classroom, this particular class, wanting to write, writing? What is your timeline for your journey to become a writer?*

When I began my journey as a creative writer, I noticed there were no books about me—a Chinese Black female who grew up passing for white in Minnesota. So, I began to write myself into existence.

Some said my stories weren't trendy; others said they didn't teach me how to write in that MFA program; and others just took pity. But along the way, mentors and friends, and even some family, gifted me with their encouragement and their support—they needed my stories, and they needed to tell their stories, which is why *How Dare We! Write* became a possibility, and now a reality.

My publisher said, *Write it.* Write the book you wish someone else had already written. But I didn't feel qualified. What did I know? Then in 2015-16 I was a mentor for the Loft Literary Center's Mentorship Program. The participating writers asked questions about my writing. I was challenged to come up with answers about my writing process, as well as how I had crafted individual poems. My first thought was, *I don't know, I just write.* But the more I strove to answer the questions, the more I realized that my writing was not without intention, but it was not all about craft, either. I realized that the textbook I sought and then envisioned needed story: the personal experience; the fear, risk, reason, and responsibility.

After carefully considering the questions from the mentorship participants and answering them, I sent my publisher, Victor Volkman, a text saying, *maybe I do know something.* He said, *It's about time you believed in yourself as a writer. Now, write the book.*

I drafted a few chapters, but the book was slow to progress. Then, something happened. I read two anthologies published by the Minnesota Historical Society: *Blues Vision*, edited by Alexs Pate with co-editors Pamela R. Fletcher and J. Otis Powell; and *A Good Time for the Truth*, edited by Sun Yung Shin. And I realized I wanted more than my story.

What about an anthology? I asked my publisher. Without hesitation, he responded, *Yes*.

I believe who we are influences our writing, just as who we are may defy those who think they have power over our writing. I knew in my heart that for writers of color, writing isn't just about process and craft, but also the challenges we face as writers, and how we overcome those challenges. I imagined a textbook that gives support and encouragement to those of us who understand that one size doesn't fit all, that MFA programs don't necessarily address our needs, nor do publishers necessarily accept stories that don't fit their agendas or economic needs. I wanted a textbook that considers the relevance of race, class, gender, age, and sexual identity; culture and language; and that by so doing, on some level, facilitates healing.

I didn't have to search far. The Twin Cities is saturated with writers, with writing classes, with MFA programs. Some of the authors presented in *How Dare We! Write* have relocated to Minnesota for their education, or their families migrated here, or they, like me were born here. Many of their stories unfolded in the Midwest, but also from beyond the Midwest. Each writer who is from outside the Midwest—from New York, New Mexico, Texas, Washington, Montana, Maine—has a connection to Minnesota as a visiting writer, a former resident, a playwright with work produced here, or a writer who just happened to know me or my publisher.

The authors included here are teachers, community leaders, activists, career writers; they are bilingual, multilingual; they are poets, playwrights, novelists, short story writers; they are established writers, they are emerging writers; they are millennials, gen x, baby boomers. What they have in common is that they have stories to tell that disrupt our most familiar white narratives about why they write, who can write, what they can write about, and how they craft their writing.

How Dare We! Write consists of 24 stories of interconnected genres, themes, challenges, and possibility. I have organized the book into five sections: Literary Gatekeepers (and other myths); The

Tyranny of Grammar; Identity(ies); Personal Narratives; Rejection Not an Option; and Healing the Heart.

Whether you identify with these writers' stories yourself and feel a little less alone, and learn how circumstances can be overcome, or you offer them as a teacher of creative writing to students who need them, this book is essential reading.

Sherry Quan Lee,
Editor

Preface to the 2nd Edition

In memory of William S. Yellow Robe (1960 – 2021)

Welcome to the 2nd edition of *How Dare We! Write: a creative writing multicultural discourse* (HDWW).

We continue to receive requests for desk copies and learn of university professors requiring HDWW as a text for composition and creative writing courses, so we have issued a second edition. Six essays, written by Carolyn Holbrook, Daralyse Lyons, Beatrice M. Hogg, Pacyinz Lyfoung, Aruni Kashyap, and Neil Aitken, have been added.

In the new and last section, "Creating Literary Spaces," writers share their experiences facilitating workshops with the homeless, with teen parents, and with writers of color who seldom see themselves in literature. Two writers examine cultural traditions and language that inform their writing and teaching. These stories reach beyond the personal, beyond the present, into unknown spaces that make a difference.

Acknowledgments

To David Mura, co-founder of the Asian American Renaissance (AAR) and Artistic Director, and Carolyn Holbrook, founder and director of SASE: the write place—thank you, thank you. David was *the* visiting writer of color during my MFA program—there were no resident professors of color at that time. He introduced me to the Twin Cities' vibrant community of Asian American artists. In 1998, David was the mentor for the Loft's Inroads Program for Asian/Pacific Islander Writers, of which I was a fortunate participant. Carolyn offered me my first teaching job after I earned an MFA in creative writing (I was the only student of color, and the only student not enlisted as a teaching assistant during my time in the program) and she invited me to participate in her Black Women Writers group. For a Chinese Black woman trying to make sense of her identity, both these writers and their respective organizations gave me a safe place to write and teach and meet other writers of color. Yet, writers of color such as David Mura and Carolyn Holbrook were the exception in Minnesota, home of 10,000 lakes—and many writers, but not much diversity. But thanks in large part to the work these two have done, not only are there many more *visible* writers of color in the Twin Cities, but their reach is nationwide.

I was fortunate to be accepted to Cave Canem in 1996, the year Toi Derricotte and Cornelius Eady established a writing retreat for Black poets, where I met writers from around the country, many of whom have since been highly recognized for their work. I will be forever grateful for the Cave Canem writers, the experience, and all that I learned that summer in a monastery on the Hudson River surrounded by poets.

Anya Achtenberg I met in the early 80s. She worked tirelessly to make the Loft Literary Center more inclusive, and its events and classes and opportunities more accessible. She is *the* writer I so vividly remember who worked amongst writers of color in the Twin Cities, and attended our readings. In 2007 Anya returned to the Twin Cities; she became my mentor and friend. She introduced her publisher, Victor Volkman, Modern History Press, to me and my work. The rest is history. Anya, I can't thank you enough for your kindness, and for your selfless commitment to writing, to teaching, and to social justice.

Victor Volkman, Ann Arbor, Michigan. We've never met, except over email and on Facebook. You have made visible the stories of three Minnesota writers—Chris, Anya, and me—because you believed in our stories and believed they fell under the auspices of Loving Healing Press' mission, even though Loving Healing Press didn't have a category for our stories. So you created one: Modern History Press. Thank you. Thank you for understanding the need for this collection and for giving voice and visibility to the writers and their stories in *How Dare We! Write*.

I tell my college students and the writers who participate in my independent workshops to get to know their writing community, meet other writers, attend readings, participate in readings, and participate in writing workshops and classes. The people you get to know, and not just writers, can move you forward on your journey in ways you may not even imagine. Also, I might add, give back, share the love.

If I were to create a writing timeline for how this book came to be, focused on the mentors, teachers, and encouragers who have in the past or continue in the present to support me as a writer, it would be filled with names such as those already mentioned, including the *How Dare We! Write* contributors; and, those, with much regret, I may have missed mentioning; and, the following people: Elsa Battica, Sun Yung Shin, Bao Phi, Eden Torres, Alexs Pate, Lupe Castillo, Vidhya Shanker, Mark Tang, Sandra Newbauer, Barbara Bergeron, Charissa Uemura, Rose Chu, Sandy Agustin, Nikki Giovanni, Nellie Wong, Linda Hogan, Alison McGhee, Ed Bok Lee; and Anne Holzman, copy editor—she came to us highly recommended and we are grateful for her expertise and generosity of time.

Synopses

What Would Edén Say? Reclaiming the Personal and Grounding Story in Chicana Feminist (Academic) Writing, Kandace Creel Falcón

As a Chicana academic navigating scholarly publication, Kandace Creel Falcón demands to push against the forces of the academy that seek to challenge or minimize Chicana, queer, and women of color feminist work. This essay details how Chicana feminists became her literary history, inspire her to add to their rich archive of work, and pave future pathways for new Latinx writers. As a Chicana feminist, writing for Falcón is: vulnerable, a call to action, and a community investment no matter where it happens.

Imposter Poet: Recovering from Graduate School, Jessica Lopez Lyman

This essay highlights the structural challenges which impeded the writing process. Internalized oppression heavily restricts Writers of Color from finding their voice. This essay addresses how the writer adapted and shifted to form a new relationship with the page.

A Case for Writing While Black, Sherrie Fernandez-Williams

There is an agony in being a black writer with slave ancestry and a long history of poverty and disenfranchisement on all sides of her family. There is a desire to give voice to those who were silenced, but Fernandez-Williams acknowledges how cut off she is from their stories and lives. Still, their hurt exists in her body and even if she wanted to shake them she cannot. It is her obligation to continue to search for them, make the connection, and search for the right words no matter how difficult it gets. For Fernandez-Williams, writing has nothing to do with gatekeepers. It has everything to do with telling the truth and resurrecting the dead.

mamatowisin: Writing as Spiritual Praxis, Nia Allery

The hidden curriculum in academe largely ignores the whole person. The author points out the dilemma for indigenous ways of being in institutions that limit learning and teaching to analyses and cognitive understandings. She didn't think she would survive or thrive within these strictures until she began teaching American Indian Spirituality and Philosophical Thought as a world religion. She found that creative writing allowed and encouraged students to describe their inward journey and spiritual praxis, known in the Cree language as mamatowisin. With this mindset teacher and students explored openly and vulnerably the expanse of mind, body, and spirit, united.

Complete This Sentence: Say it Loud!_____!, Brenda Bell Brown

Writer Brenda Bell Brown seized this opportunity to take you by the hand and walk you through the reason why she is so adamant about writing in a manner that is firmly rooted in her Black American cultural tradition. With a great big thankful nod to her teachers—both common and academic; all familial—Brenda writes from a standard of practice that does not apologize for being "too Black!," it celebrates it!

Crazy, Chris Stark

Chris Stark's memoir essay addresses how viewing as "crazy" the ideas, experiences, and foundations of writing outside of the whitemalenorm limits, silences, and marginalizes many writers of color. Stark discusses how her first novel, *Nickels: A Tale of Dissociation*, breaks down sentence structure, punctuation, language, and style to authentically convey the intersectionality of the protagonist's multiple marginalized identities.

Saying My Name with Happiness, Ching-In Chen

This is a personal essay about familial influences on writing. The essay also discusses exclusion due to racism and the power of naming and shaping your own story.

Dancing Between Bamboos or The Rules of Wrong Grammar, Marlina Gonzalez

Written from the perspective of a writer who is multilingual by historical default, this personal essay looks at how colonized cultures like that of the Philippines learn to concoct a cultural *halu-halo* (literal translation: "mix-mix"), making up words out of three (or four or five) lingual ingredients to create a vocabulary that reflects the "bifurcated tongue" and the diverging social, cultural and political impact of colonialism on writing and thought.

Intersectional Bribes and the Cost of Poetry, Sagirah Shahid

In this essay Sagirah Shahid explores her own journey as an African American Muslim woman and unpacks how her identities have sharpened the criticalness of her poetic eye.

It Happened in Fragments, Isela Xitlali Gómez R.

This piece is about how the author came to understand her writing process—in scattered particles that began to come together as she stopped forcing them. She often writes in fragmented form because that's how her memory works: unfluid, fleeting, at times not her own.

Creating Native American Mirrors: and Making a Living as a Writer, Marcie Rendon

Part how-to, part story, Rendon's essay is about how she strives to create and write the stories her people can relate to. This can serve as a guide to other writers seeking publication, audience, or ways to tell their own realities. According to Rendon, "we need to strive not just to find our own voice but the voice in us that will resonate with others like us." She writes to burst through invisibility as a Native Woman, and believes the acquired practicalness of the job of writing is how others will have access to our work.

Notes in Journey from a Writer of the Mix, Anya Achtenberg

Briefly exploring the identity issues of people of color who fall outside recognizable categories of race, and are here referred to as people of the mix, Achtenberg discusses the implications of this identity on creative writing. Interrogating creative writing truisms through this lens of identity, she focuses centrally on the instruction to "write from a sense of place."

The Thenar Space: Writing Beyond Emotion and Experience into Story, Taiyon J Coleman

A first person essay and writing exercise that considers the creative juxtaposition of past memory, present knowledge, and details from experience that work to reveal narratives that have both text and subtext. It is writing that reveals story and epiphanies for both the writer and the reader.

How Maya Angelou Empowered Me to Write, Saymoukda Duangphouxay Vongsay

Saymoukda Duangphouxay Vongsay is constantly fighting for her place within the literary ecosystem to write and most importantly, for stories from *her kind* to be uplifted. Sometimes the fight takes place inside of her head as excuses. Before she learned how to mute doubting voices, she had to defeat the idea that her story didn't matter.

Legendary Documents, Tou SaiKo Lee

Tou SaiKo Lee explores what if? What if he had access to today's social media in the 90s? Would a "basketball hoop" become a different story? His coming of age experiences influenced who he is today, a storyteller, a poet, and a hip-hop artist giving back to the Hmong community, providing resources and motivation to youth.

Stories that Must Be Told, Luis Lopez

Being brown in an all-white writing workshop. Knowing what limitations can be expected of other students as well as from the workshop lead. The importance that sincerity plays in these moments and how to account for it when no one has a similar lived experience.

Telling Stories That Should Not Be Passed On, Wesley Brown

Wesley Brown's father was the repository of his family history. And the unsettling stories he told him as a child shaped his view of the world that is often a dangerous and unpredictable place. This essay examines how, as a writer, Brown came to see that the most valuable stories are those which we would prefer not to hear.

Fear of an Apocalypse: Racial Marginalization on the Art of Writing, Hei Kyong Kim

This is a lyrical essay about what writing has meant to Hei Kyong Kim and why she writes, how her marginalized identity has been a barrier to her writing, and how the act of writing has been a form of social justice for her. Kim shares her ups and downs on being a writer of color in a challenging society and how she has worked to overcome them.

Picking a Goot' Indin (A play selection from No Res Rezpect), William S. Yellow Robe

Through an imaginary but believable situation, playwright William S. Yellow Robe renders a scene where a committee chooses which play will represent American Indians because of, or in order to get, grant money. Does it matter if the playwright is Indin?

Perfectly Untraditional, Sweta Srivastava Vikram

This is an essay about a writer's experience—someone who grew up noticing gender inequality, stereotypes, and patriarchy in different continents—and her resolve to tell the stories truest to her.

Our Silence Won't Save Us: Recovering the Medicine in Our Stories, Anaïs Deal-Márquez

The writer considers how women's stories of migration and survival in her family have defined the places she creates from. This piece looks at how mujeres have found strength in each other, their recipes, their laughter, and explores what it means to tell our stories without apology in a world that wants to silence us.

Writing: Healing from the Things I Cannot Change, Lori Young-Williams

Born to a mixed-race, black/white family, Lori grew up in the white suburb of St. Paul, MN. The death of her sister brought her to writing and it is through writing that she is able to heal from the challenges of not only being the daughter who lived, but also being the only black girl in her school and neighborhood. She learns through college, research, and family stories from her father that she comes from strength. Through writing she is able to write through frustration and hurts—and heal.

Stories from the Heart of Dark-Eyed Woman—Sikadiyaki, Olive Lefferson

Olive Lefferson grew up with an oral tradition, hearing the stories of her ancestors, feeling pride in her culture but also confusion about her identity as a Native in a white world. Criticism silenced her. Providing a space for other Natives to share their stories has helped her find her identity as a writer and as a Native woman in a white world.

A Fundamental Human Yearning, Michael Kleber-Diggs

As a son of two parents with advanced degrees and as a black boy coming of age in the 70s and 80s, Michael Kleber-Diggs was raised to see himself among the best and the brightest. In "A Fundamental Human Yearning," he reflects on how he migrated away from messages steering him toward life in the business world to embrace his true identity as a writer.

Writing Through Homelessness, Beatrice M. Hogg

Everyone has a story that deserves to be told. Women experiencing homelessness are often stereotyped and marginalized. In her writing workshop, Beatrice M. Hogg provided women with a safe place to write their stories and share their dreams. The lessons she learned from her students gave her the courage to document her own story of homelessness.

Teaching Creative Writing in an Alternative Setting: Come Clean, Be Real, Carolyn Holbrook

This essay is about a time when Carolyn Holbrook taught a creative writing class in a program for teen parents in Minneapolis and the surprising twists and turns the class took. She went in with a solid plan for the 10-week class, but quickly learned that it wasn't going to work with this group. When they challenged her ability to understand their lives, she learned the importance of and the value in changing course, when what you plan to teach isn't what the students need.

Demystifying Diversity: embracing my biracial identity, Daralyse Lyons

All her life, Daralyse Lyons has been refusing to choose between Black and White. When asked to "pick a side," she has proudly and loudly claimed "I'm Biracial." However, it was only after finding her voice as a writer that she realized that she was uniquely empowered to inspire others to honor all of who they are. Through this story of self-acceptance, you will be invited to consider your own self-conception and to unapologetically embrace all of who you are.

Hmong Origin Stories: foundation to writing, teaching, and mentoring, Pacyinz Lyfoung

Hmong Origin Stories reflects Pacyinz Lyfoung's journey to develop as a family and community modern, non-musical, but poetic bard, as she writes and teaches others to capture their stories in their daily and epic moments in accessible ways that sometimes run counter to the pursuit of excellence intended to dazzle white eyes.

Thoughts on a Queer, Indigenous, Multilingual, Multi-racial Literary Future, Aruni Kashyap

In this essay, Assamese author Aruni Kashyap discusses what it means to be a writer from India's Northeast, and forge a literary life in the United States by working in English academia. The essay also discusses how he found inspiration and guidance by closely reading the works of queer, black, and indigenous writers. What does it mean to arrive at a literary tradition from the location of exclusion and marginality? Is it possible to write creative work in the English language by borrowing from non-English print cultures, and oral, indigenous literary traditions? How does it enrich American literature by stretching the possibilities of South Asian Anglophone writing? How does it enrich the conversation about Indian-American literature?

Imagining Home: Creating Literary Spaces of Change and Possibility, Neil Aitken

Neil Aitken grew up between cultures, languages, and nations, and began collecting books to find a home for himself and his writing. In his lyric essay, he reflects on how the effort to build a library for himself became an act of resistance, a space for transformation, and a means through which he now helps others find a place and a voice for their writing. He also considers how these efforts informed his later efforts to build collaborative community libraries and archives like De-Canon.

Literary Gatekeepers
(and other myths)

What Would Edén Say? Reclaiming the Personal and Grounding Story in Chicana Feminist (Academic) Writing

Kandace Creel Falcón

Determined to find out more about Chicana feminism, I huffed and puffed as I walked up each set of stairs in the Watson Library stacks. A research project for one of my women's studies classes brought me to the library, a stately building defined by limestone and stairs, but I was digging for knowledge not assigned by my professors. Even though I was familiar with doing research in the library on the University of Kansas campus that housed the humanities and social sciences texts, my heart filled with a sense of awe, wonder, and pride every time I set foot in Watson. To think my tuition paid for the access to all these books and knowledge reminded me of the joys I felt researching in the Lomas-Tramway library as a young girl in Albuquerque, New Mexico. While a set of stairs also led up to my childhood library, it leveled out into a one-story maze of bookshelves easily navigated by patrons. The Watson Library contained five floors of books with stacks emanating from the center of the library connected by back-way, windowless, and cool climate-controlled staircases that made me feel more like a scholar in an Indiana Jones movie than a mere undergraduate in Lawrence, Kansas.

Libraries inspire a sense of belonging for me. They feel like home. Since childhood, shelves of books never judged my tastes; checking the catalogue for current library holdings and figuring out the inter-library loan systems unlocked gates I never knew were sealed. Discovering a favorite place in the library to read through the pile of books I found also brought its own rewards. The library became my sanctuary, a place where I could determine my destiny. Despite the recognition that I was often the only woman of color exploring bookshelves of texts, and the feeling that university spaces were not meant for a Mexican American like me, the Watson library felt safe.

It was in college when I learned libraries were politicized spaces, tasked with not only holding books, but also curating different ways of knowing for diverse readers. In my childhood library I don't recall coming across books by Mexican Americans, despite growing up in New Mexico. I tore through the typical (white) children's series, like *Amelia Bedelia, The Berenstain Bears,* and later *The Baby-Sitters Club.*

Rudolfo Anaya's *Bless Me Ultima*, and Sandra Cisneros' *A House on Mango Street*, books assigned to me in middle school, were exceptions, not the rule in my literary history. Stumbling upon Emma Pérez's *The Decolonial Imaginary* in the E184 call section of the 1 center stacks in the Watson Library changed me. Nearby, Carla Trujillo's edited anthology *Living Chicana Theory* lived on the shelf. Both books with rich, purple covers contained images of powerful Chicana iconography I never imagined, yet felt compelled to hold near. After admiring the covers and acknowledgments, I dug into these books' bibliographies and began searching out the other influences, stories, and voices that enabled these words on pages. Future visits to Watson encouraged a thorough search of the 4 and 4-½ center stacks where Gloria Anzaldúa's *Borderlands/La Frontera* sat next to the groundbreaking second wave feminist anthology by women of color *This Bridge Called My Back*, which resided near Norma Cantú's *Canícula*.

In the cave-like rooms in-between the library's floors that housed metal shelves crammed full of so many books, these Chicana feminist texts seemed like they were waiting just for me to find them. Upon searching them out, I devoured them with an urgency not yet felt upon other literary discoveries. As a Chicana with a brown mother and white father, Anzaldúa's ideas of mestiza consciousness, being in-between, and navigating borders helped me make sense of the experiences grounding my lived reality. By the time I came to Cherríe Moraga's *Loving in the War Years*, I emerged from her pages a Chicana. Moraga's mixed-race claiming of Chicanidad and the telling of her story of how she came to know her lesbian self inspired my confidence in claiming a queer identity too. These works not only helped me better understand myself, but they also pushed to challenge dominant assumptions that I felt deeply compelled to embrace.

Women of color writing freed me from previous assumptions I held about writing. Chicana feminists' lyrical writings fully embodied what my professors taught in my women's studies courses—that the personal is political. Except, more powerfully, Anzaldúa, Moraga and others center a Chicana experience of theorizing the personal so as to make political claims. Before reading women of color writing, my under-standing of knowledge production focused on data, on evidence collected in a methodology sanctioned by a history of white academic legacies as the only true (correct) way to make valid scholarly claims. Women of color claims, informed by the realities of what it meant to be in the world through their experiences, further released my passion for knowledge with a new recognition of the value of seeing myself in the form of the messenger. Because these mujeres connected the self to the world around them, I learned the importance of exploring histories and present conditions entrenched not only in our individual selves, but also by the collective experiences of our people. Gathering the rich history of storytelling in the form of writing then is a Chicana feminist project filled with urgency and rooted in legacy. A race to correct the record of century-long inaccuracies, a need to interrupt the narratives of domination, became my call to action and invitation to engage this shared mission.

Finding Chicana feminist authors in the Watson library stacks won me admittance into the University of Minnesota's Feminist Studies Doctoral Program. It was my archeological digging up of their words that informed my writing samples and personal statements when I applied for graduate school. It was my amplifying of their voices in concert with my urgent need to make sense of my own history that led me to the research projects and writing centering their expressions, identities, and stories. Emboldened by Chicanas reclaiming figures like La Virgen de Guadalupe as a Chicana lesbian role model, I began incorporating bold revisions and reimaginings of the intersections of my gender, sexual, and racialized identities in my writing. Along the way white scholars reminded me of how this project was not sanctioned implicitly and explicitly. I recognize it now by the way I had to make sense of these words on my own, without guidance, without classroom discussions, without the assumption that my professors would have read these works as undergraduate students. I remember how professors and grant reviewers constantly questioned my projects as a graduate student. "Is this *research*?" they would ask in the margins of my drafts. "The self and family are not valid sites of knowledge production, what is your *intervention*?" would come through in comments on my work. "There must be an archive somewhere, your job as a scholar is to find it." These demands from senior white scholars of what rigorous scholarship looks like clatter in my ears.

"Valid" academic writing and scholarship requires distance, a pretend, yet required, scenario in which the observer is supposed to be outside of that which is being observed. This is laughable. Who is behind the keyboard, the pen of your ethnographic observational notes in your field journal? Who is the name attached to your page? The assumed neutrality of whiteness translates into invisible Authorship. I do not mean the invisible authorship forced upon queer people of color where our written stories struggle to make it to page or press. I am naming the invisibility that the academy exalts, a disappearing of the raced/gendered/sexual self—operating in effort to falsely couch neutrality. White academia tries to insist the better scholarship is by those who can retain a neutral stance. (Queer) women of color writers know this neutrality is code for cis-male white privilege. I do not care for this project. I would rather my reader know this scholarship is rooted in an agenda of liberation. And women's studies as a discipline insists we push against the premise of objectivity/neutrality. Every effort challenging the establishment status quo of maintaining current power structures is the project of liberation for us all.

The PhD track is supposed to discipline you. During my time as a graduate student the process tried to beat me out of my writing. It started innocuously enough by erasing every first person utterance or inner thought. This happened in the name of "good" scholarship. I embraced the idea that through writing I should exhibit above average intelligence. So, when my professors started scratching out my "I" voice, I accepted it. I began replacing everyday words with exuberant ones I looked up in the thesaurus. Hours spent poring over difficult and indecipherable texts replicated complex (long) sentence structure in my formal writing. Soon, I could no longer recognize myself in my pages. I had been disciplined. Sometimes, in a rush to push writing out, I will revert to this distant, "objective" voice. Recognizing the strong pull of academese is not enough; I need backup.

If, like me, you are lucky, your Chicana feminist advisor will be your backup. She will give your writing back and pointedly say to you, "What is this? Where are you?" when you are missing from your stories. She will share with you that she stopped reading after the first paragraph. At first you will feel crushed, a bit spirit-broken, but later when you look again at what you gave her, you will come to agree with her assessment. You will look to her text, *Chicana Without Apology* as your muse. You will remember, you are not writing for white male academics, you are filling in gaps of knowledge, you are interrupting what has been done before. You will remember your true audience, your abuela who completed eight grades of formal schooling in Juarez, Mexico. You will remember your true audience, your mama who graduated from high school against the odds in Washington, Kansas. You will remember your true audience, your hermana who will soon graduate with a master's degree in technical writing with an emphasis in women's studies from Kansas State University. You will remember your true audience, your 4-year-old niece, and the young girl hungry for more, who is now searching for your book in the stacks of her community library.

Edén Torres, my Chicana feminist mentor, serves as the Chicana writer who most helped me bridge what I discovered long ago in the stacks. She continues to shape my writing practice even as she no longer reviews all of my work. I constantly use her as my gauge—what would Edén say about this? Where would she push me to reveal more of myself to get closer to the meat of my arguments? What story might I share to paint a better picture of the theory I wrestle and try to wrangle from thoughts to words on the page? She taught me many lessons, but the lesson I try to live most in my writing practice is that we each have an authentic voice and when we hone it, it cannot be detached from our self. When we are present and intentional about our audience, our writing sings most powerfully. My songs are only possible because of Edén's.

Basing my writing process in exposing and cultivating my authentic voice means that sometimes, most times, writing is a painful process. It is a task that requires me to lock myself away with only my thoughts. As an extrovert who thrives on being with others, writing can appear solitary at first glance. Moving the solitary to the communal takes a gentle shift in perspective and helps me feel less alone. With the successful honing of my writing craft, I bring my community into the process to counter the fears of being isolated. Feeling like the "only one" in academic institutional spaces haunts my reality when Xicanas make up such a small percentage of the professoriate. The demands of the academy constantly discipline. Women of color writers who masterfully blend story and theory bring me back into balance when the demands of academic writing conventions stifle my authentic voice.

Women of color and Chicana feminist writers lay their souls, traumas, and bodies bare for the reader. I am convinced that this practice in vulnerability is a political act of liberation. Anzaldúa reminds us of this in her famous essay, "Speaking in Tongues: A Letter to Third World Women Writers." In exploring why she is compelled to write she offers:

> Because the writing saves me from this complacency I fear. Because I have no choice. Because I must keep the spirit of my revolt and myself alive. Because the world I create in the writing compensates for what the real world does not give me.

> By writing I put order in the world, give it a handle so I can
> grasp it. I write because life does not appease my appetites and
> hunger. I write to record what others erase when I speak, to
> rewrite the stories others have miswritten about me, about you.
>
> (Anzaldúa, 2009, p. 30)

To write in this way is to be laid bare for all to consume. To write
in this way is to build community. I envision my writing through story,
like Anzaldúa's as an ofrenda, an offering, for you, my community. A
gift rooted in a vulnerable sharing of me.

Resistance defines my writing experiences. External detractors
wishing to deter my voice converge with internal thoughts trying to
shame me into not writing. Perfectionist tendencies meet lifetimes of
not seeing myself in others' words. Worries about what "counts" for
publications creep up on the need to put myself into my writing to
fulfill my compulsion to write. These tensions mark my journey in
uncovering my authentic voice. When these pressures mount, I light a
candle on my altar. The altar is my facilitator of offerings. To make an
ofrenda at my altar grounds my intention. When I light a candle to
honor the past and present, I embrace the flicker of shine from its wick.
The candlelight reminds me to face the glow of light, imagine a
spotlight and spill myself onto my screen, into my pages, whether
keyboard or pen under my fingers. When a breeze taps the flickering
light to illuminate my statue of La Virgen de Guadalupe, I imagine
how she appears in all angles of illumination. These different
perspectives of her back or side alit, harken back to my invisible
readers, my supporters, my reminders of why I write in the dark, why I
push through that which may be uncomfortable to share. Knowing
even if it is only me who needs to read these words is enough to
continue writing when it is most difficult. Rules of my craft matter less
than unlocking the process of writing for me. Finding the conditions
that best support laying myself bare for my reader took a while, but
now, when I get lost, I light a candle and make an altar wherever I am.

Have you ever moved yourself to tears when you write? In a world
where our tears may be construed as weakness, or used against us
when we call out injustice, the act of crying while writing legitimizes
my product and process. When my words move me to cry, I know I
have left something behind that cannot be consumed without leaving a
mark on the reader. I seek to move myself to cry when I write despite
feeling uncomfortable or scared. To shift myself to cry confronts the

borders within and the barriers I erect between others and myself. When I cry on my page, I know I am contributing to the archive of women of color writers who have brought me to tears through theirs. I am stretching that catalogue to embrace the young Chicanita who is searching for a glimpse of herself in the pages of a book or on the cover of a book in the tombs of a favorite library. I am honoring alternative ways for the foremothers, myself, and those not yet on this path. I learned this lesson when I revised the piece that Edén could not read. I lit a candle, scrapped the original, and opened myself to the vulnerable act of sharing myself with my page. I cried as I wrote, choking up even more when I read the new draft to myself out loud. When she gave it back to me, smiling and beaming, she said, "Now this is you."

Notes

1. I choose to use the term Chicana to signify the terminology Chicana activists and scholars used during second wave feminism, which proceeds the terms Xicana and Xicanx. While Xicana specifically references the indigenous roots of Chicanisma and Xicanx offers a destabilizing of the gender binary, my choice of the term Chicana is not to discount these interventions but rather to historically ground the terminology in the context in which I first learned of it. Chicana/Xicana/Xicanx all embody a politicized effort to challenge and correct social, political, and economic inequities Mexican Americans face in the United States with particular attention to dismantling patriarchal forms of control.

References

Anzaldúa, G. (1999) *Borderlands/La frontera*. 2nd ed. San Francisco: Aunt Lute Books.

---. (2009) "Speaking in tongues: A letter to third world women writers." In *The Gloria Anzaldúa reader*. Ed. AnaLouise Keating. Durham, NC: Duke University Press.

Anzaldúa, G., & Moraga, C., eds. (1983) *This bridge called my back: Writings by radical women of color*. 2nd ed. New York: Kitchen Table, Women of Color Press.

Cantú, N. (1995) *Canícula: Snapshots of a girlhood en la frontera*. Albuquerque, NM: University of New Mexico Press.

Moraga, C. (2000) *Loving in the war years: Lo que nunca pasó por sus labios.* Expanded 2nd ed. Cambridge, MA: South End Press.

Pérez, E. (1999) *The decolonial imaginary: Writing Chicanas into history.* Bloomington, IN: Indiana University Press.

Torres, E. (2003) *Chicana without apology: Chicana sin vergüenza.* New York: Routledge.

Trujillo, C., ed. (1998) *Living Chicana theory.* Berkeley, CA: Third Woman Press.

Writing Exercise

Gather three items that are sacred to you and place them in a purposeful arrangement with one another. Light a candle near the items. Use your writer's altar to ground yourself in your writing. Pay attention to your emotional, spiritual, and rational self as you prepare. Write a story connected to one or all of the objects you selected by starting with a story about you. If you are having trouble getting started, begin describing one of the objects and why you chose it. Think about the meaning of the object as it connects to you and the audience you most wish to reach with your words.

Imposter Poet: Recovering from Graduate School

Jessica Lopez Lyman

Spring 2011

e-p-i-s-t-e-m-o-l-o-g-y

You type the word into your biography for an upcoming performance. It is your second year of graduate school. You have been invited to read at a well-known Xicana art festival in Los Angeles. You re-read the biography several times. Overly enthusiastic to recite poetry after moving away from the Twin Cities, you press *send*. The email floats through cyberlandia.

You arrive early to the performance space. Too early. Not on Chicanx time.[1] The email said to arrive at 4 pm. You arrive at 3:55 trying to convince yourself you're not nervous. Only a few volunteers are there setting up chairs and checking lights. You walk around the stage. To the left of the stage an ofrenda made from corn husks towers above. You feel small.

Three hours later, you're in the green room. The paint is chipping and the carpet is stained. You sit on a folding metal chair. Your journal rests on your thighs. You re-read and re-read. Say the words aloud in a whisper. A few performers wander in and out. They offer the obligatory smile then turn to people they know and make conversation. Their laughter breaks your concentration. You remember when you used to laugh in green rooms with friends. Memories of home sit heavy in your throat. You swallow them down. Focus on the paint chipping.

The stage manager breaks your trance. You follow her to the main room. You sit against the wall. The MC begins to read your bio. The words do not register. You clutch your journal. You cannot swallow. The MC gets to the last line. "Her research includes Chicana feminisms, education, and episte… WHAT?!? EpistE-M-O-Logy." The crowd laughs. You drop your journal.

Epistemology. The study of knowledge. For two years you have dedicated yourself to the study of knowledge. You learn about all the "ologies." Ontology, phenomenology, epistemology. Early on, it becomes evident in your graduate seminars these words are borders.

---

[1] I use term "Chicanx" with an "x" at the end to acknowledge that gender is non-binary and to be inclusive of gender non-conforming and trans Chicanxs.

They divide the perceived intelligent from the masses. You try them on like mama's bracelets and dad's dress shoes. Loud and sparkly you shuffle around awkwardly with your new vocabulary hoping no one will recognize you're playing dress up.

Epistemology. The study of knowledge. We are all producers of knowledge they say (Bernal, Elenes, Godinez and Villenas). They call people outside of the ivory tower, people without letters after their names, organic intellectuals (Hoare and Smith, 1971). People who are not formally trained that spring up like plantain or dandelions. Organic matter. Medicinal healing. Their actions, words, theories create change. They are the bottom up. The come on up. The get on up. Intellectuals of the people.

You are not organic. You are synthetic. Polyester fabric, woven with two parts Foucault, one part Marx, with embellishments of Critical Race Theory and Chicana feminisms accenting your Woman of Color positionality (also a word you learn in graduate school).

The seminar room teaches you to critique. Through a capitalist, colonial logic most graduate programs destroy texts, decapitate theories and turn concepts and methods into loose limbs clinging onto the page for survival. What you enjoyed about a particular text becomes irrelevant, a flattened conversation develops out of "what's good." The seminar battle feasts on the graduate student performance of critique. Hour long conversations can be made out of a single line, dissected and manipulated until it no longer holds meaning. Signs reconfigured to fit the most boastful student's perspective.

You relish classes in your home department. Decolonial writers— Anzaldúa, Sandoval, Lorde, Fanon, Moraga—provide escape routes to a third space. In this space, epistemology comes from everyday experiences. Moments at the bar. Working in the fields. Sleeping next to a lover in bed. Knowledge is flesh and bone, breath and movement. Theory in the flesh (Moraga and Anzaldúa, 1983). Their words are the counter to critique. They are the solution, the method. Their essays are complex constellations. You read over and over to decode each star.

You quickly realize, however, not everyone lives in third space. Your mentor tells you people are sometimes afraid of liberation. When the door to the colonial cage opens, people will remain inside. Or people become seduced by their privilege. You understand this deeply. The previous week you attended a Chicano professor's office hours. He looked up halfway through your paper. "You know," he said, "I was really surprised at how smart you are. In class, well… I wasn't sure what to expect. You're not just a pretty face."

You felt the cage door slam. The vibration caused you to tremble. No matter your mastery of epistemology you are still a Woman of Color. Just a pretty face. You stared at his office wall. The paint slightly chipping.

Winter 2014

After you complete all course work and pass your exams, you move back to the Twin Cities. You conduct field work. Study other poets. Months later, you are slated with the task of writing. February's grey weather shines through the stained glass window in your makeshift home office. You sit with hands on the keyboard. Computer on. There is a blank screen. The white glare reflects slightly your image. You stare at yourself. Tilt your head side to side. Make sure it's really you. A rounder, emptier face mirrors your movements. You write a line. And erase. You write another and erase that too. You have been taught to critique. To destroy. Not to build. How do you build a sentence let alone an entire thesis?

Writing used to be your outlet. A mixed-race Chicana from the Midwest, you clung to journals like security blankets, rendered blank pages into survival maps. Spoken word became a talking back to yourself. At your parents' house you practiced poetry. Stared in your bedroom mirror. The Mexican white tiles of the frame surrounding your face. You recited lines to Curt Cobain. A poster of his black and white image with straight blonde hair and eyes outlined in heavy eyeliner stared back at you. If Curt could share the razorblade pain of broken hearts and worlds collapsing, so could you.

Now there are stories trapped inside of you. Voices that emerge in dreams at three in the morning, but disappear as soon as you open your eyes. You try to listen, but you can't hear them as well anymore. There are theorists and an advisor and committee members and you. Everyone speaks too loud, silences the stories. But you, you are the most powerful critic. You don't just destroy. You erase. Non-existence is the most dangerous violence. Colonialism teaches you this.

Your synthetic fabric begins to unravel. February engulfs you into a whirlwind of self-doubt, reality TV, and eating cereal right out of the box. You gain weight. You stop moving. You gain weight because you stop moving. At the coffee shop you feel the walls melt into the floor and your chest freezes. Breath stops. You are told this is a panic attack.

You don't believe the experts. Anxiety is for rich people. You pick fights with your partner. Dream up ridiculous expectations no lover could meet. Anything to avoid writing. The glare from the computer screen hurts your eyes. You cannot look at yourself anymore. You are an imposter.

Summer 2015

You buy a journal. The kind from the art stores with black sleek hard covers and blank white pages inside. You had this type of journal before in high school. At that time, it was a blank canvas that you scribbled and collaged into your tapestry of teenage angst. You consider it your open map to return to a moment before the noise. There are no lines. Not right or wrong. Just space. You need space to breathe, to sketch out the maps of stories in your head. At first it's awkward. You draw with colored pencils instead of write because the critic inside disciplines each word. The drawing is a cheap imitation of Favianna Rodriguez and Carmen Lomas Garza combined into an elementary rendition of nopales and desert landscapes. It doesn't matter. You remember, "nopal en la frente." You draw Chicanx iconography trying to find the pathway home. As a Woman of Color you know your silence is not by accident. The repetitious questioning of your qualifications from teachers has become a low buzzing sound to the background of your life.

But in the journal, there are no questions, no doubts, no expecta-tions. Just you, which is frightening enough. Journals are like mirrors, but easier to hide from those that hang on the wall. Shut them and the reflection of your life dims. You open your new journal and write a scattered jumble, your first poem in years. You write about your abuelo, an East L.A. Chicano barber. In between the graduate courses and exams, you went to his home, even spent your first Thanksgiving in California a few years back with him. The short spurts of connection rekindle your understanding of self. You remember your family's stories of border crossings, traumas, and celebrations. Slowly, you make a practice of journaling. Not every day. But enough. You remem-ber you are enough.

Spring 2016

The sharpness in your neck and right wrist is something that you have learned to live with for two years. The mantra of childhood basketball coaches repeats in your head, "No pain, no gain. Pain is weakness leaving the body. No pain, no gain. Pain is weakness leaving the body." All spring into early summer you binge write to finish. There is no more fellowship. No more money. You cry. You keep writing. You have to finish.

Summer 2016

You start to find your body again. Notice your feet on the ground. Walk barefoot in the grass and scrunch your toes into the cold soil. You eat full meals sitting down without your computer on or a chapter in front of you to edit. You watch movies at the two-dollar theater, attend Lynx games, play soccer, and work out with friends. When people talk you actually listen to them. Your mind does not keep the running list of the next project, the email that wasn't sent, the citation that needs to be added to the footnote on page forty-three. You start to recover. Even your breath is different. Lungs expand more. Instead of short shallow breaths, air now moves from your core. It's not about anxiety, you realize. It's the weight of centuries, of doubt, of other people's stories. If you do the work, write, most importantly listen to your research participants, to your family, your breath comes more easily.

You learn that writing is about discipline. Not the punitive discipline. Not solitary confinement. Not whips of mea culpa, twisted Catholic guilt. You are not a masochist. A writer's discipline is about the return. About coming to the page, the computer, even when you have nothing to say, when you are stuck. You are stuck so often. But you return. As a Woman of Color you know that writing is not about having a room of your own or an entire day. It is about returning to the brief moments in between office hours, before class, prior to a meeting. Carving out spaces in between the moments that matter. There is so much matter—the density of people, priorities, protests. You slice chaotic spaces into small segments of solitude. Writing requires an isolation, which first terrifies you. Now you crave it. The desire to come to the page. To write and write. Other writers you meet call this sacred writing time. But for you this is not spiritual. It is political because people are dying, stories go silent, and the magnitude of your privilege in the university weighs heavy. Perhaps you're still too young to realize spirituality and politics are one in the same[2]. For now,

---

[2] Queer Chicana feminist, Gloria Anzaldúa theorized spiritual activism and the role of the writer. Her work challenges me to understand the weaving between our spiritual practices and political commitments (Keating, 2015).

the discipline is about cultivating the stories others tell you. You are the word carrier. The transcriber of time, space, theory and flesh.

You no longer erase. You keep a separate file for random thoughts. One-liners orphaned, waiting for a home. Perhaps they will always remain islands in a sea of organized paragraphs or twist into new poems. But at least they exist. At least you have learned to allow them to be in all their imperfections. Now you know sometimes there are good days. Days where pages upon pages dance out of you. Other days there is nothing. Pushing out a sentence is a victory no one notices. But you. You notice. With each new essay completed, article submitted, poem copy edited you shape shift from critic to builder. Slowly, you slide one foot out the cage.

References

Anzaldúa, G., & In Keating, A. L. (2015). *Light in the dark: Rewriting identity, spirituality, reality = Luz en lo oscuro*. Durham: Duke University Press, 2015.

Delgado, B. D. (2006). *Chicana/Latina education in everyday life: Feminista perspectives on pedagogy and epistemology*. Albany: State University of New York Press.

Gramsci, A., In Hoare, Q., & In Nowell-Smith, G. (2014). *Selections from the prison notebooks of Antonio Gramsci*. New York: International Publishers.

Moraga, C., & Anzaldúa, G. (1983). *This bridge called my back: Writings by radical women of color*. New York: Kitchen Table Press, 1983.

Writing Exercise: Return to the Page

1. Find a Friend

The purpose of this writing exercise is to motivate you to begin a writing session, which for some, is the most difficult part of the writing process. Similar to weight lifting or running, I find having a partner to write with keeps me accountable to my goals. Often when we meet in person, however, we can get distracted. Instead, find a writing partner who lives far away or at the very least is not physically in the same room with you during your writing session.

2. Set a Time

The night before, choose a block of time you both will meet to write. Make sure you have no other appointments. This time is non-negotiable and should be at least 30 minutes.

3. Set up the Session

Before you begin your session have anything you might need to write—water, coffee, snack, writing utensils, computer fully charged. Log into some type of online server to chat with your writing partner or text one another. Keep the conversation short. Tell each other your writing goal for the day and agree upon a set time to work for the first session. Set a timer between 30 and 45 minutes and begin writing.

4. Post-Session

After the session is complete, check back in with each other. What was difficult? What went well? What are you getting stuck on? What can you ignore and fix later? Sometimes all we need is a little encouragement. ¡Sí se puede!

A Case for Writing While Black

Sherrie Fernandez-Williams

I am the great-great granddaughter of enslaved black people of Georgia, North Carolina, Barbados and Cuba. I am the daughter of a man who survived Jim Crow South by keeping his head in books and his eyes off of white women. I am the daughter of a single mother who was raised by her immigrant mother in a Brooklyn tenement, a domestic, whose husband, my grandfather, died too young after living the harsh life as a laborer—the only life presented to him as a poor man of color.

I consider my mother's lineage, Nada from Georgia, Angel from Cuba, Matilda from Barbados, Ralph from Miami, Hilda from Trinidad. I consider my people from pre-colonial West Africa, Dahomey, now Benin, before the Kingdom became the leading supplier of human beings for the transatlantic slave trade (Manning, 1982). I consider the time before abductions, before islands were stolen from the Arawaks and Caribs, before young British men like George Ashby "found a dynasty that endures to this day built on sugar and forged by slavery" (Stuart, 2013). Who were the creatives among them? Who were the storytellers? Who were the dreamers and which of them do I favor?

I think of my paternal ancestors from North Carolina, during the antebellum period, when slavery became more entrenched in North Carolina. The number of slaves from Africa and surrounding colonies grew exponentially during this time. Antebellum planters and slaveholders became significant financiers of our nation's colleges and universities (Wilder, 2014). So, essentially, black men and women paid the cost to educate white men and women.

While my ancestors' slave labor paid to further empower white people, laws were being passed to further disempower enslaved people by criminalizing the act of educating them. In the legislative papers from the General Assembly of North Carolina (1830-31), these words are written: "the teaching of slaves to read and write has the tendency to excite dissatisfaction in their minds, and to produce insurrection and rebellion to the manifest injury of citizens of this State." A white person would be heavily fined for breaking this law. A free black person could be whipped 39 times for the act of teaching his friends, family, or fellow parishioners to read. The State General Assembly of

North Carolina of 1830 had it exactly right because when I read and write about my folks' past nightmares and current traumas, I am also prone to intense dissatisfaction of the mind that produces the spirit of rebellion in me. Perhaps this is why, some would rather we forget the past. As my historian friend Patti Kameya says, the average American seems to have an historical consciousness of 15 minutes. I am sure America's devastation of whole groups of people, beginning with indigenous nations, has much to do with the desire of many to ignore or minimize the relationship between past and present America.

As I share my experiences as a black woman in any capacity, I must put into context the body in which I live, and the history that lives in my body. It is because of this history and in spite of this history that I have the duty to read, write and insert my voice into the world of stories. My people survived the middle passage, rape, generations of abject poverty, systematic discrimination in housing, education, and employment opportunities, so I can be here. So, dammit, I am here and I will not leave this world without having my say, with or without the help of our literary gatekeepers. I have been born with the instinct to search for the right words to compose the stories placed in my soul— though I do not always get it right, I will never quit because I know my dead relatives will never let me sleep in peace if I tried to walk away. For this fact, if nothing else, I consider myself blessed beyond measure. My purpose became clear to me rather early in life.

Like many writers, it was an early teacher who first identified my writer-self. Discovering this in the third grade was something of a breakthrough and the beginning of my emancipation. It turns out the skinny kid from Brooklyn Public Housing was not going to be spotted by Béla Karolyi while doing cartwheels in the schoolyard and be transformed into the next Nadia Comăneci. Alvin Ailey was not going to find me in the church basement learning modern dance for free with Bobby Tucker, the neighborhood choreographer. I was not going to put on a long white dress and dance, *Cry* like Judith Jamison releasing my anguish, and the anguish of my people through the movement of my back, and neck, arms, and shoulders, and legs and feet, and, and toes. Though a time or two, I thought I'd might put on that dress and Ailey would find me.

Our once bound bodies have always wanted the freedom to celebrate love and family, and to mourn our losses. I feel them occupying my frame every time I hear a drum. I just didn't know it was them—great grandmothers, occupying my limbs until it was too late—until I was too old to pursue movement as a way to tell their story.

Fortunately, for me, I found the blank page and a pencil—always available, barely costing a thing. With minimal tools and a little bit of quiet, I allowed myself to feel all feelings, even the angry ones that might make others uncomfortable. I am still a person who is concerned with the comfort of others. Empathy runs deeply in the genetic code of both sides of my family, Fernandez and Williams. My outward expression of my personality is soft-spoken, mostly affable, socially awkward—some might mistake me for being aloof. Those who love me forgive me when I say ass-backward shit because they know my difficulty in being two places at once, the internal world, and the world we can touch, smell, and taste. I have chosen to channel my disappointments into constructive pursuits, and hopefully, this will teach me how to live right.

I remember the book fair where I first set eyes on a biography of Phillis Wheatley. It was the cover that drew me; a very young black woman, sitting at a writing table, feather in her hand, her gaze forward, and the look of contemplation on her face. I admired the woman I came to know through those pages. Although she was kidnapped as a small child, suffered the conditions of a slave ship, and remained ill throughout her young life, she developed into a highly skilled poet. Instantly, her story fueled what became my secret passion. By the time I was a freshman in college, when I was reintroduced to Wheatley, I saw something else in her work, something that resembled internalized racism. I asked myself, "Did she really think it was 'mercy' that brought her from Africa? How could she not see it was nothing more than greed? Did she really see Africans as sinners because they did not worship the same god as white men? Would not the true sinners obviously be the colonizers and enslavers?" Of course, that was 20th-century me. Twenty-first-century me understands that Wheatley was quite subversive. An enslaved girl who demonstrated brilliance and a commitment to excellence automatically challenges the oppressor's justifications for slavery. She had to possess an internal reservoir of confidence to audaciously believe her words could inspire General George Washington as he led the fight against the British. Gumption was a quality the institution of slavery worked intensely to suppress in black people. Yet Wheatley had plenty of it. She was earnest in her attempt to alter the notions white people had of African people. She wanted her people to be seen as worthy of God's love. By her own existence, she knew her people had the capacity to be more than what slavery demanded if given the opportunity. She was bold enough to know that she could be a teacher of white men. I will always appreciate the lessons she's given us. I will always love her for stirring, in me, an early desire to develop a life of the imagination. This spectacular shift happened in me right there in the forsaken housing projects of New York when daily the messages I heard about myself was that I could not think. I could not write. I could not learn. I could not move beyond my circumstances. The myths I absorbed were debunked by the first published African-American female poet. She made the case for "writing while black" 200 years before I was born. Yet, every day I still live with the question, should I dare write today? Who am I to think that I should?

Starting my Master's in Fine Arts (MFA) program, I found that I absolutely loved going to school as a working adult. I romanticized all of it, the changing leaves, the red-brick pavements, and my classmates whose excitement was as palpable as mine. My program was off to a great start with courses in the personal essay and playwriting. My professors were vocally affirming. They gave me that "I see you" look. And I will not lie; I delighted in their affirmation. I became that third grader from the projects all over again. Perhaps emerging writers of all stripes experience a thrill when our potential is recognized by those we consider literary authority. My MFA experience was off to a good start.

The dust-ups began soon after. It was painful to read a novel from a white woman of the canon that oozed racist ideals and language, written with a kind of nostalgia about the good old days of slavery. The problems begin with the very title, as Toni Morrison points out in her book, *Playing in the Dark: Whiteness and the Literary Imagination*. Sapphira, the white mistress, is named. Nancy, the enslaved, is not. The pile on of hurt continues. The third-person omniscient narrator of *Sapphira and the Slave Girl*, by Willa Cather, stated: "The self-respecting negroes never complained of harsh treatment. They made a joke of it, and laughed about it among themselves, as the rough mountain boys did about the licking they got at school."

My white feminist classmates celebrated this woman's bold choices in writing and in life. Yet her portrayal of the experience of slavery crushed me. There was the beautiful slave, of course beautiful because she was "a yellow girl." Other black characters had names like Fat

Lizzie and Jezebel, and the black children of the plantations were pickaninnies. Of course, the *nigger* was everywhere. Reading the book at home, I felt as if I was being assaulted. I threw the book across my living room and cried. I argued with classmates in class, then later over e-mail. I wrote a poem from the point of view of an enslaved young woman, saying it was something I needed to do to recover from Cather. My professor critiqued the craft of the poem, but said nothing to address or acknowledge my pain. My classmates accused me of not looking at the greater genius beyond the novel's racist ideologies that were simply a sign of the times the author lived in.

Later, in another course, there was the issue of a memoir we read of a black man, an incomparable jazz musician who spent a significant portion of the book boasting of his sexual conquests of black and brown women. The narrator spoke of psychologically preying upon and dishonoring women of color, seemingly without thought or regret. This was not a life examined through the vehicle of literature because there was very little insight or reflection provided. It was hard to express my complicated feelings about *Beneath the Underdog: His World Composed by Mingus*. As much as I would have liked to defend the legendary musical genius, the woman in me, the woman of color in me, could not understand why the memoir of a black man clearly embellishing his sexual conquests would be the only required reading from a black male author that semester. By that time, Mingus was not alive to defend himself or to express how he had grown since writing the book. He would not have been around to explain to the offended that it was merely "boy talk" or "locker-room talk" or whatever sexual predators are calling it these days.

I thought of the African-American males of the CNF genre we could have studied instead—James Baldwin, Amiri Baraka, James McBride, Gordon Parks, Alex Haley, John Edgar Wideman, E. Ethelbert Miller, men seriously dedicated to craft and deeply committed to the written word. *Beneath the Underdog* was selected because my white male professor loved the book. Did he agree with the review in *Rolling Stone* magazine that said this narrator, who, for example, boasted of sex with "twenty Mexican prostitutes," explains more about "black survival than sociologists and psychologists ever can in their stiff soulless vocabulary?" Is this white imagination at its worst when imagining black men? Had the dignity and humanity of women of color held no emotional space in the psyche of my white male professor for him not to question this choice?

Later, when life became hectic with work, school and parenting—I had little ones at home by this time—I decided to fulfill a creative nonfiction requirement through an online course. The bright side was that I would be learning from a brilliant essayist. Her goal was to help us see the possibilities of creative nonfiction by reading a broad range of styles. It included *Silent Spring* by Rachel Carson and *Hiroshima* by John Hersey. Her reading list also included W.E.B DuBois, Audre Lorde, and Anne Moody, three black authors writing deeply, intelligently, reflectively about black people. I believed my professor's book selection would surely heal me from some of the poison I'd ingested before then. After reading Dubois, we were asked to watch the PBS film *Slavery and the Making of America* (2004), and my gratitude for this prof deepened further.

However, the course content was met with some backlash, primarily from one angry student who seemed to detest any conversation around diversity. She claimed that her life was diverse enough because she was connected to people from different economic classes and sexual orientations. Frequently, she spoke out specifically against black people. She felt that black people complained too much and were living in the past. She once asked why we couldn't be more like Native Americans. She felt they were more dignified in their approach to seeking justice. She never explained what was undignified about African-Americans' approach to seeking justice. As the only person of color in the class, I tried to be patient. I took precious time, effort, and energy attempting to change her view of black people. This is what Phillis Wheatley did during her lifetime, and what so many black and brown people do every day in white spaces. At night, I'd close my laptop exhausted and defeated, weary from trying to help this woman understand something she could not or would not. Sadly, it would appear as though these types of interactions are quite common for graduate students at predominantly white institutions.

Here is the thing. Even with the occasional trials I endured while in grad school, I always considered myself one of the lucky ones. Some writers of color walk away from their MFA experiences never wanting to write again. I walked away feeling like I definitely had my growth areas in terms of craft, but my strength as a writer came from the assuredness of my voice that drove the narrative forward and made the reader feel as if they were in capable hands—a young, shy, black woman, from the hood, easily rolled over by a mean enough bully, living the secret hell of an abusive marriage, one of the very few writers of color in the MFA program comprised of all white faculty, wrote with the confidence of a bad bitch much of the time. The person in flesh—vulnerable and tender. The woman on paper—bad bitch, or so I thought—perhaps wrongly.

Others have written skillfully about the difficulty writers of color have in mostly white MFA programs. Junot Diaz's essay in the *New Yorker* and David Mura's essay in *Gulf Coast* both speak insightfully about the issues and have both inspired writers of color to evaluate their experiences. In his essay, "The Student of Color in the Typical MFA Program," David Mura (2015) wrote, "In most MFA programs, the subject of race and writing about race is never considered a fundamental and essential area of study for all writers in the program regardless of color. It is never required, always an elective. This is not surprising since the majority of white faculty do not believe that such a study is essential to their own writing or to their pedagogical practices."

I would add that many programs do not even offer courses dealing with race and writing as an elective. I didn't know such a thing existed. Over the duration of my program, my writing became less race conscious instead of more. Sure everything thing I do and say leaves the mark of blackness behind. However, instead of drawing a circle around the mark, expanding it, aiming the camera directly at it, I placed translucent covering over it, not completely hiding race, but placing it in the background. Without knowing it, I was learning to write like a white woman because I must have believed that they knew what they were doing. They were award-winning authors. They were where I wanted to be. They were my teachers.

I will always give them lots of credit for strengthening my writing in many ways, I learned important lessons about reflection and insight. I learned the importance of imagistic language, the importance of symbols, the most effective ways to include dialogue in a story written from memory. However, there are critical things to me as a black writer that I did not learn in the MFA program. In creative writing, we are often taught to soften our political views on the page because we don't want to alienate some readers. Claudia Rankine spoke of this at a recent Association of Writers and Writing Programs (AWP) conference. She read aloud an anonymous letter written by an African-American student who was struggling with the decision to leave an MFA program.

In the letter, the student wrote, "Certain life experiences are said to belong to sociology and not to poetry, and that to write beyond the imagination's notion of normality is to write political poetry, sociology, identity politics poetry, protest poetry—many labels, but none of them poetry." Rankine clarified for the audience what the student's words meant from her point of view. She said that "white writers must find it relatable, and only then can it transcend its unrelatable colored writer."

The goal was made clear to me: Do not make any attempt to sound moralistic. If there is an agenda behind the writing, we must disguise it, or dilute it. However, it did not occur to me until very recently that while it is true that we might alienate some by conveying a certain point of view and exposing what we believe to be systematic institutional oppression, power and privilege, microaggressions, white supremacy and other such concepts that make some roll their eyes, by not disguising our truth, we will actually be more successful at drawing our true audience toward our work. Our true audience does not want watered down truth. When we do this, we forgo the opportunity to speak directly to the hearts, minds, and souls of black and brown readers. Claudia Rankine's *Citizen* is a prime example of this.

Readers of color have grown tired of not seeing themselves reflected in what we read. As a black reader, I know this. It wasn't until after I completed my MFA program and after my first book was published (*Soft,* the revised version of my MFA thesis) that I realized I was missing an important contextual element in my first book. My editor said she wanted to push the coming out as queer element of my memoir, but never said anything about reaching readers of color, or readers who are interested in reading writers of color. I cannot entirely blame her for that. My black identity was in the story as a matter of fact, but not very intently as a matter to examine. I thought I was doing the right thing, the crafty thing. Although as a memoirist, I now wonder how could I have not.

Currently, I am taking a class with David Mura, author of *Turning Japanese: Memoir of a Sansei.* His course at the Loft Literary Center is specifically designed for writers of color and indigenous writers who are writing about race. Over the past several months, I have wondered how different *Soft* would have been if I drafted the manuscript while taking this course. Mura would have likely reminded me that we are not living in a post-racial society. Race is a factor that determines so much of what we do, what we notice, and what we believe, and we're not doing ourselves or anyone else any favors by ignoring where we are and where we've been.

As we know, the gatekeepers are mostly white. Of publishing professionals, 90% are white. Roxanne Gay (2013) discovered that 88% of the books reviewed by *The New York Times* were written by white authors. No wonder some writers of color consciously or sub-consciously consider how they might please white readers, white gatekeepers. In the meantime, white gatekeepers are wondering about market and audience. Perhaps they are thinking, a black woman should not be writing a white woman's book. White women will read white women and white washing my stories will not erase my blackness. It only weakens my stories, making them less palatable to those who know my truth as well as I. My personal commitment as a writer is to never utter the words, *I am a writer who happens to be a black woman*. Instead, I will emphatically declare without hesitation that *I am a black woman writer*, and I will place my story squarely within the black cultural and historical context where it belongs.

References

"Act Passed by the General Assembly of the State of North Carolina at the Session of 1830—1831" (Raleigh, NC: 1831).

Gay, R. (2013, April 26). Where Things Stand. Retrieved April 08, 2017, from http://therumpus.net/2012/06/where-things-stand/Horton, J. O. (2004). *Slavery and the making of America*. New York: Ambrose DVD.

Manning, P. (1982) *Slavery, colonialism and economic growth in Dahomey 1640-1960*. Cambridge: Cambridge University Press.

Morrison, T. (1992) *Playing in the dark: Whiteness and the literary imagination*. Cambridge, MA: Harvard University Press.

Mura, D. (2015, April 21). The Student of Color in the Typical MFA Program. Retrieved April 08, 2017, from http://gulfcoastmag.org/online/blog/the-student-of-color-in-the-typical-mfa-program/

Rankine, C. (2015). *Citizen: An American lyric*. London, UK: Penguin Books.

Stuart, A. (2013) *Sugar in the blood: A family's story of slavery and empire*. New York: Knopf.

Wilder, C. S. (2014) *Ebony and ivy: Race, slavery and the troubled history of America's universities*. New York: Bloomberg Press.

Writing Exercise: Setting and Beyond

This exercise is about placing your character or your narrator squarely within an actual cultural context. The idea is not to rely on stereotypes or tropes, but to examine the lived, witnessed, or deeply and specifically imagined.

First Step: Immediate Surroundings

Think about a place, real or imagined. Sketch out one mile of this place.

What does it look like?

What is the climate? Show the terrain.

What kinds of things do you see in this place?

Who are the people/living creatures that inhabit this place? What are they doing?

What are the colors, noises, smells, and textures of this place?

Second Step: Living in a Larger Context

On a second sheet of paper, write the name of your protagonist in small letters at the center of the page.

Draw a ring outside of that circle. In that ring write a few of the most important traits of this character.

Draw a ring outside of that circle. In the next ring the most important aspects of the immediate environment.

Draw a ring outside of that circle. In the final ring include what is happening in the world/or country on a larger scale: historical, political, social.

Somewhere on your sheet write two goals of your character, an immediate goal and a long-term goal that is connected to the immediate goal.

Obstacles: What are the obstacles in the way of your protagonist reaching their goal?

Begin writing a story about your protagonist on a particular quest. Describe the immediate and specific goal/desire with which they are preoccupied. What is the larger long-term goal/desire with which they are preoccupied? Let the reader get to know your protagonist by showing their personality, beliefs, hopes, and dreams. Describe their immediate environment. Help the reader understand their life and lifestyle. Who else is part of that world? Weave in the objects that serve as images and symbols. Place your story within the social context of time and place. What is happening in the larger world? Is there war? Is there political unrest?

You do not have to write any of this in any particular order. Let it flow and watch what happens.

mamatowisin: Writing as Spiritual Praxis

Nia Allery

As an indigenous person, I struggled trying to find personal meaning and connection in higher education—its "academic canon" shaped by cogitation. Plodding through the cerebral terrain of vast amounts of information is thought to be part of "academic rigor." Its paradigm is largely influenced by philosophers such as Descartes, whose famous line *Je pense donc je suis* captures the essence of the predominant way of being in higher educational institutions today.

The mechanics of such a paradigm were disturbing to my holistic view of the world, a world shaped by the integration of mind, body, and spirit. I was thrown off balance when I encountered the hidden curriculum of the academic canon—a curriculum that demanded clearly defined, categorical parameters, demarcating disciplinary fields of study. Could I separate and categorize my way of being in order to fit in? Was I asking the impossible when I aspired to transcend this hidden curriculum of separation?

Like the Tinman in *The Wizard of Oz*, I could not find my heart in what went on in the classroom until I taught a course entitled American Indian Spirituality and Philosophical Thought. It was an upper division course with a mix of students from across the spectrum of disciplines, beliefs, ethnicities, and physical abilities. My goal was to teach this course as a world religion and to integrate the various disciplinary approaches into a holistic experience—an experience of the mind, body, and spirit. Above all, I wanted to use the indigenous ways of knowing. I wanted my students to explore the metaphysics of inner space. We were going to practice what is described in Cree as *mamatowisin*, "the capacity to tap the creative life forces of the inner space by the use of all the faculties that constitute our being—it is to exercise inwardness" (Hart, 2010, p. 104).

Through the design, development, and teaching of American Indian Spirituality and Philosophical Thought, the classroom became the touchstone of dramatic inward changes for me. I could now freely expose my soul in a course that demanded full payment. In many respects the classroom reflected my innermost convictions about life. "The kind of classroom situation one creates is the acid test of what one really stands for" (Tompkins, 1990). I needed to know: What were the students thinking? What were they feeling? How were they processing and understanding core concepts?

I needed a strategy to unlock these hidden mysteries of the heart. Initially, I decided to have the students write short papers (1-6 pages). They were to academically and personally respond in writing to key questions related to readings, lectures, videos, and classroom discussions. There were three parts to these responsive writings: In Part 1, they were to paraphrase key ideas and concepts from the readings; in Part 2, they were to respond to key questions based on the readings; and in Part 3, they were to reflect and comment on their personal reactions to the readings. Parts 1 and 2 would be "graded," and Part 3 (not graded) was to be a confidential exchange between us. Actually, Part 3 was of most interest to me because it would reveal the students' innermost responses to the concepts and ideas in the course.

These written responses (mostly in Part 3) became the key to finding out how they were creating meaningful connections to the readings, discussions, and the general content of the course. It required an inward look. It required clarification of one's purpose. It required finding a sense of meaning. It required *mamatowisin*—the connection of mind, body, and spirit.

It was from their writings that I realized the students were being additionally challenged to "see with a native eye" while suspending their own Western worldview that viewed human beings as dominant over nature and separate from nature. In short, it was critical for all of my students to learn to see the world differently. They had to view humans as integral to nature rather than dominant over or separate from nature. Otherwise, they would misunderstand and misinterpret nature-based ceremonial and ritual practices. I had to switch to an experiential modality. It meant that I had to challenge myself to practice *mamatowisin* in teaching.

In teaching with *mamatowisin*, the heart is aroused. The atmosphere is electric. A student is typing. Her braille machine clicking at a faster pace as the room gets caught up in the moment. The person signing for the hearing impaired student is equally excited. It is a classroom setting that allows spontaneity yet encourages the reflective pause as one ponders newly formed ideas.

More and more, I began to understand and realize that my students had to traverse new conceptual terrain. They had to understand a relational worldview and experience "the manifest and subtle power running through all [of] nature" (Versluis, 1992, p.15). They had to experience *theophany* or divine revelation (Versluis, 1992, p.10). From this profound and critical vantage point, they could further their knowledge of the indigenous way of knowing, which was personal, oral, experiential, holistic, and conveyed in narrative or metaphorical language (Hart, 2010).

Gradually, I broadened writing to encompass all manner of creative response. For example, I gave students readings on the rites of passage of the Kwakiutl tribe (from the Pacific Northwest) and the Dine tribe (from the Southwest). These ceremonial rites of passage marked the transition from being a child to being an adult. After the students read the assigned readings related to these rites of passage, we discussed them at length in class using video, interactive lecture with Power Point, and small and large group discussion formats.

Not wanting them to regurgitate this specific information related to these ceremonial rites of passage, I asked the students to describe in a reflective journal format (6 typewritten pages) their rites of passage. They were to highlight their major, life-changing events and personal experiences that served as their "rites of passage." Their responses were amazing. One of the students (English major) wrote 85 pages in her journal entry! She told me her entire life story with a note letting me know that I could stop reading at the end of page 6. She had me spellbound.

As the students deepened their understanding and spiritual praxis, their writing became much more descriptive and metaphorical. What they were experiencing was beyond the linear and cognitive. It encompassed more than mere understanding and cogitation. They were entering *mamatowisin.*

As an example, here are some excerpts from a student's journal entry on his rites of passage:

> These personal journals are like lancing an infected boil; the psyche leaks all over the place. Suddenly there is the attempted suicide, half-truths about heroin and opium, death of a friend. The rites of passage are often stained with pain. I have a certain animosity towards confession and the alleviation of guilt, probably because of my background in the United Pentecostal Church. Some thoughts and experiences are best left unsaid.

* * *

Because this course is focused on spirituality, I've decided to tell three different stories, each with a definingly different spiritual frequency. These aren't necessarily rites of passage, but they do reflect seasons of spirituality, transitions, the dying and being born, the putting down and picking up.

* * *

...It took us the better part of seven hours to reach the final plateau before we reached the peak of the mountain. We were exhausted. We all knew we had to go on but we felt a little defeated. The last climb was going to be difficult as it was covered with ice and snow patches. We pressed on. I entered into the pain and the lack of breath. I was both calm and insane at the same time. As I got nearer and nearer to the peak, I felt my energy reviving. We climbed the last 100 yards quickly and nimbly. The top.

* * *

We sat silent in the cold wind.

Next is a poem written by another student who chose to participate in an Inipi ceremony, also known as the "sweat." It's a ceremony where one physically and psychologically detoxifies and is embraced in the "womb" once again. It is a "rebirth." This particular cold November night was white with snow and quite cold but it clearly was transformative for this student.

The Home Journey
1

This time I entered from the East
after a road that was strange to my hands
a mood of an already started ceremony
proving sweetly, my inner side.
A rare evening
conspires with my heart
to move in unison.

And there was something
definitely in the way
the twilight played in me
melodies I didn't know I had.
In the darkness

I hear the sounds of mother earth
the rhythm that generation after generation
 of rape
by the stranger thought to be Quetzalcoatl
have not erased.

11
Wakan Tanka, mother earth, great spirit;
allow me to take communion with you,
to transcend,
to become you.
Let me rest in the warmth of your womb
in the micro cosmos of which I am part.

Heal my wounds
for my journey has been long
and the battle debilitating.
Allow me to be born again
in the midst of your sacred fire
so I can reconnect with all other nations
as one.

111

I exit from the West
sandwiched in the brief moment
between the acts of physical and spiritual realms
I let spirals of sacred smoke
rise from my body
to the starry sky.
I let a tear go down
while the world resounds in my chest
as I realize I've finally
come home.

These excerpts were not the exception. Students embraced the opportunity to expand their horizons, to listen to similar journeys from their peers, and, above all, they enjoyed being in relationship—embracing their humanness and the other than human world. They had "finally come home."

When evaluating the students' papers/entries, I encouraged them to initially write freely. Then they were to go back and edit their final product before submitting it. A prerequisite for taking American Indian Spirituality and Philosophical Thought is a facility with the mechanics of writing. In general, my rubric is simple. The guiding assessment questions are: Was this written response a true measure of the student's understanding? Is it a cyclical measure of how far the student has traveled in his/her inward journey of the heart—a truly reflective/spiritual practice, encouraging a lifetime commitment and transformation? Above all, does the writing reflect *mamatowisin?*

In conclusion, these reflective and creative writing strategies gave me glimpses into the hearts and souls of the students (regardless of ethnicity and cultural background) from whom I learned so much. That is to say, instructional strategies that integrate mind, body, and spirit are consistent with the need to be fulfilled as a human being. Such integrated practices are reflective of the perennial wisdom of indigenous peoples. As I continue to explore the different facets of teaching and learning, I know that creative writing in its various formats will continue to reveal the hidden dimensions of the human heart and will gradually impact systemic change from the inside... as we practice *mamatowisin.*

References

Ermine, W. (1995). Aboriginal epistemology (pp. 101-112) cited in Hart, Michael (2010). "Indigenous Worldviews, Knowledge, and Research Paradigm." Journal of Indigenous Voices in Social Work, 1 (1), pp. 1-16).

Neuliep, J. W. (2015) *Intercultural communication: A contextual approach*. Sage: Los Angeles.

Tompkins, J. (1990) "The pedagogy of the distressed." *College English,* 52(6), pp. 653-660.

Versluis, A. (1992) *Sacred Earth: The spiritual landscape of Native America*. Inner Traditions International: Vermont.

Writing Exercise: Suggestion for Journal Writing

Journal writing is unique in offering you the opportunity to deal in a very personal way with the content of a course. You'll long remember the connections you've made to an idea or concept that made an impression on you in class. Below is a suggestion that may be helpful to you.

The Big Questions Journal

There are some courses that lend themselves to asking the big questions about humanity and the universe—the tri-world of humans, nature, and the supernatural, and their relationships. They pose questions such as *Who are we? Where have we been before birth? Where will we go after death? For what do we live? How should we relate to other humans, nature, and the spirits?* This level of questioning is where I would like to reside permanently because these can lead to immediate insights that are imaginative, creative, and enlightening. In the end, these questions are probably the most transformative for yourself as you progress through your creative writing experiences.

The Tyranny of Grammar

Complete this Sentence: Say it Loud! _____!

Brenda Bell Brown

> It is not without heart that we write narratives that make you cry, "It's so hard to decipher." Why, we tell our stories with such fluid phrases that demand you stop (a long time) and think (those who wanna, gonna). We are the writers who don't mind the critique that "most readers just won't get it." We have to admit, it's no fault of ours, we just ain't thinkin' 'bout you.
>
> —She Sine Do, *This Is Why I Write: And You?, in the present tense*

Though a fictitious author, She Sine Do sums up the passion and sentiment conveyed by many-a-writer-of-color (like me) who no longer stops to ponder any questions pertaining to the who, why and forthwith of their writing output. These writers now write with the fury of those on fire, replicating the urgency of the #BlackLivesMatter movement with equal regard for Chicano-Latino, Asian, Native American, other disenfranchised and Allied people who are pressing for dramatic, socio-political change for humanity's sake. Their... our writing bears the impress of self-actualization that has become more noticeable, on the whole, because the love of self, kin, and friend has been, as the young folk say, "put on *blast*" with this hyper-culturally conscious movement. And there is no indication of it coming to a slow roll any time soon.

These... *us writers* are writing with a vengeance.

Me? Actually, I thought that we had always done so. I can boast that sensibility based on the up-bringing that I was privileged to receive as a child growing up in a historically Black suburb in Memphis, TN. My ninth birthday came two days before the assassination of the Rev. Dr. Martin Luther King in my homeplace. I don't know about you, but as a child who declared themselves an artist—poet, actress, crafter— early in life, from that point on a lot of emphasis was placed on me and my fellow child artists to be raised up in the correct aesthetic. My teachers, both within and without of the classroom—at home, in the church, at our youth social clubs, in the theatre—my teachers, they chose well the work that we were creatively-teethed on. It was an imperative of the Movement, and we were caught up in the flow.

Recitation of James Weldon Johnson's "The Creation" was my go-to piece for many special occasions or when called upon to "recite something nice" for a church or civic group. "Ego Tripping" and "The Great Pax Whitie" by Nikki Giovanni became the spoken-word pieces interpreted by me and other young, Black Memphis girls. We danced to it in scoop-necked black leotards, while Nikki's voice blended with the spirit-filled melody of the Reverend James Cleveland's choir. We worked that Black-themed choreo-poem on stages in schools throughout the Mid-South.

My junior-year History class, taught by the very learned Ms. Ora Rockwell, opened every session with readings from her personal copy of *Dark Symphony: Negro Literature in America*. We chose the lit to be read and she found the historical context for the subject matter in our text book and guided us through our learning and discussions with some very candid and personal lectures. That teacher. Ms. Rockwell.

So many of my teachers set a high bar for learning and execution when it came to the literary arts. And they used, as guiding principle and form for most of my secondary-school subjects, the Black cultural aesthetic. So, when I left my cocoon of Black culture and pride to study at a predominantly White college up-North, I was armed.

So many folk had taken me aside to inform me that "things would be different." However, they added, "don't you change." So, I didn't. I couldn't. The Movement was still going, and I had been literally equipped for the charge. At the university, when I was introduced to the man who would become my mentor in theatre and literature—Professor George Houston Bass—I was effectively and most efficiently passed from my teachers in Memphis to the man who was the former secretary to Langston Hughes, and writer in his own right.

He was also a native of Nashville, the home of the historically Black Fisk University with its celebrated Fisk University singers; where the celebrated art professor Aaron Douglass' Black Renaissance murals graced walls in its Administration Building; where the schooling of Nikki Giovanni and Judith Jamison and Roland Hayes, and so many others, took place.

Under Bass' mentorship, I maintained my voice and reinforced it with the life and lifestyles of Black America that I grew up with in my birthplace and beyond.

That voice has persisted, to this day, because I know for whom I write.

Laughing out loud, I will share this, an excerpt for a work-in-progress...

CeeCee ran so fast that her flip flop broke. Man! Right beside the pig pen. She held her breath as she propped herself against the black walnut tree, struggling to get the thong part through the messed up incised hole that made her dust-stained, sky blue rubber slipper keep coming off her foot! After a few minutes of stench-assailed frustration, she kicked both flops off. She chucked them into the field by the road and ran barefoot, all the way home.

MayMay, May-Ree! May-Ree! Mayyyyy-Ree!

Chile'! I'm right here!

CeeCee didn't see her Mama on the side of the house, tending her spring tomatoes. May-Ree liked to hunker down low when she worked in the garden, hidden from sight, deep into the vines of her prizewinning tomatoes ripening red in the sun. She popped up quick, for an old woman most known for her slow, steady ways.

I'm here!

CeeCee waved her bony arm at her Mama as she kept on running up to their front porch. By the time she had reached the house, CeeCee had clocked 6 miles (4 barefootin'); seen pigs sloppin', horses chewin', cows grazin', chickens steppin', 1 coon, 2 green snakes sunnin', and a lotta' bird, mostly raven; she had skimmed over many a sharp stone until one finally got her. She tracked ruby red blood from the front door way to the bathroom. Grabbing a bottle of peroxide and a vial of mercurochrome out of the medicine cabinet, she rushed back to her mother, swabbing her toe prints of blood with a wad of wet Scott*sch* that she had jabbed between her toes.

All done,

May-Ree declared when finished with her doctoring. She scooped CeeCee up like a baby doll, and treated her to a piggyback ride to her favorite chair on the porch. Fussing a mile a' minute, *talkin' 'bout how CeeCee sure to get flat feet for going barefoot so much*, May-Ree bent over her baby and placed a Band-Aid that she just happened to have in her apron pocket over the cut on CeeCee's sole. She sported arms akimbo when she straightened up and asked

Now, what was you runnin' for?

An even longer excerpt from this piece of speculative fiction that places the heart and soul of the "The Movement" in the nature and nurture of a Southern town named Justice had caused my classmates undue consternation. They cite my persistence in writing in the Black Southern vernacular, using phraseology that is steeped in Black phraseology with its African roots quite pronounced is what makes this work as intriguing as it is difficult. As with any workshopped piece, you take notes and thank your critics for a) taking the time to read your work, and b) taking additional time to think deeply enough to provide constructive criticism. It truly helps.

However, it is still up to you, the writer, to decide whether or not to hold firm on those elements which make your story intact and its messaging hit home for the audience you intend. It is better for your sanity and your time to go into the project with a strong grasp of your intended audience and your commitment to their reading satisfaction. It saves you a lot of rewrite time even with all the technical aspects considered because, most importantly, it keeps the text true to you. Truth will provide context, making relevant those technical flaws on any given day. Just be mindful of those consistent, contextual flaws that persist in the process of honing your voice, your craft. They may very well be the diamonds in your rough drafts.

As for my insistence on "writing Black," my literary attitude is based on the fact that I love it. Do tell, I am in good company: Nobel prizewinner Toni Morrison, my revered elder in the discipline, welcomes the term "black writer." Says Morrison,

> I'm writing for black people... in the same way that Tolstoy was not writing for me, a 14-year-old coloured girl from Lorain, Ohio. I don't have to apologise or consider myself limited because I don't [write about white people]—which is not absolutely true, there are lots of white people in my books. The point is not having the white critic sit on your shoulder and approve it.

The "white critic" that Morrison references alludes to writer James Baldwin's embodiment of his self-critical angst, "a little white man deep inside of all of us." Morrison disavows the need for such a critic, noting that she "never really had it.... I just never did."

There is a Movement.

It is a constant.
It is gaining Momentum.
It is evident.
Drum majorettes like Morrison are keeping time.
We writing to the same beat.

References

Bell Brown, B. (in progress, unpublished) O'er Roun'da Hightower: Makedo The Source Of The Power.

Elbow, P. (2012) *Vernacular eloquence: What speech can bring to writing.* New York: Oxford University Press.

Emanuel, J. A. (1968). *Dark symphony: Negro literature in America.* New York: Free Press.

Giovanni, N. (January 01, 1970). The Great Pax Whitie. *Black Feeling, Black Talk, Black Judgement.*

Hoby, H. "Toni Morrison: 'I'm writing for black people... I don't have to apologise." *The Guardian*, online, April 25, 2015.

Johnson, J. W. (1994). *The creation.* New York: Holiday House.

Sargent, E. & Paraskevas, C., eds. (2005) *Conversations about writing: Eavesdropping, inkshedding, and joining in.* Toronto: Nelson Thompson.

Writing Exercise:
For You, For Us, For Them: an exercise in inkspilling & inkshedding

In his book *Vernacular Eloquence: What Speech Can Bring to Writing,* Peter Elbow urges writers to employ the "wisdom of the tongue" to produce writing that is both natural and strong. Citing aspects of tone and voice, Elbow reveals their relationship with writing in terms of "the language activity most people find easiest—speaking—for the language activity most people find hardest—writing."

Think of one of those times when you have lapsed into speech patterns that only your family or close friends are ever privy to hearing as you excitedly talked, free and strong. Spend 10 minutes "free-writing" about your topic of discussion, employing unplanned speech practice in this rigorous writing exercise. Note that this type of writing helps ideas to flow unfettered and is known to facilitate invention. Remember: take just 10 minutes to *freewrite*, a term that Peter Elbow uses to describe writing that flows from your pen as intensely as free speech rolls from your tongue—the natural one.

Segment what you wrote into three distinct passages:

- a personal message that is just meant for or that would only be fully understood by a very close friend or family member;

- a passage that could be shared with a large group of people with whom you share a particular affinity—interest, racial or ethnic identity, cause, etc.; and

- a segment intended for the public-at-large.

Note the ways in which you used language in each segment. Was it done in a manner that clearly indicates who is being talked to/to whom this particular passage is directed?

Then, take those segments and write a full, cohesive paragraph that incorporates each category using what Elbow calls "inkspilling" for singular, personal composition. Note the relative level of ease *and* difficulty that went into writing for each audience, and the connective sentencing that you are now using to make those three segments flow into a singular paragraph. No matter your topic, you may find yourself second-guessing the ability of one or all, each separate group, to under-stand exactly what you are trying to share in this comprehensive paragraph. If the underlying purpose of writing is to communicate via the written word, why make the act of comprehension difficult for any potential reader? *Do not be tempted to censor yourself.* Merely write to make your message understood, as you craft your passages with your various audiences in mind.

To take this exercise a step further, share the first draft of your inkspill with one or more other writers and "inkshed" or workshop your paragraph to incorporate their responses. In this day and age of "pile on" social media messaging, the practice of inkshedding is yet one more way to share experiences outside of your own via the written word.

Crazy

Chris Stark

Crazy, one of the white male MFA students laughed as we sat in our graduate fiction class waiting for the professor.

Definitively, another agreed—the straight white man with long dreadlocks who'd recently admonished one of my stories featuring a homeless, lesbian teenager protagonist for being "too outside the mainstream." He said I created a character with multiple oppressions to get attention.

A handful of white male graduate students joined in the laughter. The rest of us sat mute.

A well-known Native woman writer was the target of their ridicule. She'd been brought in for a week of workshops culminating in a reading the evening before our fiction class. She is one of my favorite writers. The white male graduate students went on to mock her description of her writing process and her views of the power and place of stories in culture. Mostly, I remember them laughing at her as I sat there, horrified at their disrespect and privilege, and immobilized by the word "crazy."

That was not the first time white male graduate students in my program denigrated women-of-color writers. In the same room, during a class on first year composition pedagogy for teaching assistants, another white male graduate student had lectured us on how, in his undergraduate Composition 101 course, he, an unpublished teaching assistant, would fail all of the poems of a prolific and well known African American woman poet and professor who'd worked with us in the same visiting writer series as the Native woman. He said her poems would not meet the standards of his freshman composition class. His delivery was animated. He strode around the classroom. He gestured wildly. He took up space. He wrote on the chalkboard in his lilting, curling cursive that had previously been identified by another male student as handwriting "obviously by a female." He detailed the reasons why her poems would receive Fs. No, he was not the lecturer. No, he was not supposed to deliver a sample lesson for the day. He seemed to feel *moved* to drive home how inferior this Black woman's poems were. He just could not sit still. He just could not be silent.

No one silenced him.

My ancestry is a crazy quilt—different patches from across the world brought together by migrations, immigrations, emigrations, colonization—all made possible by the attempted genocide on Turtle Island. As a mixed Native lesbian whose family hid our Native ancestry, or spoke of being Indian but did not participate in Native culture, and never discussed our missing family murdered in the Shoah until my grandmother was on her death bed, I felt what was not there, what was tangible yet invisible. I felt it through my grandmothers' confusion, loneliness and grief. I felt it through the loss they carried. I felt it through my ancestors' spirits—always present but not real to the world I lived in. I knew to hide the spiritual experiences and knowledge I had as a child. I knew, instinctively, I would "get in trouble."

I knew I would be viewed as "crazy."

As a mixed Native lesbian who grew up in a violent home and was told repeatedly by the rapists in my family and outside my family that if I told anyone about the abuse, no one would believe me—people would think I was *crazy*, all those decades later I tucked myself into the desk I sat at, surprised, mildly shocked, angry. Silent. That chord of silence followed me from my childhood, that chord of silence came to me from my grandmothers and their grandmothers before them back to the beginning of the murder of the people on Turtle Island, back to the slavery of Indigenous people, back to the sexual and physical violence, back to the stolen land and houses and crops and iron kettles left boiling on the stoves when Native families fled their homes because the military was coming, back to the Two-Spirit people torn apart by dogs the Spaniards set on them, back to the death marches the U.S. government sent the Cherokee, Dine and others on and that Hitler later used on Jewish people. The silence and shock traveled backwards and forwards, disrupting time and space until the threads found their current place: in a dismal, basement classroom in southern Minnesota where straight white men continued the ideology that began five hundred years earlier, that wiped out over 90% of the people on this land, that scattered my Indigenous relatives into whatever crevice and crack they could find where they had to hide to live. I sat in that classroom like someone had my tongue.

Someone did have my tongue. A lot of someones, over the course of my lifetime, right down to the way my DNA is written. Epigenetics is a new field of study in "Western science" (which, of course, does not include Native science present on "Western" land for tens of thousands of years). According to "Western science," ancestors' emotions, such as

depression, become written into our DNA. Historical trauma, something frequently discussed in Native, Jewish, and African American
communities is not only this "thing" that happened *X* number of years
ago, but ways of knowing and being in the world become embedded in
descendants' bodies. The experiences of our grandparents and great
grandparents are written into our DNA—the library of our bodies.
Spiritual connection with ancestors is not unusual or supernatural in
Native communities. It's a given. It's a pressure, a presence, a
knowledge, a knowing—their loss and screams written in me, their loss
and screams and pain and murder and rape merged with my own as a
child, a girl pinned to my bed as the weight and rage of the world
forced its way into me. I never screamed out loud. I screamed inside,
where I met my ancestors, and our screams became one and so I
carried them forward in that way. We carry them through time. We
remember.

I wrote the bulk of my first novel, *Nickels: A Tale of Dissociation*,
while I was in an MFA program. It's a novel of prose poems with very
little punctuation. Written in first person, present tense, the book
immerses the reader in the mind of a young, white and Native, lesbian
girl whose father rapes her for years, and whose parents both
participate in abusive and frightening homophobic behavior toward
the girl. The book gives voice, or rather voices, as the girl develops
dissociative identities to survive, to a character who is silenced in the
novel, and by extension to people from those social groups in our
society. The protagonist belongs to some of the same social groups I
belong to, but she is not me. The few times I workshopped the book in
my MFA program, I was criticized for writing about someone similar
to me, for writing about myself. Never once, in the MFA workshops or
in other writing groups I have been in has a white man been "accused"
of writing about himself, even when he clearly is writing about himself
and his experiences. I remember sitting in a poetry class, filling up with
bitterness, as I had just been "accused" of such a thing while the white
male professor read his story about a white man hiking in the forest.
We all knew he drew upon an experience he had for this story, but no
one said a thing.

It seems that for those of us considered "outsiders," we cannot own
or define our own writing. Implicit in that is that we are not to tell our
own stories, fictionalized or not. Implicit in that is that we do not get
to have stories. We are to listen, be silent, and be awed by the "right
way" to tell a story, as defined by those in the ruling class going back

to Aristotle. Native writers, specifically, are criticized for not having a climax, for telling stories in a cyclical fashion, for not following that checkmark structure we were taught since elementary school. As a writer, I have experienced this many times, and as a teacher, I have watched my Native students struggle with these issues as well, but without an understanding that it is a cultural difference being expressed through the very structure of their stories. In the classroom, I always bring up the culture of "how to tell a story" or "good writing."

One day on my way to teach at North Dakota State University I heard an Asian writer discussing the cultural differences between what she called "Asian writing" versus "Western argumentative writing." She said that the linear style taught in Western cultures would be thought of as stupid in Asian cultures. She said an argument paper is written in a cyclical style until the writer arrives at an answer. Even the literary concept of "conflict" is culturally based. Man versus nature. Man versus man. Man versus Self. Man versus Society. This is not "truth." It is not the only way to write, to view the self and the world. It's a viewpoint. An aspect of an individualistic culture in love with the idea of a white, straight, male hero who exerts great strength and willpower despite all the odds, i.e. despite nature, despite other men, despite his own demons, despite society. It is, in a nutshell, the ideology of manifest destiny, of white male Amerikkka—the outcast hero conquering all. So if you don't belong to a culture that idolizes those traits, or you want to tell a different kind of story, and you want to write, what do you do? Your writing won't be considered by many to be any good. You might even get slammed in some dank classroom somewhere by an overzealous teaching assistant.

Just like when I was a girl, and knew to keep the spiritual experiences to myself, I did not share anymore of *Nickels* with my classes. It was not that the professors and all my classmates were hostile or mean spirited, but they did not know what to do with the writing. They did not know how to make sense of it. They had no *place* for it. Therefore, I had no place in the classroom to explore and share my work on the book. I knew their reactions would stunt, disrupt, and perhaps stop my ability to get down the story. For example, parts of *Nickels* consist of a chorus of voices commenting on the protagonist's experiences. During a workshop, a professor asked, *Is it like a Greek chorus?* Perhaps it is *like* a Greek chorus, but it is not a Greek chorus. It is something else that I don't necessarily know how to articulate. It does not have a name in English. It does not exist in English. Therefore, it does not exist in literature either. It is like music. It is like a pounding in the head. It is like a surge of energy. It is like all the hair on your head standing on end, connecting with unseen.

Some Western psychologists would say it's the dissociative selves of the girl. Others would say it is any variety of other disorders. But indigenous ways would describe it as something beyond the girl's psychology, beyond the individual self of the girl. It is the voices of spirits watching over the girl. Spirits. *Manidoog*. Ancestors. Those with the girl. I have a sensation, an indescribable knowing, about what this is, something I know in my being, but something I cannot convey in the English language. I have experienced this with elders when talking about dissociation and trauma. More than once, elder Native women have broken down during these discussions, sobbing. They say they lost their language when abused in boarding schools or the public schools systems. And when they lost their language, they lost their ability to experience or understand or convey Native concepts, because English does not have those same concepts and therefore does not have words to describe what is beyond the parameters of the English language. I feel this myself, although I never spoke Tsalagi Gawinhisidi or Anishinaabemowin as a girl. Yet descendants know and feel beyond the parameters of English. Therefore, when writing *Nickels*, I had to bend, twist, and break the rules of English to best get at different cultural experiences, realities, and awarenesses beyond "white ways."

While writing, I took the lid off of "the grammar rulebook" and at times I "found myself" (versus had a conscious thought and followed that thought) combining sentences in a way I do not recall seeing or thinking about previously. The last word or few words of a sentence would end up being the beginning of the next sentence. Later, I read that this structure is similar to Indigenous languages. Again, I was astonished. In the process of writing *Nickels*, I was unearthing buried aspects of my Indigenous ancestry. When I first began writing *Nickels*, I wrote with punctuation, and then removed it. Obviously, punctuation would make connecting sentences in this manner impossible, so I dropped any thoughts of including punctuation. Once I made this final decision, it was like my writing bloomed from one brightly colored beaded Woodlands flower into an entire forest scene of flowers with twirling green tendrils connecting them all. Another downside to using punctuation is the way it would separate and disrupt the girl's thoughts as they sometimes tumble around each other, come out in rapid fire, and weave and twist around each other. I wanted this to be as experiential as possible to the reader—I wanted the readers to hear the girl in her own style, not translated into "proper English." So the punctuation had to go. Such that when I showed a "prose poem" section of *Nickels* to my class, and the professor asked, seeming somewhat perplexed and somewhat intrigued, *Is that like a Greek Chorus,* I simply said, *Yes.*

Although I stopped workshopping *Nickels*, I wrote, and I allowed myself to write with freedom, in a way that is true to someone with dissociation, is true to someone who is Native, is true to the protagonist who, in my experience, existed somewhere, she and her story, and it was my task to find her and it, and get it down on the page.[1] When I sat down to write, I had to find and grab the protagonist, as she and her story already existed in my experience. The Native woman writer my classmates ridiculed also discussed stories in this way. As I remember it, this was the main reason they referred to her as "crazy." Upon release of *Nickels*, I was honored to be part of the reading series at my alma mater. When asked to describe my process, I said that for me, it is like the story exists elsewhere, and I have been charged with going to find it, and bringing it back as intact as possible. No one said anything derogatory, but it felt the same as it had five years earlier. Saying a story has a life of its own that exists alongside the "writer," of course, questions issues beyond "the writing process." It challenges the foundation of Western philosophies: the emphasis on the individual and *his* will power to bring into being versus something more complex, a co-creator relationship with the story that acknowledges the story as its own entity, as having its own essence, or spirit.

This is crazy, when considered while perched on the lip of the dominant culture. However, many indigenous cultures have world views similar to this (as do some white writers). One of the graduate students at my alma mater told me privately that she'd heard a well known white woman writer express her writing process similarly. In writing my second novel, *Carnival Lights*, the experience is the same although the story and style are different. A year ago I thought I had the novel completed. As I prepared to send it to my publisher, a character emerged with his entire backstory, set in the late 1800s. He is a Native teenager violently murdered by three white men. He, Leonard, emerged along with his backstory in a few minutes. It sprung out of me, as real as anything in my life, and then I sobbed, unable to write for a week. Grief poured through me for the teenage character, who felt more to me like a long-lost ancestor, buried in an unmarked grave in Little Falls, Minnesota and written into my DNA, than a figment of my imagination.

In *Nickels*, sentence structure, tense, point-of-view (switches among her different "parts"), repetition (common among trauma survivors and in oral storytelling), and punctuation work together to disrupt white, Western notions of time and space. They work with the themes of the psychological state known as "dissociation" in "Western" psychology and with the Indigenous understanding that we are one with our ancestors, including the idea that when we heal ourselves, it works "backwards" in time and heals our ancestors too. My *we'ah*, Earl Hoaglund from the White Earth reservation, told me that what the dominant society calls dissociation, or Dissociative Identity Disorder, is, in Anishinaabe culture, viewed as a gift. He said "dissociative" abilities are gifts from the spirits and were given to me so I could survive my childhood. He also said he had to travel throughout the U.S. and Canada for years, meeting with elders and traditionalists, so that he could gain these gifts for the people. In other words, these abilities, viewed as a pathology in the dominant culture, are in Anishinaabe culture gifts that helped him to conduct ceremonies. Therefore, what are viewed as "gifts" that allow some to help others heal, are considered "crazy" by white culture.

Given that these are Anishinaabe ways, it is not an enormous leap to say that the dominant culture in the U.S. views Native cultures as crazy, or mentally ill if you are "sensitive" and "politically correct." Another elder told me he is careful about what he tells to whom, given how the dominant society views traditional Native ways. Indeed, the association between Indians and insanity is evidenced by The Hiawatha Insane Asylum for Indians, built in Canton, South Dakota, in the late 1800s. Native people, especially leaders, were brought to languish there. Eileen Hudon, an elder from White Earth, said the only time she ever heard an adult say something mean to children was when the adult would tell a child who was acting up that s/he would be sent to St. Peter Asylum for the Criminally Insane. Canadian Native people were also sent all the way to St. Peter, located in southern Minnesota, ironically about 20 minutes from where I did my MFA program. So all these threads from the past, present, "real" life, and novel writing weave into one large tapestry. Differences, in Anishinaabe ways, are considered to be gifts that make a person valuable and gifted to the rest of the tribe. Differences are honored. In white ways, most differences are pathologized. Crazy.

Notes

1. I am not saying all people with dissociation and all Native people are the same, but rather that I was writing from these identities.

Writing Exercise

Choose 4-5 songs from musicians you have not listened to before. I choose a variety of male and female singers, styles, and cultures. For instance, when I do this exercise with my classes, I might play a song from Big Hat, an ethereal 90s band from Chicago; Tanya Tagaq, an Inuit punk throat singer; Monkey, a Chinese opera adapted by Fred Ho and the Afro Asian Music Ensemble; a song from a Finnish "alt" band from the 80s singing in Finnish; and The Wallets, an 80s alternative band from Minneapolis. Listen to each song and, using "associational logic," jot down whatever comes to your mind, including colors, place, people, images, events, time, and so on. After having listened to all of the songs, choose one, create a narrator associated in some way with the music—perhaps a janitor at a venue where the music is being performed, or a person riding public transportation while listening to the music on her/his headphones. Then, write a short story incorporating the music in one way or another.

When I use Fred Ho's music, I also play a traditional Chinese opera so the students are able to see and hear the opera. Chinese operas are melodic instead of harmonic, are sung in Chinese, and often employ different instruments than Western operas. Hearing (and watching on You Tube) a Chinese opera is, for me, a mind expanding experience (as is listening to music sung in Finnish). When I listen to music outside my cultural norms, I can practically feel my neurons growing. Hearing music radically different from our norm makes us consider how "beautiful" in one culture is not necessarily experienced as beautiful in another. This is a powerful reminder about (not) using descriptors like "beautiful," "awesome," "good," and so on as what is "good" or "beautiful" to one reader is not necessarily considered "good" or "beautiful" to another. This exercise can also be a good opportunity to pay particular attention to avoiding clichés and stereotypical characters in our writing. For me, writing is like being in semi-trance state, as is listening to music, especially music from other cultures. Combining the two makes for alchemy.

Saying My Name with Happiness

Ching-In Chen

I grew up with my mother's tightlipped lack of curiosity (her non-response to my million *Why? How? Where? What?* questions) and my father's opposite practice of bullshitting his way through and flourishing the bare bones of a story into an entertaining saga. They were my first writing teachers, teaching me hunger and desire, how to follow a story beyond its original borders.

When my mother told a story, I listened close. Like going out to eat at a restaurant, it was a treat because it was so rare. My mother's stories were usually instructive. There was the story of the man who was so lazy, his wife worried about him when her sister got sick and she had to leave him to go and take care of her. She made him a big pancake which she draped around his neck so he would have something to eat while she was away. He was so lazy that after eating the ring of pancake around his neck, he starved to death rather than lift his finger to move the other bits of pancake where his mouth could reach them. There was the story of the daughter who cut into herself and used the blood to make a broth to feed to her mother to make her well. My mother told me these stories to teach me how to be a good daughter, to chide me into action when I wanted to be lazy. For everything else, especially when it came to stories about our larger, extended family, I was on a need-to-know basis.

My father, on the other hand, liked to chat—and loved being asked *Why this, Why that*. My father would test out hypotheses and What Ifs on his listeners—but my brother and I only figured out as we got older that he might not always be completely accurate in what he relayed to his listeners.

I kept these bits of story from both my parents and tucked them away, this connective tissue I imagined between the bones of the worlds I navigated—the inner story, inner world which my family constructed—and an outer one which I visited in school. And I started narrating my own stories to myself—keeping myself company as a lonely child knows how.

As I grew older and learned more English at school, my mother started putting her written words in front of me for correction. I read her strung-together words, at her request, smoothing them over into generic sentences that would not betray the way she formed her words.

I learned that the ability that I had to re-shape language and to intuitively pinpoint what sounded correct to the ear was one which could gain me power. The child I was in the hallway at school—who tripped over and swallowed my own words—could re-imagine each scenario with dreamt-up friends who would stand with me and not be ashamed of who I was, not be ashamed of my family.

This shame began at a young age, when nobody could say my name correctly. They called me ChingChong, ChickenWings and ChopSticks. I wanted so much to be rid of my name that I asked my family for my birthday for a different name. A WASP name, Elizabeth, which would make me normal. My mother did not say anything, though my name meant Happiness. Instead, she quietly and fiercely took me by the hand to the courthouse for my birthday and granted my request. At school, not much changed. I still was different, colored, unfashionable, ugly, strange. At home though, my parents had acquired a flexibility with my identity—calling me Yee-Lah-Sah-Bai, Elizabeth (if in front of white people), and Ching-In. They honored my wish, yet didn't leave my other identity behind.

Looking back now, I realize that I learned much of my internalized hatred and shame at school—in social situations, but also in the classroom. I never read a piece of writing by a writer of color or a writer who identified as an LGBTQIA writer—and only one piece of writing by a woman in any English class throughout elementary, middle or high school.

I loved to tell myself stories, but I didn't see myself as a writer, just a weird lonely kid trying to get through to the end of the day when the last bell rang and I could go home. In fact, I learned that writing could be dangerous in the false impressions that it might give others of an inner world they did not have access to.

I did write a fictional story about a girl my age whose mother had passed away. When my father picked up the page and started reading and relaying what was written on the page to my mother, they both became angry, though I tried to tell them it was just a made-up story. *What if someone picked it up like me and thought it was true, or worse, that you wanted your mother dead?* asked my father. He asked me to not write such things in the future. I learned then the possibility that writing had to call into being what you might want to see in the world.

When I was 16 years old, I was pulled into the guidance office at my high school and told about a community which would change my life. I was told about CAPAY, the Conference for Asian Pacific American Youth, which would draw Asian American youth all over Massachusetts to come together to talk about Asian American youth issues as a community. This was my first inkling that I might belong someplace outside of my tight-knit family—and going to the CAPAY conference connected me to other Asian American young people, many of whom shared my experiences. After CAPAY, I got a letter in the mail, inviting me to apply to an Asian American summer youth leadership program called YouthWrites.

That summer of my 16th year, I learned about Asian American history, and civil rights issues, and got to know the other Asian American youth. I met some who had similar experiences to me, as one of the few Asian American students in the school. It was just as important to me to hear stories very far from my own lived experience—such as escaping war or being put in an English-only classroom without understanding the language.

I learned to name my anger and my pain—and that I could choose to shape and write my story. I learned that there was much I wasn't being taught in school and learned to search out other kinds of knowledge. I created my own reading lists, each new author I discovered leading me to others—in their thank yous and acknowledgments, in their locations and in the journals which had given them space for their words. From this kind of research, I constructed a list of writers who I hoped could give me insight into my own histories.

This is still a principle that I adhere to in my own writing life—a realization that I can harness what I taught myself—that I had to learn on my own how to shape and write my own story. I have to remind myself that I've been doing this since I was young. My past experience with rewriting syntax, with surviving to the end of the last school day bell, helps me now as a poet. These experiences gave me a set of experiences to pull from as part of my writer's toolbox.

Those early days of writing—of discovering my own voice—led me to take back the name I was gifted as a child—Ching-In, which means Happiness. And I keep this story with me and offer it as a gift to those around me—to tell them that I found my way back to a place where I could say my name with happiness.

Writing Exercise

1. **Write an origin story for your name(s).** If you want, you can look up the definition of your name and borrow some of that language and/or imagery for use in the origin story, but it's not necessary.

2. **Write a tender letter to your name**—acknowledging any wounds or hurts or pain—and creating an intention or desire for another path your name could take into the world.

3. **Create your own reading list.** Include at least one writer who shares an identity you have, but also a writer who doesn't. Try to include a writer you wouldn't normally read.

Dancing Between Bamboos or
The Rules of Wrong Grammar

Marlina Gonzalez

> I still live in you /Mga kundiman, balagtasan, and harana /
> Music of bandurias /Beat of bamboo stalks
> > —Marlina Gonzalez, "Pilipinas Hindi Kita"

My challenge as one who speaks and writes in more than one tongue is having the puzzlement of a two-laned writing brain. I want to repeat the unforgettable stories chattering inside me. Stories spoken and written in the slow, thoughtful voice of our late *Inang* (my grandmother). Visually vivid memories shared by my *Mader* (mother), occasionally punctuated with the lilting *punto* (accent) of Nueva Ecijaños. The meandering, energetic, gestural, cinematic mind of our late *Fader* (father) whose pronunciations could zigzag from Laurence Olivier's British to indigenous *Pangasinense*[1], often told with his hands framing the world so you can see the movie screen in his mind.

In some way, seeing paragraphs like the one you just read, written with words from and with different languages, dialects, and diacritical marks, is a visual delight for me.

But my attempts to capture their indigenous vocabularies—multi-syllabic, rhythmic, deeply poetic, entertainingly naughty—are often interrupted by the grammatical imposition of my English Mostly education. My writing fingers wish to defy the language barriers between my first and second language, wishing to preserve the metaphors of the first—Tagalog. I find myself writing between two clapping bamboos. I wish I could offer single-language readers some magic potion to drink so that you too can skip with agility between my clashing languages.

Tagalog is derived from the word *taga-ilog*, meaning "of the river" or "one who hails from the river." I was born in Manila. The name itself is derived from the phrase *may nilad,* which literally means "there is a nilad (flower)." *Nilad* is a flower often seen floating or growing along the Pasig River. Even the name Pasig is a derivative of *"Paz, sigue me..."* , a final cry from a drowning Spaniard calling out to his Filipina lover Paz. "Paz, come with me!" Paz. Peace in Spanish.

So when I am asked, Where are you *really* from? What language do you speak?

I oblige with simple answers, albeit with a secret belly laugh. "I was born in Manila. My first language is Tagalog."

If you are satisfied by that simple response, you would have only heard a third of the answer. Because these simple sentences really carry three stories.

> I speak the language of the river that flows through the city
> where the flower *nilad* floats
> and where, legend has it
> a drowning Spaniard uttered a final request to his Filipina lover
> named Peace.

Jose Rizal, the revolutionary Filipino renaissance genius of literature, science and politics, wrote in one of his earliest poems, "Mother Tongue" (at the age of eight):

> Because by its language one can judge
> a town, a barrio, and kingdom[2]

Taglish, Engalog, Spanglish and My Bifurcated Tongue

Writers are the navigators of untraveled human voyages, the daring namers of cultural unmentionables, the audacious explainers of thoughts and sensations and emotions not readily explained by the puzzled soul. Add to that puzzlement the choice, if you are so privileged as to be multilingual, to speak in one or more languages.

I am not a willful multilingual. I am really multilingual by historical default. I dream/speak/write/love/swear in three languages, speak in 2.5 of these languages, write in two out of the three but can only speak or write one language at a time as a result of three centuries of Spanish rule (1521 to 1898) and just under five decades of U.S. occupation (1898 to 1946). Of the 170 languages spoken across 7,107 islands, there are only two official national languages. Filipino (based on Tagalog). And English.

Willful multilingual writers make a conscious choice to write in one of their chosen languages. Being a multilingual writer by historical default, my conscious and unconscious languages flow into and battle each other, with one language (English) wanting to dominate the narrative while the language of my heritage (Tagalog) insists on asserting its irresistible eloquence. But together, Taglish or Engalog is/are the language/s of my soul. One cannot exist without the other.

In October of 2013, autumn in Minnesota, *tag-ulan* (rainy season) in Luzon, I returned to the Philippines after 23 years, to immerse myself in Tagalog and to do research for my play about language and colonialism entitled *Isla Tuliro* (Island of Confusion), commissioned by Pangea World Theater[3] and Teatro Del Pueblo.[4] I wanted to capture the absurdly unique world of Tagalog using my multi-cultural languages.

The visceral experience of being surrounded by the language-of-the-river upon arrival in Manila presented a most powerful epiphany for me. Many questions were awakened inside me. Words and expressions, dormant for decades, sprouted out of me. Words with *malumi and malumay*[5] accents flooded my ears. Delicious, colorful, imagistic Tagalog had been lingering beneath my skin, floating like *nilads* along the synaptic rivers of my imagination. I wanted to use these words, eat them like a feast, share them like a blessing. But how does one struggle through the lingual clashes when English now comes more naturally but Tagalog comes more poetically?

Intentional wrong grammar/syntax/spellings have become my tool, an acrobatic verbal exercise fueled by an indigenous mental process that allows me to traverse the vocabularies of in-betweenness that is effortless, that is, until I write.

In *Isla Tuliro*, there is a collective character, the *kayumanggis* ("ones with brown complexions"), who have the chameleon-like ability to adapt to any culture and any language that is thrown their way. Through the *kayumanggis*, I am perhaps trying to make peace with my clashing, conflicting, colonized selves.

Kastila: Conquered by the Krus [6]

My Spanish is not real Spanish. It is Spanish learned through the rote memorizations of the rules of conjugation... *Yo soy, tu eres, nosotros estamos, vosotros estáis, el/ella está, ellos/ellas están...* coupled with years of committing to memory poems and songs in the colonizers' languages written by writers who also wrote in Spanish and English as their second and third languages.

In elementary school, we had to memorize Jose Rizal's "*Mi Ultimo Adios*" ("My Last Farewell"), properly reciting it with hard Castilian "R"s:

> Adiós, Patria adorada, region del sol querida,
> Perla del mar de oriente, nuestro perdido Edén

Outside our school, *jeepneys* (surplus WWII American GI jeeps spray-painted, rococo style, with primary-colored curlicues) whizzed through overcrowded streets, sprayed with fake snow at Christmas time and displaying plastic Jesuses on mini-altars hanging from rearview mirrors. Christmas carols blasted through overly woofered or tweetered loudspeakers, weaving between English and Spanish with a Filipino accent:

> Mamacita (yeyeye)
> Donde esté Santa Klaus?
> Oh where is Santa Klaus
> Dis Christmas Day-hey?

This is what it was like growing up in a country whose national anthem was first written in the language of Spain (Colonizer No. 1) then translated for the convenience of the Americans (Colonizer No. 2) before it was finally (finally!) translated to Filipino. It took two centuries, from 1898 to 1956, before the national anthem landed in its own language. There was a time and a generation of school children (my parents) who had to sing the anthem in three different languages during the daily school flag ceremony, with the colonizer's flag being raised first before the Philippine flag could wave freely in its own sky. (Today, this still happens at Filipino immigrant community gatherings, except for the Spanish version.)

> Spanish:
> Tierra adorada, Perla del Mar del Oriente
> (Land adored, Pearl of the Orient Seas)
> English:
> Land of the morning, child of the sun returning
> Filipino:
> Bayang magiliw, Perlas ng Silanganan
> (Beloved country, Pearl of the East)

For centuries, we pledged allegiance to ourselves by pledging allegiance to another. The Philippines was, and for the most part, continues to be, a country in search of its lost self.

Inglis: Conquered by the Pen

I went to a school run by Belgian nuns who forbade us to speak any other language but English. Their first language was Dutch Flemish (which they decided *they* were allowed to use). They couldn't speak a word of Tagalog to save their souls. Student language monitors were deployed at recess to fine anyone who broke the English Only rule. They would step on our toes so we would yell out *Aray!* in Tagalog, and they would meet their quota of offenders before the end of recess. Eventually, we learned to combine *Aray* with *Ouch!* (the acceptable way to scream in pain) and we would yell *Arouch!*

My first childhood poem (published by the school's literary journal) was written in English. *Letters Have Faces*, written in first or second grade, described each of the letters of the English alphabet, based on what they looked like to me as a 6-year-old. Looking back, I realize that even their faces and personalities were Anglo. "Letter A is a Lady of Taste."

My favorite game at recess was a card game called Author Author, where we had to identify American or European authors by their portraits or name the author based on their writing. Elizabeth Barret Browning... *I love thee to the depth and breadth and height my soul can reach.* Edgar Allan Poe... *Once upon a midnight dreary, while I pondered weak and weary.*

This was the breeding of my English-speaking self. The ability to speak like "Amuhrken" indicated that you came from a wealthy family. To write like Elizabeth Barrett Browning was the mark of high education. To recite *To Be or Not To Be* like Sir Laurence Olivier meant you were cultured and sophisticated. Wealth, education, sophistication—all the marks of a highly cultured privileged *colegiala*.

Taga-ilog

When I started writing scripts and plays in the language-of-the-river (Tagalog), they were written bilingually. Each page was divided into two. The left side showed the stage directions or camera shots in English. The right side contained the Tagalog dialogues (but with actors' directions in English). Looking at these scripts makes me realize (once again) that this is the mapping of a divided mind, living between the folds of two vocabularies.

Bilingualism and the Rules of Wrong Grammar

When I choose to write poetry, I am aware that my true self comes out when I am compelled to weave in and out of English and Tagalog, resisting to make it convenient for English Only readers. This poem is entitled "Pilipinas, Hindi Kita / Pilipinas, I Did Not."

Pilipinas
Hindi kita iniwan
I did not leave you
Amerika
Hindi mo ako inimbita
You did not invite me

And yet here I live
Not in Caloocan
Tarakatak ng kalesa
Click-clack of horse-driven buggies
I no longer hear
Here I am
Amerika
Not
Pilipinas

I want to write bilingually. I have always written bilingually. But how does one do that in a culture that insists on erasing my bilinguality, which, by the way, is the result of expeditions and conquests by the very same culture?

Let me try to bi-explain myself in bilingual metaphors.

Tinikling, Dancing Between Vocabularies

Tinikling is a traditional Filipino dance between bamboos. It mimics the movement of the *tikling* bird trying to avoid being ensnared by bamboo traps laid out by rice farmers. Legend has it that Spanish colonizers punished native farmers who reaped small harvests by having them stand between two bamboos riddled with thorns, and the farmers had to learn to avoid being caught between the punishing thorns. Though there is no historical basis for this, the existence of such a legend is more telling than the truth.

The *tinikling* offers a visual explanation of how bilingual writing works. Like the agile dancing feet of a *tinikling* dancer, a bilingual writer's mind is connected to her feet at all times, transferring and translating the beat of clapping bamboos from a hearing experience to a whole body experience. Living in a predominantly English-speaking culture means you cannot stop to think or even attempt to explain your actions and your meanings, or you will lose track of the dominant beat and find yourself caught in the thorns of misunderstanding. I can't help but relate this to the spate of recent attacks on black bodies we have witnessed. There is never time to explain your black skin or your brown skin to someone intent on eradicating your black or brown body because he or she feels threatened by the mere sight of you. You have to keep dancing between the clapping bamboos of race perception. Those who tried, hands up or not, have ended in tragedy. Is this a far-fetched metaphor? If it is to you, you've never had to dance/write between bamboos.

But I digress... or do I?

How does one speak or write or exist, survive or even dare to thrive in an environment rich with diverse cultural perceptions, when our cultures are blind to each other and one culture insists on taking over the dialogue?

McKinley's Magnificent Dream

In my play *Isla Tuliro*, there is a scene where two flamboyant creatures who call themselves Encanta and Encantado fall from the sky and land on the island of the *Kayumanggis*. Seduced by the flora and fauna of this newly discovered paradise, they decide they should stay, inspired by what they call their Magnificent Dream. Based on the real text of President William McKinley's 1899 speech defending U.S. expansionism as Manifest Destiny, I wrote a scene that rewrites his speech from the perspective of the colonized *Kayumanggis*.

Here is an excerpt:

ENCANTA and ENCANTADO
(finishing each other's sentence)

...A golden light just shone over our worried little blonde heads... somebody died for US so WE could be saved. It's our Responsibility to do the same for you! We should stay here! And help y'all have a Better Life. Because it's our God-Given Right to Teach y'all. And to... Uplift... y'all and... to Civilize... y'all so we can save your Pagan souls! So y'all can go to heaven.... Because y'all came to us as a Gift From God... Our little brown brothers and sisters! ...someone died for us... to save our souls and now we have been cleaned! And we can clean you too... And teach you to talk like this. Not like (mimicking   KAYUMANGGIs)   Abararararbararaa (patronizing)... You deserve to know how to... enunciate and to... pronounce your words clearly... to be, you know, be...

Civilized... And once you've learned all that? Then you'll be just like us, you know?... if someone made a movie about our dream, it should be called "Our... Magnificent... Dream."

"The problem is the Englishness." That is a quote from Tsitsi Dangarembga's novel *Nervous Conditions*. This "Englishness" is my greatest challenge, even as I write in English.

The other problem is we are considered The White Man's Burden. You see, the full title of this 1899 poem by the British poet Rudyard Kipling is "The White Man's Burden: The United States and the Philippine Islands," in which he refers to Filipinos as "Your new caught sullen peoples / Half devil and half child."

Take up the White Man's burden --
Send forth the best ye breed --
Go send your sons to exile
To serve your captives' need
To wait in heavy harness
On fluttered folk and wild --
Your new-caught, sullen peoples,
Half devil and half child

I am constantly jumping in and out of the bamboo trap of "Englishness" by trying to re-invent the rules of English grammar, intentionally misspelling English words, writing in broken English on purpose. This is my literary rebellion, as expressed in my poem "Pilipinas Hindi Kita/Amerika, I Did Not."

Land op di morning
Child op di sun returning
'ika nga namin
That's how I would really speak
My borrowed tongue
Amerika
Pinaawit mo kami
You made us sing
Our national anthem
In your language
You offered, gave me
Bahay, home, anak, child, love, property, heartache
Sawing puso
Amerika

Dito ba? Dito ba?
Is this where
I belong?

Sifting through my writings, I find this entry in my e-journal from when I took my trip back to the Philippines:

October 21, 2014
I am realizing the invaluable wealth I have in my life. Being re-immersed in the culture I was born into is like becoming "un-baptized" from the borrowed religion imposed on us through colonization. We had a highly spiritual, sophisticated pre-Hispanic culture, replete with symbolism, living insights, a closeness to nature and a deep understanding of our true souls as First Nation peoples.

Sa dibdib ko, tumitibok ang masalimuot na kasaysayan ng pag-aalipin, pakikibaka, nguni't matibay na paninindigan. Sa ugat ko, dumadaloy ang katapangan ng kanununuang hindi magpapatalo sa agos ng kasaysayang pilit tayong nilulunod, pilit tayong hinuhugasan. Hindi mawawala ang bakas ng pintado sa aking kaluluwa. Nagpapasalamat ako sa pagtuturo ng Ama, si JUAN FELEO. Ama, buhay na buhay po kayo sa amin! Buhay na buhay po, Ama!

ENGLISH TRANSLATION:
Pulsing within the core of my being are the intricacies of a history of enslavement, struggling but strong in its own self-conviction. Flowing through my veins, I feel the valor of my ancestors who never backed down from the strong waves of historical injustice that tried to drown them out, that insisted on cleaning us out. The mark of Painted People shall never vanish from my soul. I am grateful for the teachings and example of my grandfather, Juan Feleo. You're very much alive, Ama. You are very much alive in us po [7], Ama!

Notes

1. From the root word *Pangasinan* meaning "land of salt"

2. Mother tongue.

3. Pangea World Theater is a Minneapolis-based theater arts organization founded in 1995. It works with artists from many

communities locally, nationally and internationally to create new aesthetic realities for an increasingly diverse audience.

4. Teatro Del Pueblo is a Saint Paul-based Latino theater company that promotes Latino culture through performing arts. Pangea World Theater and Teatro Del Pueblo received funding from Joyce Foundation to commission three national playwrights to create new work as part of their Latino/Asian Fusion. See www.pangeaworldtheater.org.

5. Malumi words are pronounced liltingly with the accent on the second to the last syllable. Maragsa words end in vowels pronounced with a glottal stop to the throat.

6. Cross (English); *Cruz* (Spanish)

7. "Po" is a word that is a term of respect added at the end of a sentence when speaking to someone you respect. It is not a noun, pronoun, adjective, adverb, verb, article, conjunction, or a kind of Vietnamese soup. It has no equivalent in the English language."

References

Dangarembga, T. (1988). *Nervous conditions*: A novel. New York: Seal Press.

Kipling, R., Wise, T. J., Carpenter Kipling Collection (Library of Congress). (1899). *The white man's burden*. London: publisher not identified.

Rizal, J., & Salas, R. V. (1957). *Mi último adios*. Kalibo, Filipinas: s.n.

Rizal, J. (2004). Our Mother Tongue. Retrieved April 10, 2017, from http://www.joserizal.ph/pm05.html. A poem originally in Tagalog written by Rizal when he was only eight years old

Rusling, G. (1903, January 22). Interview with President William McKinley. *The Christian Advocate*, 17.

Writing Exercise

For bilinguals:

- Write an essay about a word or form of expression in your first or second language that has no equivalent in the English language.

- Take a poem you have written in a language other than English and translate it into English. Then write a short essay about the challenges you faced in the translation.

For English-only writers:

- Invent a word and write a prose or poem about its meaning.

Identity(ies)

Intersectional Bribes and the Cost of Poetry

Sagirah Shahid

In his essay "The Negro Artist and Racial Mountain," Langston Hughes (1926) wrote:

> The Negro artist works against an undertow of sharp criticism and misunderstanding from his own group and unintentional bribes from the whites. "O, be respectable, write about nice people, show how good we are," say the Negroes. "Be stereotyped, don't go too far, don't shatter our illusions about you, don't amuse us too seriously. We will pay you," say the whites.

What strikes me about all this is how relevant this essay still is. Nearly 100 years later we are still writing about the roles race and identity play in our creative practice. I think about the ways in which I encounter these "bribes" in my own writing as an African American Muslim woman. With my Muslim identity, there is certainly pressure to conform, to write in such a way that either distances myself from the faith—so as not to offend other Muslims with my "racy" subject matter, or to give in to sensationalism and co-opt the identity in such an exaggerated way that my faith becomes a prop to lampoon. There is also a third option, which is to romanticize the identity in a way that is simplistic and refuses to engage with the identity critically.

These bribes are coupled with the realities of my Blackness. Though I come from an expansive and rich artistic tradition, there will always be attempts to either erase or invalidate the creative contributions and the phenomenal history of that tradition. There is also an urgency to resist and respond to the oppression that literally snatches away our lives, either through bullet, or jail cell, or classroom.

Being a woman further complicates things if you are Black and Muslim and American, because all three identities carry with them unique and familiar expressions of misogyny that often get ignored. Sometimes the misogyny gets called out, but usually this attention is utilized to scapegoat one identity whilst enacting the very same oppression in shiny new ways. My favorite example of this is hijab.

I started wearing hijab when I was 6 years old and decided to stop wearing it when I was 20. This is of course taboo. When you start wearing hijab you're supposed to keep wearing it. Naturally, folks from both within and outside of this experience either frowned upon or congratulated my life choices, as if to say the ways in which I choose to clothe or not clothe my body had anything to do with them in the first place. This narrative of policing women's bodies gets championed as a desire to "free" "oppressed" women from "radical Islam" or to "protect" a woman's "virtue" in the eyes of God and from the eyes of men. Personally, I find it hard to believe the gates of "freedom" or "virtue" rest entirely upon the shoulders of a piece of cloth—but that's just me.

When I write poetry, identity is a reoccurring theme in my poems because it's a reoccurring theme in my life. There's no avoiding it. When I wore hijab, people assumed I wasn't American.

"Where are you from?" people would ask me—an innocent enough question right?

"But where are you *really* from, *originally?*" they'd ask again, taking in my hijab, my light brown skin, and my Arabic last name and gleefully awaiting my real answer, because lord knows I couldn't possibly be from here, snowy Minnesota—right?

"I mean your parents, where are *they* from?" Usually at this point I'd debate internally if I should give a mini history lesson about the trans-Atlantic slave trade, reconstruction, Jim Crow, the Great Migrations which just so happened to coincide with the conversion of a substantial portion of the African American population to Islam, many through the Nation of Islam at first and then many more, my grandparents included, eventually converted to Sunni Islam—but usually I just say, "Chicago, both my parents are from Chicago."

The good news is, when you grow up swatting away the White people who go from exotifying your religion in the 1990s to trying to liberate you from your religion in the 2000s, when you grow up experiencing anti-blackness racism from Arab and Asian Muslims in the 1990s to Islamophobia and anti-immigrant racism from other Black people in the 2000s, when you grow up feeling like you're the only one noticing how the whole "40 virgins" thing from 14 centuries ago, feels an awful lot like that commercial where that perky bikini-clad girl is selling a car or a hamburger or a beer—really it's hard to tell these days—when you grow up seeing those things, you can't but raise a skeptical eyebrow at the world. And this is important because creativity is a critical practice.

As a poet, I must stretch the possibilities of language—I must bend it, shape it, interrogate it, and play with its moldy texture and musky scent if I expect to encounter a poem; I must do these things with

respect and integrity. My identities sharpen the criticalness of my
poetic eye. Even before the poem is born I have to engage on some level
with my identity and all of its luscious complexities and contradictions
if I'm going to attempt writing a poem. I have no choice in the matter.
Perhaps you do? That's cool. I still don't have a choice in the matter.
Here's why:

- I'm writing the poem in English. Yes, if I tried really hard I
  could probably learn a non-imperialistic language that
  didn't colonize or oppress half the world, but at this stage in
  the game, who am I kidding? So when I write the poem, I
  write the poem in English. On a subconscious level I am
  acknowledging the violence of the poem's very existence.
  This is painful because I know somewhere in my heritage
  my African ancestors were force fed this language.

- The poem can't decide who it wants to be in conversation
  with. Is the poem pushing back against the racism that
  brought it into existence—and if so, does that mean the
  poem is actually pandering to the "White Gaze" as Toni
  Morrison (2013) so aptly described it? Or, if I am critical of
  the other Muslims who socially shun Muslim women who
  don't wear hijab, will the secular Christians in this country
  take that as an invitation to hijack our conversation? Does
  any of this even matter? Because chances are I'm going to
  have to bob and weave the hell out of myself if I'm going to
  somehow build an audience to be in conversation with while
  also avoiding the pit falls of tokenization and racism.

- In every poem I will debate whether or not I should insert
  the following phrase: "This poem is only a single poem,
  written by a single poet who carries these identities—you
  are not allowed to manipulate this art into some sort of
  warped and overly simplified generalization of these
  people."

Even if I'm writing a poem about the cheery little birdies perched
along the power lines, the poem is still an act of rebellion. It's
rebellious because I'm alive and writing it. I'm alive and writing in a
body that is living proof of the hypocrisies this country was built upon.
When I write, my body becomes a weapon, each syllable a reminder or
argument professing the resilience of my ancestors. When I walk into a
classroom, when I prepare to give a reading or submit a poem for

publication, I feel the weight of my body, which will most likely be one of the few bodies that look and pray like mine in that space. So I channel that great heritage I carry within me and tap into the resilience of an ancestor I refuse to forget. I channel her strength when I occupy these spaces because I don't need a textbook to know, she channeled me while she occupied the spaces she was forced to occupy.

The birth of the poem then, is costly. It's emotionally and psychologically taxing. There are no guarantees that the poem itself will survive or withstand this process. I make peace with this in small and largely insane ways:

- I don't take the poem for granted. I treat each poem like she is one of my many teachers. I listen to her and the ways she is instructing me on how to converse with identity. Most days I am a mediocre student—but I don't berate myself when I fail, I just keep trying. It is important not to judge this failure, but instead learn from the process of that failure. I ask the poem question after question after question until I feel confident in mastering the lessons of that particular poem. Each poem and arguably, every draft of a poem carries in it a number of lessons. You must commit your life to learning them.

- The poem is not my only teacher. Life is my university. I try to consume the world in as many ways as possible. This is especially important if like me, your identity is intersectional. There won't be exact road maps or curriculums for you to relate to unless you devote your life towards searching for them or creating them. Contrary to popular belief, learning is the practice of receiving and giving some of yourself to the world who is also your teacher. Read widely, certainly across disciplines and absolutely beyond the United States and Europe and without a doubt within your own cultural traditions, but also listen to the album, the chapbook, the holy book— listen to that textbook that actually is not a textbook but is the person sitting right next to you on the bus ride home. There is a lesson there, that might also be a poem but you will never arrive to the poem if you aren't listening. I cannot emphasize enough how vital the act of listening is in the poem's process.

- Respect the poem, but also utilize the criticalness your identity and life experiences have equipped you with. Challenge the poem. Persuade it to try something new. Above all remember that the debates you have with your poem is not happening in a vacuum, both you and your poem are participating in a discourse that is larger and older than either one of you. You must honor this discourse, even when it is painful or lonely you must honor that discourse.

I can't predict the future, so I have no way of knowing if in a hundred years from now there will be billions of African American Muslim women writing poetry into the world. I have no way of knowing if the poetry of Tasleem Jamila el-Hakim or Nayyirah Waheed (2013) will become just as prolific as that of Amiri Baraka—but I certainly hope so. I also hope if you are unfamiliar with any of these poets that you seek out and study their work. And if you are familiar, revisit the work again. You might find who you were looking for.

> listen to my poems
> but do not look for me
> look for you.

—Nayyirah Waheed

References

Hughes, L. (1926) "The Negro artist and the racial mountain." *The Nation*, 23 June 1926.

Morrison, T. (2013) "Toni Morrison on language, evil and 'the white gaze,'" https://www.youtube.com/watch?v=FAs3E1AgNeM

Waheed, N. (2013) *Salt*. poetry collection, 24 September 2013

Writing Exercises

Occupying Space

Ride a bus or a train or a subway to a place you have never been before (if there isn't an accessible mode of public transportation in your town, walk to a part of town you are least familiar with). On your way there listen to your surroundings. Make mental notes of the smells and textures of the space. When you arrive to your destination, turn off any electronics you may have on you and engage with the space—you can interpret this loosely, but essentially have a conversation with the space. When you are ready, go home and write whatever comes to mind for at least 5 minutes without interruption (if you feel stuck, write about the ways you occupied space). Repeat this entire cycle as many times as necessary.

Fasting

Commit to reading the works of Black authors for at least 30 days. Abstain from reading or listening to anything that is not engaging with Black culture during the 30 days. Your goal should be to read at least two novels, two works of nonfiction and four collections of poetry written by Black authors. As you are reading these works, set aside five different times throughout each day to free-write for exactly 10 minutes (do not exceed the 10 minutes). I recommend spreading out these free-write times as follows: Morning, early afternoon, late afternoon, sunset, and evening. After the 30 days, repeat this practice as necessary.

It Happened in Fragments

Isela Xitlali Gómez R.

Few frames in my mother's house match each other. The brackets don't matter. The picture does.

* * *

In eighth grade, when she asked me about the C on my report card, I told my mother that I did not enjoy reading. Correction: I told my mother that I did not enjoy the reading assigned in my English class. Mrs. Schultz and the California English Language Arts Curriculum had us studying tons of Johns, plenty of Roberts and an Ernest. On the regular some Annes and some Emilys, and in March more Sylvias. A Langston here and a Pablo there. On a lucky day an Amy. On 28 days a bit of Frederick and a Maya, but never a James and never an Audre. On the fifth of May, an Octavio, maybe a Sandra. Onward, never a Louise or Maxine, a Joy, Jhumpa, or Julia.

"Ma, it's not what you think. I do my homework. But they only got us reading American literature. They're all old and they write about snow. I like Chicana literature, you know like *House on Mango Street*."

She might have honked because some guy in a raised pick-up truck had just cut her off and made her miss the left turn signal. She might have honked because that's how Californians both sigh and shout, especially when their daughters reveal to them the miseducation of middle school Mexican kids in a land that grows more cactus than apple. But my mother was in the driver's seat while I sat in the back with no access to the look on her face—disappointed or heartbroken, thoughtful or reacting, impatient or insouciant.

"Chela my child, Chicana literature is American literature. That house on Mango...? It's in Chicago." In that moment, my mother gave me a gift, not unlike the surprise piñata at my quinceañera—necessary in spite of our forgetfulness. She reminded me that we belong, that we are here, embedded in the soil that nourishes seeds that grow into trees that sliver down into pages of books, newspapers, and journals. That we read, that we make history, that we write.

* * *

Cut time. Genre need not apply. My father's cassette collection cut category corners. Santana. Prince. Ronstadt Rock. Dylan. Ronstadt

Mariachi. Mariah. DeeDee. Cue. *I got rhythm. I got music. I got galán. Who could ask for anything more?*[1]

* * *

In seventh grade, when she asked me who wrote the song I sang throughout my 25 minute shower, I told my sister, "yours truly." Xochitl looked me in the eye, called it a poem. Six months later, I walked on stage by myself for the first time and read the lyrics to that debut single of mine—which, by the way, is pending release from a major music label, as soon as one of them listen to the mixtapes I keep sending via snailmail and gives me a record deal. Unplugged, uncut, and unusually unblemished for a preteen, I opened for the "Fifth Annual Chicano Poetry Night" at East LA College (ELAC), footage of which will likely appear in my "E! True Hollywood Story," also pending release, and confirmation.

In her first semester, my sister had filled her schedule with every Chicano Studies course in the college catalog, joined ELAC's MEChA chapter, and started spelling Chicana with an X. One month later, she's giving stove-side speeches on Saturday mornings. "We, the Mexica, we survived. No, we thrived on corn," she says to my brother when he complains that the tortillas de maiz from the new mercado are too small to make breakfast tacos the way he likes. By the time Xochitl finishes her lesson on this particular power crop of our people, she has briefed us all on the Treaty of Guadalupe Hidalgo, the making of Dodger Stadium, and the medicinal properties of garlic, onion, and tequila. So in case anyone was unclear up to this point, she was Brown, proud, *and down.*

All this had earned her a role on the poetry night planning committee. When it came time to find a "featured youth" for the noche de poesía, she bribed her baby sister with some Hot Cheetos and Starbucks. She said, "we'll do it together," reminding me that she would also have a 5-minute spot at the mic. The night of, I went up and did some Jesus rhymes. She went up and let it shine a la Mexican sonnet, three quatrains and a couplet about raspados, guisados, and our traumado family.

Partaking that night dubbed Xochitl and me the second generation of Gómez Ramírez girls to whirl words on that campus. In 1975, our mother started taking three busses each way for her commute from El Sereno to ELAC, also known as the holyland since the late 1960s for

---

[1] With apologies to George Gershwin.

all Brown ones born north of the border. That 80-acre campus was one of the pilots to clear space for Chicano Studies as a discipline, which meant that by the autumn my ma arrived as a fresh faced first year, multiple cohorts of students had graduated in the literary tradition of Martha Cotera, Corky Gonzalez, and Tomás Rivera. It was early on in the movement, so the Lorna Dees, Glorias, Cherríes, and Lucha Corpis of the world labored away to tackle the canon, pushing for recognition and publication of women's work—a task we still trying to topple. Three decades after her stint there, our mother watched both her daughters find voice in that small community college auditorium with black flaking paint, heavy velvet curtains, and an audio video system that was state of the art technology in 1988. This was 2004. Xochitl and I still argue over which of us was the Selena and which was the Suzette of the Quintanilla family in that particular set list, but for now let's just say we were Lola and Chavela, each divine in their own right and ranchera.

* * *

Lunchtime specials at the Gómez house:

Tuesday—tin can tuna tacos
Wednesday—pastrami and aguacate on a French bun
Sunday Before Church—menudo
Sunday After Church—Costco chicken and spaghetti with feta cheese

Piecemeal concoctions make for ideal nutrition.

* * *

In sixth grade, when she asked me about the story I wrote for our statewide writing exams, I told my teacher it was loosely autobiographical. Mrs. Jiles nodded, "these scores are off," and handed me my paper, a giant number 3 scratched across the top. A committee of district staff and teachers had loaded up on Folgers coffee, prepackaged mini muffins, and optional antacids, in a tiny conference room with a failing air conditioner, to grade all the creative tales drafted by every elementary student in 26 schools. These harsh, unspeakable, unfathomable even, workplace conditions inhibited their capacity to score objectively. This offers the only logical reason as to why they gave me three out of six possible points. I was heartbroken, yes. But really, 11-year-old me was baffled at the blatant bias of the educational system. I knew it, even at a young age. I knew they wanted certain types of characters. That in 2003, my decision to not concede to the norm, to not reify the literary establishment would risk my chance at success by industry standards.

On the other mano, this exam could take me to new heights. I thought, maybe this will catch someone's eye, open puertas, make me a commissioned artist. So I vowed not to shoot for some synthetic spinoff of the era's principal protagonists. I said no to the clownfish, the wizard, the ogre. My shit would be new, authentic, edgy. For my headlining hero, I went rogue. I wrote a rabbit. Later I learned that Thumper, Roger, and The Hare had lived in the canon for quite some time. But I decided that those lagomorpha leporidaes were manufactured versions of the truth. My bunny would be *real*—a cottontail with no fluff. Packed with all sorts of issues: an orphaned only-child in a city where neoliberal capitalism tries to take claim. As I pressed No. 2 pencil to wide-ruled paper, I understood this could make me vulnerable so early in my career. And I knew there would be no taking it back; I had just chewed off my eraser.

When the grading team of sugar-high public school staff returned our stories, I felt disappointed despite my nuanced understanding of the submission process. Then, as in every epic journey, came the twist, the turn of events, the setting-in-motion. Mrs. Jiles announced to the class that mine was her favorite story and, without revealing the identity of the unjustly disregarded aspiring writer, read aloud one of my earliest works, "Bumble Bunny's Adventure."

> Preview: Born Bernabe Benjamín Conejo, he picked up his epithet from a classic case of the system miswriting names for their convenience. The office lady at his preschool asked Señora Conejo to spell their names for the registration forms. When she responded, "uppercase C-o-n-e-j-o," the office lady smugged. "Coh-what? Isn't that *bunny*? He looks like one. That's what you are, right?" She glared at the boy and back at his mother, "I will write Bunny. Trust me mam, it will make life easier." Then on the first day of class, his teacher took one look at the roster and dismembered the pupils' names to fit through her tight dry lips. That's how Bernabe Benjamín Conejo became Bumble Bunny.
>
> A few years later, Bumble lost his parents, Chava and Concha Conejo, to the local ranch town's most recent round of guisado de jackrabbit. Alone and nearing puberty, he struggled to trust anyone, including the teachers that butchered his name

and the guidance counselors that slaughtered his sense of self-worth in coded messages about rabbits multiplying and bunnies burglarizing gardens. A quippy child's story of trauma masked in farm animals and bright colors.

I remember rejection and I remember recovery. Yes, all from a sixth grade writing assignment, but one that reminds me of the possibility to write a story, get ignored, then get encouraged, and end up with something like *The Chronicles of Tortilla Hija* or *A Series of Chuleta Events*[2].

* * *

My grandfather built a house. First it sheltered dolls. Then it roosted books. Dr. Seuss. *The Bible. Silverstein and Berenstain Bear. Caperucita Roja.* My father's lost poems. My mother's unpublished play.

Wood chunks. Discarded nails. Leftover paint. Eventually they come together to stand for something.

* * *

It fits that my writer origin story happened in fragments; my memory and vision function in similar fashion. Focusing on creative nonfiction in recent years, everything I write comes out in crumbs, once from a solid loaf of bread but no matter now, an accumulation of them will still feed me. For those who call this approach lacking or deficient, sufficient but not nourishing, I can guarantee they don't know how to make something from nothing, how to make ten different salsas from one type of chile or how to fill chocolate with heat to make mole. But I can find the nutrients in scraps. I can make mother's lesson, sister's encouragement, my first experience with evaluation connect like chain-link, twine like rope.

My origin fragments do not fall in straight line nor follow conventional dramatic arc. Instead, each a ceramic chunk, glass shard, or metal bead—some grey, some bright, some fading—they piece together in mosaic, an art form that recalls beauty from afar *and* beauty up close. I am no visual artist but I still borrow from this medium that engages micro and macro intuition. I remember miscellaneous details from random childhood moments that have nothing to do with my goal in a given writing project. This frustrates me until, several months later, I realize why it matters that I sang loud enough in the shower for

---

[2] Las dos de these titles son forthcoming publication, tu sabes, once I write them. ¡Échale ganas!

the whole house to hear me, why it matters that my teachers sliced my name. On their own, these memories tell tiny tales of a Mexican kid reading, performing, writing. Side by side, it's a story of the same Mexican kid learning from her family how to survive the literary world.

Alongside these moments, I came to writing by the blessing of trauma and all that it fractures in brain, body, and blood beating heart. When I was 5 years old, my father committed suicide. I have spent every year since then not knowing what happened but knowing what happened, absorbing his polished image, forgetting he was gone, forgetting he was real, reminding myself to remember, forgiving myself that I didn't, slapping myself for losing clarity, forcing myself to find the truth, learning that truth does not exist.

How do I even begin to write this?

I have trouble deciphering dream from reality from fable. I stumble when describing him, unsure whether the source of detail is my recollection or someone else's. I remind myself that blurred memory makes for magnificent malleable material. Trauma can seep into veins and camp inside joints in gradual, subtle ways and the person won't notice. Whether generational or personal, it impacts storytelling, both subject and process. My dad's death, the cutting of our names, my sister's attempt, my brother's coma, the lack of healthcare resources, the erasure of these stories, the weight of sharing this knowing some White writer will fetishize it, some White writer will co-opt it, some White writer will declare it false or fatuous, some White writer will profit from it—it all creates fractures, for me at least. And that, is part *and whole* of the story. It took me a long time to see that, to accept that, to love that, to get to a place where I can write that.

How do I go about the craft of it?

I consider my short attention span another blessing. As a kid, I had little interest in the standard novel. I instead spent my days flipping through *Where the Sidewalk Ends* and *Calvin and Hobbes*, listening to Selena in English and Christina Aguilera in Spanish, watching *SNL* and *I Love Lucy*. Short attention spans allow for exposure to more forms and the eagerness to mock them, merge them, mushroom them.

I once found myself on an Air Canada flight with one goal: write a new piece for the public reading I had the following night. After an hour of useless scribbles, I discovered that Air Canada had a great selection of movies for in-flight rental, including *Air Bud, Castaway,* and *Death at a Funeral,* the Neil LeBute version. I convinced myself that the latter cinematic masterpiece was well worth the $6.99 in Canadian dollars, considering I would view it purely for research purposes. In the film, Chris Rock gives his father a somber eulogy in a scene of comedic genius. Several years prior, I gave the eulogy at my grandmother's funeral, the kind that makes people cry and makes her look like Mrs. Doubtfire and Dolores Huerta at the same time, a sweet baker with "huelga" tattooed on her forehead. But my grandmother was not that person. Maria Nico had a vulgar sense of quiet humor and made survival into art.

When I realized that Canadian inflation was not in my favor, I made use of my in-flight film field notes and wrote a new homage to the woman that no language can capture. The next evening at my reading, I shared the first draft of "Uncut Eulogy of Our Grandmothers," a piece that is 100% accurate and 100% embellished, a piece that blurs the edges between my sister's memory and my own, a piece that takes advantage of the fact that my great aunt was too drunk and grandmother is too dead to correct me, a piece about what grandmothers and granddaughters share with each other *off the record*. My grandmother would be proud of this eulogy, but perhaps also glad that I waited to share it until after she passed.

* * *

Fragmentation finds many forms and takes new shape when piecing together. Remember to accept that brokenness enhances story, grounds story, challenges common understanding of story. If you forget, forgive yourself. Collect the pieces.

* * *

On the second story of the green house we live in, a stained-glass window breaks the sunrise into nine colors of light. From 5:58 a.m. until 12:49 p.m., they land on the grey wall beside the staircase. Shifting portrait of a bird that disappears each day.

Tomorrow, at 6:02 a.m., with more clouds in the sky, pay attention to that window. The shards have something to tell you.

Writing Exercise: In Memory for Creative Nonfiction Writers:

1. Pick a blurry memory of yours.
2. Without questioning yourself, write everything you can about it.
3. Who is there?
4. Smells. Sights. Tastes. Touch. Sounds.
5. Identify, to the best of your ability, what you know is true, what is made-up, and everything in between.
6. What do you wish you knew?
7. Evaluate how the blurriness impacts your writing process. Do you feel stuck? Frustrated? Apathetic?
8. Research alternative shapes for storytelling. Spend time mulling over other art forms: landscape photography, ceramics, tap dance. Hint: In photography, artists will take a photo of the same image with different lenses, filters, lighting. Sometimes they'll place several of the versions side by side in display. Sometimes they chose only one for the final cut in a gallery exhibit. Either way, they worked it in 360 degrees. That perspective will sharpen your art.
9. Create mockery. Who said it's a bad thing? Write this blurred memory from several lenses. Imitate another art form to do it.

Additional rules and tools of my craft:

- Rule: Do not italicize language in Spanish, unless for critique of that common practice. Many multilingual writers agree these days that italicizing non-English languages contributes to otherizing our tongues. My thoughts: *I do not walk with a slant in my body. Nor do I speak with a slant in my tongue. Why write that way? I aint the crooked one.*

- Rule: My audience must always include someone I grew up with, perhaps even teenage me. My writing has a mission: make the world of words accessible and applicable to my folk.

- Rule: Make White people uncomfortable. It's really not difficult. Even when paying them no attention, as in no mention of Whiteness in my writing, they get uncomfortable.

- Rule: Keep it tight. The writing that is. Eliminate unnecessary words: limit adverbs, limit use of passive voice. Make five lines into three lines.

- Tool: Music. Listen with intention. Take a piece of your writing and list songs and albums that remind you of it. Incorporate lyrics as transitions between fragmented sections.

- Tool: A Letter to My Therapist.
  In self-reflection pieces, speak directly to someone in a pseudo-therapy session. Choose anyone: actual therapist, favorite writer, bartender, your old lady neighbor and her dog Molly. One potential benefit of the form: for those of you who've been in therapy, you know that your conversation with the practitioner does not need to stay focused on one topic.

Creating Native American Mirrors: and Making a Living as a Writer

Marcie Rendon

I write to create mirrors. As a Native American child who loved to read I searched the school bookshelves, the Bookmobile and other public libraries for books with pictures that looked like my family. I looked for books that told stories I could relate to. Growing up in the 50s and 60s in the United States, those books did not exist. There were books about cowboys winning the west and the *Little House on the Prairie* series, which held my interest for about all of two seconds. I remember reading every word in Britannica Encyclopedia about Geronimo and Cochise once I learned they were real people who did heroic deeds on behalf of their people.

Given the scarcity of reading material that interested my young Native self my first goal as a writer has always been to create stories my people can relate to. Stories, poems, plays and articles about Native Americans, about mothers, about young people, about poor people. My plays for theater tend to also include my understanding of a spiritual realm that exists simultaneously alongside and with our human existence because that is how my spirit sees the world.

A second goal I have is to write stories that present Native people as living people today. We are not a Curtis photograph. We are not a Disney cartoon. We are not a prop for every wannabe Manifest Destiny movie star seeking a credit roll. We are so often locked in the past, and then most often as a Plains tribes person. We are so much more. And so much more alive than that.

I remember one of the first times I read my poetry publicly at an honoring for author Meridel LeSueur. In the front row were five Lakota women. I read a poem about our grandmothers being erased from history's page. When I saw one of the women wipe tears from her eyes I knew my poem reached her—one Native woman to another. My poem mirrored our existence, validated our lives.

There is nothing more life-affirming, writer-validating than having your audience, your people, the ones who look like you, the ones who have lived a similar experience, crack up laughing, wipe a tear from their eye, or elbow the person next to them in a "hey, that's us" kind of way.

My third goal is to make a living as a writer. This is where many writers balk. People get so focused on having a book published they forget that almost every aspect of our lives requires a writer. Newspapers, magazines, blogs, advertising, signage, songs, scripts, the list goes on, all written by someone. A writer can get paid for each and every one of those endeavors.

I have written since I was a child in grade school. Everyone always told me I was a wonderful writer. No one ever told me I could make a living as a writer. It wasn't until I decided to write full time that I realized if writing was my goal, with three children to raise, then I had better start making money at it. I do not have an MFA degree and consequently started writing for a living with no knowledge of how to write a novel, write a play, or prepare a poetry manuscript.

With the realization of where my limitations were I set out to read every "how to make money writing" book I could get my hands on. And I tried any number of those "how to" suggestions. Five things stuck with me that have helped me continue to make money as a writer.

One. Submit for publication. You cannot get published, and paid, if you do not submit. Submit. And submit to paying markets. It is important to submit to markets that will pay you for your writing.

Two. Never say never when offered a writing job. We live in the digital age with unlimited access to information at our fingertips— provided we have wifi access. So what if your only knowledge of meerkats is from watching *Madagascar* with the children on Netflix? If a magazine or an educational company asks for a 500 word article on meerkats by next Wednesday for $75, my only answer is yes and I get to googling. I get that publication credit and cash the check.

Three. Know where, when, and how you are willing to compromise. A work for hire is a work for hire. If they don't want me to use the word evolve I won't use the word evolve. I don't even ask why. I just Google *evolve thesaurus* and find an acceptable word. However, when the editors asked me to not write "when we lost the war in Viet Nam" in my children's book *Farmer's Market: Families Working Together*, we had a go-round. We had numerous go-rounds. It wasn't until I enlisted the written support of author Jim Northrup, Viet Nam Vet, Marine, who emailed saying, "We lost the blank-blank war," that the editors relented and left my sentence be.

Four. Do what you say you are going to do. Make that deadline.

Five. Ditch the fear of rejection. Along with that, learn to actively seek constructive criticism. None of us writes perfectly all of the time, if ever. We can always learn more, and we will always improve if we are open to listening to more experienced writers.

Those five rules that I hold myself to have helped me make a living as a writer for the past 26 years. However, there are other aspects to the writing life that can be challenging.

Non-native queries might be the most interesting. A to-remain-unnamed company once asked me to write a traditional Native American Christmas story. I replied, "We never had Christmas before white people came." I was then asked if I could possibly re-write a traditional Native story as a Christmas story. I replied, "That would be impossible because we never had Christmas before white people came." They then asked if it might be possible for me to *sort-of* turn the White Buffalo Calf Woman story into a *sort-of* Christmas story. I replied, "That would be impossible because I am Ojibwe and that is a Lakota story and maybe I could just find you a Christian Indian to write a Christmas story for you?"

As a Native American woman on my home continent, complexities exist in relationship to all other cultures. I have found myself on stage explaining to new immigrants that we as Native people have always been here and that I am sorry the United States educational system doesn't teach them about our existence. I have been at spoken word events where I have felt compelled to say, "If you are asking for land reparations, you are asking the wrong people. Stolen land is stolen land." After 9/11 a liberal, white Minnesota crowd booed me off the stage when I suggested that folks stop fighting in my living room and that maybe they should all consider going home. It bears repeating, and arriving at an understanding, that everyone in the United States receives the same mis-education about Native Americans as everyone else.

As a writer, who is Native, it is important to know myself, my history, and what I am willing to handle in my relationships with other people. This can take courage, integrity and continual education of current issues within my own communities and my relationships with other communities.

Among Native people there are many viewpoints about our responsibility as Native writers. We have to measure up not just to some literary standard but also to an imaginary, undefined or constantly in flux, at least to my knowledge, Native cultural standard.

Ojibwe author Mark Anthony Rolo (*My Mother Is Now Earth*) and I had a heated argument years ago about writing. He was of the opinion that as Native writers we had a responsibility to strive to write "good literature." My argument was I thought we should just write stories our people wanted to read and whether those stories were deemed good literature or not was irrelevant in my opinion. I argued that it was important that our people read and be able to see themselves in the writing. The argument ended with me yelling I was going to write a Native American Harlequin romance and to hell with literature. He has since won a Northeast Minnesota Book Award, and Harlequin rejected my romance because it "lacked sexual tension." In my defense, I had never read a romance novel before attempting to write one and there is still hope for publication because they did say "we like your writing." If I can ever stop laughing over "lack of sexual tension" I might have another go at it.

At a Native writers' retreat in 2014, talk turned to the history of Native writers. It was the consensus of that group of writers, most of whom were writing educational works, that Native writers in the 60s and 70s were writing to reach Native readers and we owe our current successes to the inroads they made for us. Writers and works mentioned were: N. Scott Momaday's *House Made of Dawn*; anything by Vine DeLoria Jr.; Leslie Marmon Silko's *Ceremony*; James Welch's *Winter in the Blood*; Joy Harjo's *The Last Song*.

This group of writers postulated that most high-profile Native writers today have two things in common. One, they are Ivy League educated; and two, they tend to write for and to a white audience. The one exception they agreed on was Sherman Alexie. Although some did not like his use of sweat lodge ceremony and alcohol in his books they all agreed he writes for a Native reader.

Because these complexities all exist, it works best for me to write in my own voice to my own people. I write in many genres across many disciplines. I write poetry, plays, stories, songs, fiction, and creative nonfiction. When possible I take writing classes on topics I feel will be helpful to me in upgrading my writing skills. I attend writing work-shops of writers whose work I admire or who are regarded as experts in their field.

My mentor, Anishinabe writer Jim Northrup, told me early on in my career that if I wanted to make any money with my poetry I needed to learn how to speak in public. Saying hello to people used to reduce me to tears but I took his advice to heart and signed up for performance art classes, spoken word classes, and got on stage with knees quaking and voice quivering, determined to follow his advice. It has paid off, both monetarily and with publication credits.

My personal reading material tends to what I call airport murder mysteries. Following the adage "write what you know," I searched for a mystery writer's group to join in the early 90s. I found an advertisement in the Loft Literary Center's newsletter for a group that was meeting at Blue Moon Coffee Café on Lake Street. I forced myself beyond my shyness and went to the introductory meeting. While there my writer's imagination took over. I was with a group of people I didn't know, several men and women who all seemed to know a whole lot more about murder than I did. My mind said, "These people write what they know. One of them might be a serial killer." I was the last one to leave the meeting that night. But the next month, my will to write overtook my fear and shyness and I returned to the meeting.

I continued in that group, organized and hosted by writer Babs Lakey (creator/author of *Futures Mystery Anthology Magazine*) until we disbanded when two members moved overseas. I then joined another group, hosted by Chicano author Diego Vazquez Jr. (*Growing Through the Ugly*, 1998). In this group everyone writes for publication, often sharing calls for submission notices with everyone in the group submitting to the same call. Cooperation is better than competition and fear of rejection is minimized with others' continued encouragement and support.

Today, I also belong to a loosely organized women's writing group. Most are women of color, who are all published writers. When we meet we read and critique each other's work and support each other to find avenues of publication.

In addition to my writing groups, the biggest asset to my career was participating in a Native American Journalism Internship at the University of Minnesota in 2001. Twelve aspiring Native American journalists had the opportunity to work with Native American editors at both the *Pioneer Press* and the *Star Tribune*. My internship was at the *Pioneer Press* under editor Art Coulson. I learned to write succinctly, rapidly, and accurately and to meet a deadline—in other words, to write straight through any imagined writer's block.

I love to write. For me, writing is playing with words. I love listening to the voices around me, the voices in my brain, and I love putting those conversations and creations down on paper. Writing, for me, has always been a fun challenge, something that I truly enjoy engaging in. My best advice to aspiring writers is to find your voice that will reach your people, learn to scorn rejection, submit and submit again, find a compassionate but challenging writers group and write a few newspaper articles just for practice.

My artistic statement reads:

> We are kept in their mindset as "vanished peoples." Or as workers, not creators. And what does this erasing of individual identity do to us? Can you believe you exist if you look in a mirror and see no reflection? And what happens when one group controls the mirror market?
>
> As Native people, we have known that in order to survive we had to create, re-create, produce, re-produce. The effect of the denial of our existence is that many of us have become invisible; the systematic disruption of our families by the removal of our children was effective for silencing our voices; however, not everyone can still that desire, that up-welling inside that says sing, write, draw, move, be. We can sing our hearts out, tell our stories, paint our visions. We are in a position to create a more human reality. In order to live we have to make our own mirrors.

References

Alexie, S. (1992). *The business of fancy dancing.* Brooklyn, NY: Hanging Loose Press.

Harjo, J. (1975). *The last song: [poems].* Las Cruces, N.M.: Puerto Del Sol.

Momaday, N. S. (2010). *House made of dawn.* New York: HarperPerennial.

Rolo, M. A. (2012). *My mother is now Earth.* St. Paul, MN: Borealis Books.

Silko, L. M. (2007). *Ceremony.* New York: Penguin Books.

Welch, J. (1981). *Winter in the blood.* New York: Penguin Putnam.

Vázquez, D. (1998). *Growing through the ugly: A novel.* New York, NY: Henry Holt.

Writing Exercise

The year is 2030. Write a three-paragraph news article detailing how the water shortage is impacting your people.

Notes in Journey from a Writer of the Mix

Anya Achtenberg

> I want to rediscover the secret of great speech and of great burning
> —Aime Césaire,
> *Notebook on a Return to My Native Land*, p. 49

Where to begin, whether in essay or story's complex weaving, may be simpler for some—the spark arrives from the creative firmament—but that spark is shorthand for the multiple sources of and entry into story for writers of the mix and writers of color.

For writers of the mix, the mix inhabiting me, that spark is never the actual beginning. For those for whom identity is a kind of way station, whether providing a bit of breathing space, or imposing a cloak of suffocation—the beginning of a work is a challenge beyond that of craft, complicated by more than some generic writer's block, or anarchic resistance to conventional structure. But, why? Perhaps, for writers of the mix, writers out of category, some thin "beginning" to our own stories is an inexhaustible lie.

Our truest stories come forward in a voice that is not "performing" its identity but IS it; and somehow fully holds all that we know and all that remains mystery, without possibility of breaking down voice into DNA percentages.

Have issues and experiences regarding race and identity affected me as a writer? Yes, profoundly, cellularly, word by word, and into every bit of craft. I'll explain, but first let me indicate the blinding sandstorm and blinding snowstorm into which my full history and identity have disappeared.

I know clearly what I am not. I know light skin privilege, as real as the clubs of angry cops coming down toward my head, but not landing. My skin privilege is indisputable, though undercut by gender and poverty, homelessness and violence; by trauma, individual and intergenerational. My skin does not speak to the true complexity of my race and the ways I have never been white, nor to the reality of my maternal grandparents—who were brown skinned, black of eye, hair indigo; hers, straight and braided; his, curly like mine, which dreads if let be. They point to all those before, whom I cannot name, whose bones I cannot find.

Here is my identity confusion—Jewish origins include significant percentages of DNA—ancestors—from North Africa, the Saudi

Arabian Peninsula, from Siberian indigenous people, the Fertile Crescent, the Caucasus (*not* equivalent to white[1]), the Iberian Peninsula, with only the most recent stops in Russia and Ukraine before 20th century migrations. I am light-skinned, green-eyed, with African hair—in Cuba some call me *jaba*, a form of *mulata*. The complexities of genetics speak also in bones and hair; hold migrations and rape. The ill-informed racial categories of the U.S. constitute just an instant in the histories of my lineages. Only one of my parents was born here; none of my grandparents.

The centuries of persecution and genocide of Jews throughout Europe were effected on a racialized basis—called an inferior race, polluting the medieval waters to bring Bubonic Plague—"Black Death". (The sadistic Inquisition and Expulsion punished heresies, the "darkness" of the soul.) Called "subhuman mongrels"[2] in the twentieth century, classified as racially inferior to the Aryans, considered animal-like for experimentation and genocide; sexualized for rape; burnt alive—*until* crossing the Atlantic into whiteness, or some creation of "whiteness". Suddenly we're white? History stripped? No one-drop rule[3] applied? This confusing wash of whiteness remurders my ancestors, drowns history. My story with its DNA, in its difference and its parallels, connects me to people of color and their histories.

A tale of whiteness negates not only the truth of my story but its form, its shape of constant rather than building tension; this white tale wants a perfect screaming climax and gentle leaf-falling denouement; wants comfy resolution. The false tale of my origins swells in opposition to the complexity of the real story which mirrors and holds my writer's opposition to conventional story structure, and my embrace of truer forms. In my work with writers, I want to clear a path for each one to go beyond the old prisons of story form.

What are you? When I hear this chorus, demanding a straightforward story of origins, I hear the same notes as when others chorus, "Write what you know." You see my dilemma? What I don't know—the many silenced threads of my identity—is truly my story. And using my beautiful Sephardic name that I have only orally—Sefara-rabi, spelling undetermined, would again shift my identity.

As a teacher of writing I tell my students to look for the silences, the threads that disappear into the cloth and need to come forward in the tapestry of story.

The work

Writers of the mix and writers of color have been beaten over the head with simplistic instructions I've always had trouble following.

Find your writer's voice, they say, but my voice is ghost, one or many, including the long back family of ghosts that know me. My voice is occupied, inhabited, speaks to story from shifting, bleeding boundaries. Like many in a racist society, I sometimes do the wrong thing, but all manner of beings come to me, sit with me at the edge of things, in the chasm of the boundary I cross everyday without reaching the other side. While I have lived with a sense of placelessness, of permanent exile, sometimes I become a land for the beings I meet; the disembodied ones, the exhausted ones, the ones wandering, searching, in flight, in trauma. In being displaced, I become a land for my characters, a road for my students. I am on the map. But, blink, and I am gone.

ancestral bones scattered in more places than I can ever know

Writing is possession. Possession by those I am, or by those I am not? Both. Which is which? Unknown. Nothing is black or white here.

Perhaps the most difficult instruction for me to follow, the one I want to focus on, is this:

Write from a sense of place

But I live in the chasm between origins and address. I found comfort in this passage: "Writing is born from and deals with ... the impossibility of one's own place," from Michel de Certeau's *L'Ecriture de l'histoire* (p. 327).

Language spills over the banks with the rhythms of those I cross with, and the endless crossings within me. My bones speak. The fist in my voice tells me I will never listen to another categorization of me or the voices I carry. When they come to me, however they come to me, I stand with them as they refuse another burial of soul and spirit, voice and gift; of their true mix of races, and the long migrations that brought them to the crossing.

I'm an interlude, an in-between, a liminal being; portal more than edifice.

My identity lives in a multi-voiced story, a chorus of intertwined narratives that move toward what's still invisible. My particular chorus comes to me at least in part because of my roots. As writers, we know this: characters inhabit us, possess us. But it may be that how truly they come, how deep their revelations of self and world, is connected to our long journeys, the crossings, the multiplicity, the being taken, the hard flight.

Can we make a place in language for the crossings within our identity? Without a single linear narrative of race, ethnicity and origins, the self has permeable borders; many voices can get out into air; many voices can get in, at home in the spinning disk of a self not anchored to place, to oneness, to category.

Since I write from such a way station, I slip into characters; they slip into me. Unasked, unpursued.

That my history and racial mix are in good part invisible, gives me my task: make visible the invisible; chip away at historical amnesia; show the interconnectedness, disappeared to cover how power works.[4] While not particular to me, this is, for me, unavoidable.

Writing from a sense of place seems a simple directive, unless you lack such a sense, at least as conventionally implied. Nothing has ever told me, *You are safe. You are named. You are at home. You begin here and proceed through story.* The standard rising and falling of tension we are told should structure our stories has a kind of disciplined yet masturbatory logic; but for those coming from generations of trauma, for instance, from the complexity of a thousand dangers in war or in the inner city, I understand tension in narrative as constant. It never goes away. It is high blood pressure and early death. It calls for seeking other story structures that work with that consistent level of tension, and open story to the spectrum of experience of life *in this tension*, rather than, simply, *in place*.

Trauma, Place, and Story Craft

What does a sense of place in story mean to those traumatized out of place and present, those for whom trauma is a lifelong negotiation? Issues of trauma—intergenerational, ancestral, current—snake intimately around and through the issues we face as writers of the mix and writers of color, whose generations have long held trauma in body and memory, causing epigenetic mutations in our DNA; expect, then, "mutations" in our language, in our ways of telling story. Trauma and dissociation knock us out of body and place into wandering and liminality; knock us out of time into unbearable unlocatable hovering and intensity. As narrators in many ways "unbordered" and permeable, we become ourselves a "place", a site of possession by characters who live and tell their stories through us, as we tell ours through them.[5]

Trauma affects language down to the simple sentence. Breaks it. Makes silences; blurts, rants. Our words haunt, race, are buried, unfold. Dislodged by trauma, our narrators see from many places, even from the grave, whether in earth, fire, air, or the waters. What we know is not simply what is on our resumes.

How to have voice, tell story, when one's place has been stolen, flooded, razed, cut down, bombed, colonized; the storytellers raped, killed or kidnapped? If we cannot write from a conventional sense of place, we can still tell story by affirming that mobile running flying narrator and its landlessness. A well of creativity and powerful language opens as we undo or defy conventional story structure.

How can we sing King Alpha's song in a strange land?[6]

My go-to guys for critical language expressing what I had long sensed and practiced are Deleuze and Guattari in their slim volume, *Kafka: Toward a Minor Literature*. A minor literature is "that which a minority constructs within a major language. ... [T]he first characteristic of minor literature... is that in it language is affected with a high coefficient of deterritorialization." With physical displacement comes a severing from one's social, political and cultural practices. Writers of the mix live this loss within the "cramped space" of placelessness, where, *of necessity,* our individual stories connect to the political at every point (Deleuze and Guattari, pp. 16-17).

Life within such cramped spaces births uprising. In other words, writers of the mix/writers of color, with this high degree of deterritorialization in our language, exhibit high potential for radical and revolutionary work. With language less "representational", more expressive, marked by intensity; there is "a whole other story vibrating within" the story (Deleuze and Guattari, pp. 17-18). This critical language speaks of a condition perfectly familiar to me, and offers a way to refute those judging our works within old, biased parameters.

We must never listen to those who say, *Every story has already been told.* Having no stable place on the associative web of place and privilege, driven to the edges of that web by the engine of what we contain that is explosive—a liminal or marginal vision; a language of intensities; a story told by displaced, wandering narrative voices—we arrive at the invisible, the untold stories.

The contradiction of placelessness is that writers who have been knocked out of place, body and time by conditions of history and trauma, are, in a sense, present in more than one place at once, as well as in no place, but rather in flight. They have a gift at narration that does the same; narration that is fragmented, multiple, in motion. These issues of narration need to be recognized and explored, rather than feeding writers of the mix, writers of color, writers out of category—or imprisoned in incorrect categories—simplistic explanations of reductive forms of narration and story structure.

Placelessness and Intensity

The nature of our language: its intensity, density, wildness and far-ranging associative power, connects to our being writers in search, in flight, out of migrations and in hiding, seeking place when there is no place. The judgment "so intense!" is tinged with insult, from those standing firm in their place and privilege, who perhaps cannot long tolerate feeling dislodged, uncomfortable, challenged. Indeed, writing from a sense of place can imply writing from privilege. But the language of many of us—even those from communities long in place, but at the site of trauma—moves in a wandering line of journey, culturally dense and not cleanly obedient; associatively charged with a pileup of factors that work toward expression, factors that press. And pressure can make diamonds, no? Such language, in moving beyond the narratives that exclude, distort, and disappear us, can illuminate the finest threads of story. Critiques of our art must not be Procrustean, cutting off what's "too long" to fit the monster's bed, or stretching it to fill that bed of expectations.

Narrators of diaspora, of the mix, of color

Fragmented, diasporic experience often births a fragmented story structure with multiple narrative voices. Part of our work is finding narrative forms to hold the fullness of our story and reveal the interconnectedness of its shards. With that associative ability to move expansively in time and space, narrators develop who can hold the story, shamanistically revisit trauma, rejoin the fragments of a trauma-tized and amnesiac history, and explore what is hidden in the ragged seams of story.

Writers out of category and placeless can be embodied for an instant as boundary jumpers, border crossers, shapeshifters, in flight and magical appearance; we can disappear into the whirring of atoms that move together in form that is permeable; the membrane of the self, permeable. Stories and beings pass through us, take up residence. Lack of boundaries, as with trauma, pose difficulties for the psyche, yet opportunities for the birth and development of characters. The fuel of the dislodged narrator can push the story to repeatedly jump borders of place, time, character, and shift narration from voice to voice.

As a writer of the crossings; identity partly unknown, shifting and slowly revealing; I understand our preface to conventional "rules" of craft as this—do *not* buy the "rules" we've been force-fed, though they sit in us, but work with and against them through maximum exploration. Simply, interrogate the "rules", or step over them.[7]

Identity for writers of the mix lives in the truth of crossings, not in debate about "what" we are, or with imposed classifications that disappear us. Sometimes I ask my students to simply tell a story of being recognized, which helps them locate their voice.

The full exploration of identity is not over until all the bones are found; all history, known; all faces reconstructed; all migrations revealed; all the lovemaking and all the rapes recorded genetically; and even then... This is the condition of writers of the mix; perhaps, the human condition.[8]

Simultaneously, at every moment, populations with recognized and marked identities are under constant and vicious attack, and I stand with these struggles. While our vast unknown histories remain so, the identities of people of the mix cannot be fully recuperated (or disappeared) into categories, but lived as a mode of being, a connecting strategy; a tool for recuperation of history. Our literature of crossings is a practice of crossing that carries value, danger, and revelations of connectedness.

Whose instructions, to write from a sense of place?

Is being "placed" synonymous with privilege? It is fertile to interrogate it as such; to suspect these harping instructions hold (narrative) strategy that obscures and congeals concepts of hierarchy and power; distorts and mutilates our stories. The "placed" are the head of this order, the ruling class of story; the "norm". All else: deformed, overdone or falls short. One popular "story authority", Ron Carlson, says: "As we know, nothing happens nowhere" (Carlson, p.73). (Nowhere is where many people live, and from which they tell stories.) These words suggest why those placed may have less compassion for those who are not: "A woman in a vague place may not suffer. No real camp, no mental anguish" (Carlson, p. 73).

For many, our experience of place is surreal, dissociative, a wall already up between self and the place we find ourselves. It is not that those without place do not suffer, but that many with privilege of place cannot see them, or see "nothing happening", nothing they can perceive in writing with a high degree of placelessness; fluid, de-territorialized narration; "intensity" that perhaps disorients and dislodges the privileged reader; sacks his comfort; even terrifies him.

For this writer of the mix, "the secret of great speech and of great burning" is not in congealed formula. There is no straight line from identity to story, from genetics to voice, from the generations' cries to the beginning of our story. As I am not contained in one of 5 boxes absurdly claiming to hold identity, but call myself for now a writer of the mix, I must go with story finding its unconventional organic form in motion and constant tension. What we contain upsets, affects, confuses, celebrates, complicates, expands, sits in dense strata below the story surface, and cracks open story. We hold the key in our tangle of language and chorus of voices to the shape and structure of story's living clay; to its intentions, its vivid life in brokenness and harmonies, its true music.

"The man who couldn't understand me couldn't understand the roaring of a tiger."

(Césaire, p. 49)

Notes

1. See Razib Khan's article, "Stop using the word 'Caucasian' to mean white," at Discover/Blogs, at blogs.discovermagazine.com

2. "Subhuman mongrels" can be traced back to Adolf Hitler's 1925 book, *Mein Kampf,* used to fuel genocide against the Jews. Singer Ted Nugent used the term referring to then-President Barack Obama (Terrill, 2014).

3. The "one-drop rule" (hypodescent) "dates to a 1662 Virginia law" re: mixed-race individuals (Bradt, 2010).

4. Césaire's net of association, stretched agonizingly by colonialism and racism, arrives at shocking truths and beauty, suggesting it may be fruitful to ask writers: "What do you want to rediscover?"

5. Of course, some of us reside long at the sites of captivity, trauma, resistance, and creative rebuilding of community, and write wondrous stories, deeply placed (Hurston, 1985).

6. This line from Psalm 137 was adapted in lyrics by Renford Cogle, "Rivers of Babylon," sung by The Melodians, Jimmy Cliff, Bob Marley, and others.

7. John Gardner (p. 8) writes, "There are techniques—hundreds of them—that, like carpenter's tricks, can be studied and taught... but there are no rules."

8. The Jewish Multiracial Network and Jews for Racial & Economic Justice held the first national meeting of Jews of Color, May 2016, with African Americans, Latinos, Asians, Sephardic and Arab Jews, and others (Samuel, 2016).

Research confirming stories of the presence of Jews globally is voluminous and surprising; for example, Sephardic Jews mixed with the Lenca tribe in El Salvador (Chevez, 2016); and the Lemba people of Zimbabwe and South Africa descend on the male side from Jews from the Holy Land (Vickers, 2010).

9. See title story of *All Stories Are True*, by John Edgar Wideman (1993). In the few steps it takes the narrator to reach his ill mother, he has wandered, digressed, returned home as jazz does. This writing exploration comes from *Place and Exile; Borders and Crossings*, from my *Writing for Social Change: Re-Dream a Just World Workshop Series* (Achtenberg, n.d.)

References

Achtenberg, A. (n.d.). Writing Story / Finding Poetry / Freeing Voice. Retrieved April 12, 2017, from http://anyaachtenberg.com/?page_id=24

Bradt, S. (2010, December 09). 'One-drop rule' persists: Biracials viewed as members of their lower-status parent. Retrieved April 12, 2017, from http://news.harvard.edu/gazette/story/2010/12/one-drop-rule-persists/.

Carlson, R. (2007). *Ron Carlson writes a story*. Saint Paul, Minn: Graywolf Press.

Certeau, M. (1975). *L'Écriture de l'histoire*. Paris: Gallimard.

Césaire, A.; trans. by Berger, J., & Bostock, A. (1969). *Return to my native land*. Harmondsworth: Penguin Books.

Chevez, L. A. (2016). Indigenous Rights in El Salvador: The Legacy of a Great Lenca Woman. Retrieved April 12, 2017, from http://revista.drclas.harvard.edu/book/indigenous-rights-el-salvador

Deleuze, G., & Guattari, F. (2012). *Kafka: Toward a minor literature*. Minneapolis, MN: Univ. of Minnesota Press.

Gardner, J. (1996). *The art of fiction: Notes on craft for young writers*. New York: Alfred A. Knopf.

Hurston, Z. N. (1985). *Spunk*. Berkeley, Calif.

Khan, R. (2011, January 22). Stop using the word "Caucasian" to mean white. Retrieved April 12, 2017, from http://blogs.discovermagazine.com/gnxp/2011/01/stop-using-the-word-caucasian-to-mean-white. Discover Magazine blog

Terrill, D. (2014, January 18). What if Ted Nugent were president? The Nuge explains (VIDEO). Retrieved April 12, 2017, from http://www.guns.com/2014/01/18/ted-nugent-president/

Samuel, S. (2016, May 04). Jews of Color Get Personal and Political at First-Ever National Gathering. Retrieved April 12, 2017, from http://forward.com/opinion/340018/jews-of-color-get-personal-and-political-at-first-ever-national-gathering/

Vickers, S. (2010, March 08). Lost Jewish tribe 'found in Zimbabwe' Retrieved April 12, 2017, from http://news.bbc.co.uk/2/hi/africa/8550614.stm

Wideman, J. E. (1993). *All stories are true*. New York: Vintage Books.

Writing Exercise

Wandering and Digression: a writing exploration that implicitly questions the privilege of placed narration; expands the concept of place in diaspora writing; and honors the power of the placeless and displaced narrator to break conventional story form. We affirm the roving, wandering consciousness; the split and dislodged narrator who, through associative power fueled by the need for flight and ache for return, breaks open story to the invisible, hidden, suppressed—to its fuller context. Such narrators are characterized by permeability, liminality, motion, multiplicity and compassion.

First, write as jazz that wanders and returns, starting with a place, or a place lost, that is important to the narrator, character, or self. Give us a glimpse. Stay for a few moments, in that one street, house, forest, that office or bar—in that one image of place.

Second, write freely away from it. Digress! We know the broken story. We know rupture; we know flight. We know what it is to be knocked out of place, out of body; to travel in time. Wander—jump—digress—far away, to the opposite side of town, or of the globe; even to the most distant part of the universe, quickly! Write from that place. Use the music of your language—arabesque, drumbeat, cantor's song, celtic harp, wild salsa—and keep the miracle of your rhythms to carry the story far away in the time it might take the narrator to walk just a few steps.[9] Digression adds context, and opens the road to the invisible, and to the secret sources of events and emotions.

Third, write yourself (or your character) back to the place you started. An entire story might form with its own bone and muscle; no attention paid to "conventional" form.

Personal Narratives

The Thenar Space: Writing Beyond Emotion and Experience into Story

Taiyon J Coleman

> When I was just eight years old, "... [a] thousand injuries of
> my... [auntie] I had borne as I best could, but when... [she]
> ventured upon insult, I vowed revenge."
> —Edgar Allan Poe, "The Cask of Amontillado"

"You're too stupid to ever write about anything," is what my auntie
laughed and said to me in response. I had announced in my grandmother's house at the dinner table that I was going to write a book, my
first novel.

From calling me stupid to teasing me about my weight and laughing
about my loud asthmatic snoring in the middle of the night, I was
determined to write about all the injustices that I had suffered at the
hands of my wicked auntie with her skinny-ass Jordache jeans and a
early 1980s feathered haircut.

Although she was my mother's baby sister, she was only six years
older than me, and she viewed me as her nemesis. Earlier that morning,
she hung the multicolored living room rug out to dry on the wire
clothes line directly facing me and all my neighborhood friends, including the one brown boy that I liked as we played run-in-bases in the
adjacent yard. As the area rug dried, a round darkness demarcated the
space where I had an accident as I slept on the floor pallet the night
before; at my grandma's house, I wasn't allowed to sleep in a bed nor
on her couch). Hanging that carpet out to dry announced to all my
friends that I wet the bed, and like the Montresor in Poe's "The Cask
of Amontillado," I vowed to take vengeance, a writer's payback, with
the utmost impunity against my auntie for her insult. I would write a
novel telling about her evil ebony black ass.

During the month of June over that summer of my eighth year, I
dug through my grandma's green flowered couch cushions like a
Peabody coal miner searching for the daily coins that my Papa let slip
nightly from his drunken pants pockets. With my shiny pilfered money,
I made a bike trip to the Sparta Pharmacy. I purchased Bottle Caps,
Lemon Heads, Jolly Ranchers (we called them wine candy), a big shiny
black binder, a Bic blue pen, and the biggest freaking packet of white
notebook paper that I could find. I think it was a paper packet of one

hundred pages. I know. It was so lovely. I still get excited when I encounter empty writing paper today. Once home, I ran into my grandparents' house, and like any serious author, I sat down to use their coffee table to ceremoniously prepare my writing materials. Even at 8 years old, I believed that procedure and process was everything.

I stuffed all my candy into my sweaty grey white bra distributing it evenly between my breasts lest I be subjected to my big sister's "finders are keepers and losers are weepers" law. I know I was only 8 years old, but I was a big black girl, and yes, I was wearing a bra, and no, it was not a training bra.

I took the blue Bic pen out of the store bag, and I placed it gently on the coffee table next to my grandma's hoarder stack of *People* magazines. Jesus himself help you if you tried to throw just one away, especially the ones that were at least 5 years old. My momma always wrote with a blue pen in her checkbook, in her word circle puzzles books, and on little sheets of white paper that I occasionally found crumbled up on top of the kitchen garbage can where she had obsessively, what seemed to me at the time, added and subtracted the same numbers over and over again in order to arrive at a budget number greater than 0.

I wanted to be like Momma in any way that I could, but according to my grandma, my skin was too dark, and I was too hardheaded, and as a result, hard pressed to get any lighter. During my summers in Sparta, I didn't do a good job of taking grandma's sage advice to stay out of the sun and to always wear a pair of shoes on my feet. They didn't carry skin lightener cream at the Sparta Pharmacy, but they did sell single blue Bic pens. So if my skin could not be as light as my Momma's, at least my writing ink color would be just like hers. Grandma didn't know anything about genetics back then and neither did I; to her, I had fucked up my skin color, my weight (too heavy), my hair (too nappy), my height (too tall), my mouth (too loud), and my feet (too large).

No worries. There was room for Grandma in the retribution novel narrative too.

Removing the plastic wrap from the notebook paper, I sifted the stack of white paper with red lines directly on top of the coffee table (to even it out of course) before placing the paper inside the black binder. I oscillated between holding the stack of paper up to my nose and breathing deeply of its woodsy scent and pounding it back on the table. The steady hard and loud whacks of tightly held one hundred pieces of paper repeatedly hitting my grandma's wood coffee table, recently polished with asthma inducing Pledge furniture polish, reverberated throughout her shotgun house and made my heart race in anticipation of my first written words.

"What the *hell* is that god damn racket?" my grandma yelled at me from the kitchen.

I didn't answer.

"Olon!" she called for my Papa trying to figure out what the hell was going on. He had already escaped the house to Micheaux's, the locale watering hole on the west end of town via his red riding lawn mower at about 6 miles an hour. The sun would fall before Papa would return to find my grandma asleep in her room, me on a pallet on the living room floor, and him on the couch for what was left of the night. I don't think the Sparta police gave out RLMWUIs (Riding a Lawn Mower While Under the Influence) back then.

"Cut that shit out girl!" Grandma followed up with even louder when she didn't get a response from my Papa, and it didn't even faze me.

I had 100 new and even empty white sheets of paper with a new blue Bic pen awaiting a rendezvous with a new black shiny binder, and I was going to write my god damn novel. I was in heaven, and not even my grandma's shouted threats of a fresh green tree switch with my full name written all-up-on-it torn from the front yard oak tree could take this moment away from me. The second chapter of my novel was going to be solely devoted to grandma's mean ass in detail, and remember, the first chapter was destined for my auntie (a.k.a. Fortunato).[1]

The last piece for my materials assembly, the shiny black binder, lay flat and open with its even shiner metal clips in the middle. Leaning over the coffee table, I placed a hand on each end clip of the binder, I pressed the metal tabs, and the circle clips "popped" open. Smiling wide, I grabbed the pack of paper like I used to grab my 2-year-old brother that I raised from a baby, and I lined up the notebook paper circles with the open circular metal clips. I replaced my hands on each of the clips and pressed the tabs. The tabs "clicked" into space and closed.

It took a second for me to realize that my skin, the fleshy webbing between my left index finger and thumb, which I now know is anatomically called the "thenar," was shooting daggers through my left hand and up the left side of my body.[2] I looked down, and I realized that I caught my hand inside the lock of the binder's metal circle clips. For a moment I was stuck as I couldn't pull my flesh from the metallic circle's hold, or I risked tearing a complete hole into my skin. Breathing deeply, I used my right hand to press down on the left tab of the binder and "pop." All the metal circle clips opened.

"Well ain't that shit a bitch," one of my grandma's most popular catch phrases, ran through my mind, and I was able to gently remove the flesh between my thumb and my index finger from the death star[3] grip of the binder's metal ring. Small red, almost black, dots dripped across my fresh white paper before I could place my hand inside my mouth to suck the blood in order to solve the next writing challenge facing me.

To conserve paper, I decided to write on both sides of the notebook paper because I didn't know when I would be able to raise enough couch coins for the purchase of more paper, and I just knew that I had a lot of shit to write because, in my 8-year-old mind, these people had been doing me dirty for 8 fucking years too many. There was not enough small bags of spicy hard pork rinds and bottles of homemade root beer in the world to soothe my mind, body, and spirit of their perpetual slights.

Steve Perry's heartfelt "Don't Stop Believing" played in the background from the ajar door of my auntie's bedroom where her brand new 1980s blue stereo set with matching speakers sat directly in front of her queen size bed. As the metallic taste of blood from my left hand soothed me, I used my right hand to start my retribution masterpiece and oscillated between writing with my right hand and picking and eating my candy out of my sweaty bra, as my grandma repeatedly complained that the house thermostat for the air conditioner was set on hell.

I wrote sitting on the couch in the living room in Sparta, Illinois, for what seemed like hours in front of the TV. *The Young and the Restless* had started, and by the time I came to the bottom of the back of the first page, the soap opera was over, my left hand had stopped bleeding, my candy from my bra was all gone, I seemed to have exhausted my injustices, and my right hand was severely cramping.

Today, no matter how hard I try, I can't remember anything after that moment, and I don't ever recall returning back to that shiny black notebook to finish my handwritten novel. I do, however, still carry the pain from all the bad things that my auntie and grandma said about me and did to me. When those memories become really bad, I now know that writing, believing in myself, and having the courage to tell and write my stories was and is a powerful weapon that no one, not even my grandma and my auntie, can ever take away from me. Of course, I hope that my craft of good writing has grown from simple Edgar Allan Poe reckoning and justice stories to narratives of the human condition with the complex and creative ability to weave empathy and compassion into individual and specific characters and their infinite conflicts that work to resonate beyond the personal.

Hopefully with craft, empathy, and compassion, my writing grew to craft beautiful and tragic tales of what possibly happened to a young black girl born in the 1930s in a small rural town on the Mason-Dixon line that could make her grow to be so mean and ugly to her own children and grandchildren, and my writing now explores the social and family dynamics of generational addiction, racial oppression, sexual abuse, and poverty that easily turns the soft-rock of the late 70s, a featured haircut, and a pair of bran new Jordache jeans into a stone cold inhumane bitch before the age of 16.

So what does this have to do with alternative approaches to creative writing?

As a writer, I learned early in my life from the people closest to me, my family members, that writing and being a writer would be an extremely challenging thing for a poor black girl from Chicago to do and be. It's one thing for Frederick Douglass to write about the curse of new knowledge upon acquiring literacy while enslaved[4], and another thing to actually live, in "free times," and have literacy, and to still have to act against silencing from your family members, society, culture, and institutions as a woman writer of color.[5] Negative experiences have first and foremost come from my family and the struggles of a belief in myself, struggles affected and compounded, like really high interest on bad debt, by structural and cumulative racism and sexism, and it manifests at a micro, individual, level. As a black female writer, I have had to fight against my family, community, self, and institution while writing simultaneously. In this vein, my literary culture is a proud culture of struggling against silencing to result in the power, art, agency, beauty, and self-actualization that comes from speaking, writing in spite of.[6]

Overcoming my negative writing experiences is a daily practice of consistent writing and self-love through individual work and effort and community. The rules for my craft are simple: just read and write when and where you can about what you want. In *On Writing*, Stephen King says that "If you want to be a writer, you must do two things above all others: read a lot and write a lot. There's no way around these two things" (King, 2000, 145). Turn off those negative self-voices, those negative people, and negative situations and do the positive you, which is believing in yourself and your writing through direct action: reading, writing, and loving yourself—challenges and all!

As a partnered woman with three kids and a full time job, I try to not write when my hair is on fire, and I am always working to develop a routine practice. In lieu of a routine practice that may be challenging in the face of prioritized responsibilities like kids, work, life, etc., I join writing groups and make contracts with my writing friends in my writing, creative, and artistic communities to challenge one another and keep ourselves on task through being accountable to others about our writing and writing processes. Ultimately, my goal as a writer is just to produce writing that tells my story and has utility for readers; I want to always connect outside of myself and my world to the equally valuable worlds and experiences of others. In this way I am connected, connecting, and never alone.

Notes

1. The Montresor cleverly uses Fortunato's hubris against him and outwits Fortunato into the catacombs where the Montresor buries Fortunato alive. I in no way advocate that writers use violence and/or violence against family members in this, my, essay. I am using Poe's short story as a writing metaphor and making an attempt at levity. As a writer, I subscribe to the saying that the "pen is mightier than the sword."

2. "...The root is the Greek verb *thenein*, meaning to strike, and thenar was that part of the hand with which one would strike, or the palmar region...." See Lyons (2008).

3. A reference to George Lucas' *Star Wars* (1977) and its Death Star seem appropriate here, as in this moment I truly understood what the Force meant. I was trying to work in the light, but clearly, my grandma and auntie were using their Force for dark side, and my hand injury was the result. My real parents were dead, I was in the wrong fucking family, and I just needed to wait for my Ben Obi-Wan Kenobi, C-3PO, and R2-D2 to show up, and then, things would be right with the world.

4. In *Narrative of the Life of Frederick Douglass*, Douglass speaks of the ironic epiphany that literacy brings to his condition of slavery and ignorance. Once he can read, he learns how enslaved he is mentally and physically, and ironically, he also becomes more dangerous as a slave that is literate because his agency increases.

5. Patricia Hill Collins (2009) argues, "The convergence of all these factors... the suppression of Black women's voice by dominant groups, Black women's struggles to work with the confines of norms of racial solidarity, and the seeming protections offered by a culture of dissemblance influences yet another factor shaping patters of silence." (p. 135). Also see, "Crooked Room." in Harris-Perry (2011).

6. Hurston, Zora Neale. "Characteristics of Negro Expression." (McKay and Gates, 2004, pp. 1041-1053). See also, Hughes, Langston. "The Negro Artist and the Racial Mountain." (McKay and Gates, 2004, pp. 1311-1314). See also, Wright, Richard. "Blueprint for Negro Writing."(McKay and Gates, 2004, pp. 1403-1410).

References

Collins, P. H. (2009). *Black feminist thought: Knowledge, consciousness, and the politics of empowerment*. New York: Routledge.

Douglass, F. (2001). *Narrative of the life of Frederick Douglass, an American slave written by himself*. New York: Penguin.

Harris-Perry, M. V. (2011). *Sister citizen: Shame, stereotypes, and black women in America*.: Yale University Press.

Hugo, R. (2010). *The triggering town: Lectures and essays on poetry and writing*. New York: W.W. Norton.

King, S. (2014). *On writing: A memoir of the craft*. New York: Scribner.

Lucas, G. (1977). *Star wars episode IV: A new hope*. 20th Century Fox.

Lyons, J. (2008). Etymology of Abdominal Visceral Terms. Retrieved March 26, 2017, from https://www.dartmouth.edu/~humananatomy/resources/etymology/Forearm_hand.htm

MacKay, N. Y., & Gates, H. L. (1995). *The Norton anthology of African American literature*. New York: W. W. Norton & Company.

Morrison, T. (1993, December 7). Toni Morrison - Nobel Lecture. Retrieved April 15, 2017, from http://www.nobelprize.org/nobel_prizes/literature/laureates/1993/morrison-lecture.html

Poe, E. A. "The Cask of Amontillado (1846)." *American Studies Hypertexts*, University of Virginia, 01 Jan 2004. http://xroads.virginia.edu/~hyper/poe/cask.html Accessed 07 Nov. 2016.

Writing Exercise

As a prose and poetry writer, I would like to leave you with a writing exercise that uses an object to facilitate the creative and objective writing experience, which often leads to discovery of new and exciting writing content.

I find that writing about a seemingly arbitrary object from one's own memory tied to other details of that memory helps to balance the emotions that can sometimes be overwhelming and obscure the creative craft and component needs of writing and the story itself for readers. Sometimes good writing is intentional, but most often times, it is an act of discovery while writing.

Richard Hugo (2010), in *The Triggering Town*, believes that the best writing resides within a trigger or a detail, which is usually a concrete image that the writer discovers in the early drafts of their writing. Hugo believes that the trigger in the writing, like a light in the dark, is a sign that signals the writer regarding the direction and the development that their writing content and structure should take. The vehicle in writing is the concrete detail and/or image that can carry infinite themes and meanings to the readers. Tenor is the infinite themes and meanings carried to the reader through the vehicle of the writing. Put differently, the vehicle is like a car that can carry the passenger (tenor) in a narrative. The value of your own writing often resides in the irony and tension between details of the past (revisited memories and feelings), knowledge of the writer (subject) juxtaposed to the hindsight (present details) contemporary view, and knowledge of the writer and their readers.

As you work through the exercise, I respectfully ask you not to think too much because over-thinking can disconnect us from ourselves and others, and as a result, stifle creativity. Never stop writing because like Toni Morrison (1993) said in her Nobel Lecture in Literature, "We [writers] die. That may be the meaning of life. But we do language. That may be the measure of our lives."

Part #1—A Warmup

Please write 10 sentences in 10 minutes. Your sentences must include the following:

- A detailed description of your favorite object; please make sure you use any applicable senses to fully explain your object: touch, sight, hearing, taste, and smell;

- A personal memory and/or an event in which your favorite object was included;

- An explanation of how that object makes/made you feel, so please name (write) at least one emotion (feeling), and answer this question: How did that event make you feel, and why?

- One sentence and/or detail that is entirely false (a complete and total fabrication... a.k.a. a lie)!

There are no right or wrong answers, so have fun!

Part #2—Juxtaposition of point of view and time in personal narrative writing

Spend one minute finding and thinking about a childhood/younger memory about something that you wanted but that you did not receive. It can be a tangible object or something intangible.

Now, write three sentences from your memory explaining what that "thing" was that you wanted and did not receive. Don't explain why— just explain what. Don't censor yourself.

Write three sentences from your child's and/or younger point of view explaining why, then, you actually wanted that thing that you did not receive. Please try to use a child's (younger person's) logic, and please include (reference) your age, at that time, somewhere within the three sentences;

Now, write three sentences from your now, adult point-of-view, explaining how you feel now about that situation and how you believe it affected (or still affects) you, and why. In order for irony (tension) to result, the adult's answer to why should be different than the child's answer for why. If the answer is not different, explain why you think your answer has not changed.

If there is time, talk, write, and reflect about how this exercise felt to you and why.

How Maya Angelou Empowered Me to Write

Saymoukda Duangphouxay Vongsay

This personal essay comes from a place of frustration. It comes from calling out a literary ecosystem where racialized representations and pleas for diversity and equity are largely dismissed. Muffled are voices from indigenous, transnational, and diasporic writers who are left to their own initiatives. So we create spaces for ourselves because it is necessary while inadvertently creating spaces for one another too. It happens this way because we've all felt isolated, dismissed, or silenced at some point in our career. We are asked to consider our place in this largely white male dominated (WMD) literary ecosystem. Some of us give in. Some fight on. When we are invited into WMD spaces, we sometimes have to be more than just the writer. We become interpreters, cultural navigators, and negotiators for the words written in our native language to not be italicized or footnoted. It can be exhausting.

As a young girl, I went without reading, seeing, and hearing stories about the Southeast Asian refugee exodus from the mainstream. Lao Americans have resettled in the United States for more than 40 years and yet our stories are not widely known. My fight as a writer has been about normalizing my refugee identity in my poetry and my plays. For some, *refugee* has negative connotations. It's associated with trauma, shame, violence. But there is also resiliency, survival, hope. I want my work to honor the trauma, violence, resiliency, and hope.

This essay comes from an alternate vision of whose story is appropriate for amplification. As I'm writing this from the non-WMD nook that my husband has created for me, I'm reminded that my work is not *play*. He has seen and felt my sadness in no longer having a workspace. He emptied a corner of his recording studio, leaned a futon and coffee table on one wall and bordered the five-foot window with string lights. *You can write as much as you want here.* He gets it. He fights for me to write.

It took years for me to understand and fight (even myself) to claim my place in the literary ecosystem as a writer. I used to not have the courage to ask for it until others showed me how, through their writing, their presence, and their insistence, they mattered. I credit Maya Angelou for my awakening.

* * *

In 1993 I was a cocky 12-year-old whose poem was published in the school newsletter. The 15-line *Oranges* was a declaration of love for citrus. No one in my seventh grade class had positive words about the poem after reading it except for Lin. She was my best friend, my girl crush friend, and if she liked it, then well, I'll have to write more just like it. Just for her. 1993 was also the year that I stopped going to English as a Second Language sessions, declared myself a writer, and decided to pursue writing as a career. When I told my parents of my intentions, they said, *You can be whatever you want as long as you make it to college.* They followed that with a laugh. *Laughter* when translated from the Lao refugee lexicon meant *affirmation.* It was better than yelling. Their laughter was all the oddly-supportive blessing I needed.

My science teacher, Mr. Martin, advised me to do proper research if I wanted to be a writer and to read titles outside of my comfort genres. Venture away from my beloved adventure, horror, science fiction, and comics? *All great writers do it,* he said. I trusted him. He was a scientist after all. Lin and several other girls recommended *The Baby-Sitters Club* and *Sweet Valley High* series while some of the boys tossed *Maniac Magee* and *My Side of the Mountain* to me in the hallways. I accepted the stories of the babysitters and the teenagers at Sweet Valley High for the soap operas that they were. In an honest attempt to be adequately thorough, without being dismissive of each series I read several books. I contended that although white girl drama was completely out of my realm of understanding, I was intrigued by their parents' divorces, their obsession with school dances, and the level of intimacy they developed during sleepovers. I thought, *If these are the stories that take up all the room on the bookshelves, then where will my stories fit?* I grew up with five rules that if broken, had hefty punishments including: being sent back to Laos to live with my father's relatives. Unlike the teens in the *Baby-Sitters Club*, I wasn't allowed to talk on the phone, attend sleepovers, or date. Those books were in no way a mirror to my reality. My English teacher told us, *Write what you know.* But would anyone find my stories about migration, food stamps, and multi-generational household-living fascinating? I never saw stories like mine in bookstores so I wasn't able to even imagine that they could be one day. I ranted to my English teacher, *Why are there so many white people stories?* She nodded her head, sighed then said, *Come back here after your lunch period and I'll have something for you.* An hour later she gave me an alphabetized hand written list of writers of color.

> Letter A—Angelou, Maya.
> Letter B—Baraka, Amiri.
> Letter C—Chin, Frank.

In January of 1993, Maya Angelou, as Poet Laureate, recited a poem for President Bill Clinton's inauguration. I'm embarrassed to admit that I didn't watch it in real-time but remember thinking, *A former "night lady" is reading a poem at the White House,* and seconds later, *A refugee like me could be there someday.* She was accepted fully for all that she's experienced and for all of the work that she has done to help others find empowerment in their experiences. Knowing that she, with all of her graceful messiness and honesty, was honored by an entire nation and welcomed to tell her story—I developed an interest in her work and started reading her poems.

During a bus ride home one day an eighth grader sat next to me. In her hand was Maya Angelou's *Wouldn't Take Nothing For My Journey Now.* I thought it was pretty sweet that I was sitting next to another book worm so I pulled out *Maniac Magee* and started to pretend-read, hoping that she'd notice a fellow book lover and—most importantly—befriend a seventh grader. Fifteen minutes had passed since we pulled out of the school yard and she hadn't opened her book. *What book are you reading,* I asked with a high shrill voice. *I'm reading Maniac Magee. He's a runaway,* I said. *That's cool,* she said. *Thanks! What about you? What about you,* I repeated, trying way too hard. She lifted the book from her lap, *It's not for me. My older sister's school library didn't have it so I'm borrowing it for her.* I didn't know what to say except, *That's smart.* She smiled. *Uh-huh,* she nodded, *my sister's smart. She's a junior and she's studying essays. This book has essays about being a black woman.* I felt, strongly, the desire to read those essays and so the next day, I went to our library searching for the book. It seemed that the Eighth Grader checked out the only copy. I was told to wait two more weeks for my chance but when that time came, I had forgotten about it.

The season changed and so had my reading interests. No more were teen soap operas taking space in my backpack. I was finally reading Angelou's book. The essays, stylistically, were like nothing I had encountered. I felt like I was reading my friend's journal. I took my time with the book—I literally had to because of my dyslexia—and went over passages, sentences, and certain words over and over. Angelou's writing helped me to understand how politicized my existence was (and is) in this society. She wrote about taboo topics like her husband's affair and sexuality. I didn't know that those stories could live in *real* books. Between you and me, I hadn't menstruated and my friends were nervous for me. They said that I may never bleed. Some said that the tuberculosis I suffered through the fourth and fifth grade canceled my period. I half-believed them, but part of me was also grateful for the slow blossoming because it meant that males averted their eyes from my body. I didn't have to navigate the horny boys in the hallways or at the bus stop. No one wants to kiss sickly. All of this tragedy is literary gold and I intended to be empowered rather than shamed by it.

That spring, I started a journal. My mom bought me a composition notebook and stickers from the dollar store. My first entry was an imagining of my first period. I wrote for a long time that night, almost a full hour. I carried my notebook close to my body. I wrote in it when I felt inspired. Those pages were my confessionals. I made superficial entries like my dislike for Noah's love confession or getting new shoes for volleyball. I also bled on those pages. I wrote about my mother's depression and how ill equipped I was to help her. On her good days, I made sure to write too. It was urgent for me to memorialize her happy days. But I mostly wrote list poems. Sour mangos. Afterbath Splash. Mt. Airy. Tiger Jack. Tuberculosis treatments. I filled two composition notebooks before the end of the year. I felt empowered each time I wrote a new entry or poem. I haven't stopped writing since. I do it mostly for legacy. I am hoping that someday, a young person may hear me speak or recite a poem at the library, open mic, or in a classroom, and feel inspired. They will think to themselves, *If that tuberculosis-surviving dyslexic refugee menstruating woman can do it, I can too.*

Excuses are for losers

It took me a long time to understand that I was sabotaging myself with excuses. I'm not lucky enough to live in a bubble where it was just my voice asking me, *Who am I to dream?* Although I exist independently from others, I'm still an essential part of a literary ecosystem operating as a writer and a reader. My inner voice contended with other voices. Sometimes, the voices joined forces and became a singular Supreme Voice that guilted me out of writing. There were just so many excuses! Some of which you may recognize as your own:

I forgot to bring my laptop. This pen doesn't write smoothly enough. The internet isn't working and I need to get online to do research. I'll shower first. The laundry needs to get done. My nails are too long for me to type comfortably and I'm too tired to trim and file them today. I need a writing partner. Fifteen minutes is not enough time. I don't like any of these writing prompts. Inspiration isn't coming to me. This story idea is no good. No one is even going to read this. There's nowhere to write. I have to do this other stuff first. I can't write on an empty stomach. I ate too much so I better let my belly go down before I start that poem. I can't decide on which book to read. If they had given me that grant, I could've worked on my poetry manuscript. This doesn't even make sense. I quit. I need a smoke break. I should watch some Netflix to get inspiration. My computer doesn't have Microsoft Word. That submission fee is too much. Those panels will only pick their friends. I forgot grammar rules. My English degree has become pointless. Why am I doing this again? I don't have a writing community. I'm the only Lao writer in this city. What if I don't have an audience for my work? I don't have a proper writing space. It's too loud. It's too quiet. I can't find the right playlist on Spotify for me to write to. This isn't the right time for the project. It can wait. I can't afford that writing workshop. I should spend more time with my family.

It took some practice for me to squash those excuses. As the years passed on, voices of support and inspiration became audible. They took shapes as mentors and even rejection letters! But I learned how to train my ears to recognize these voices. Eventually, I learned how to amplify the positive voices and the excuses came up less and less.

Writing Exercise

You are a superhero. What are your own unique gifts and talents? What powers do you hold to help make yourself, your community, and the greater community better?

Think of an issue that you care deeply about. How does the issue negatively impact you, your community, or the greater community? What are the far-reaching implications of their actions? Now, imagine that issue as a Super Villain. What does it look like? How does it move around in this world? What are its strengths and weaknesses?

In every superhero narrative, there comes a moment when the villain is finally caught. The superhero usually gives an epic monologue before slaying the bad guy. Write your epic monologue.

Legendary Documents

Tou SaiKo Lee

I was thinking about a scenario of how it would have been if I had today's access to social media like YouTube, Twitter, Facebook, and Instagram when I was growing up as a teen in the 90s.

For example, I would take Instagram photos of my specialty growing up, ramen noodle soup with hot dogs and boiled eggs. Post pictures of the time when I tried to fry bologna and it just bubbled up and got burnt around the outlining. Maybe capture the time when I made macaroni and cheese for grandma and she scolded me about why I needed to put cilantro and green onions in it to make it taste festive for her.

During my high school days, I used to stroll around Frogtown looking for something to do and saw a bunch of other kids just kicking it with no place to go. I was looking for a program to join or to get a job but never found anything. Maybe back then, if I posted my frustration as a status on Facebook, other people would make comments with suggestions of places I could work or programs I could join. Just about every kid I remember seeing in that neighborhood ended up in a gang… eventually.

I remember when someone stole my basketball hoop and I found out it was a neighbor that took it and he lived about a block away. I saw it on his alleyway and when I went to go get my hoop back, his friends started saying all this gang stuff to me that I didn't understand. One of them did these weird formations with his fingers like some type of gang sign language to me. That's when I called up my cousin who was in his own gang to come over and do some… gang translation. My cousin got me my hoop back… then told me to join his gang. And now that I think back about it, *I joined a gang because of a basketball hoop* and it became a life-changing situation that shaped my pathway to this day.

I was thinking about how in grade school, random kids would say racist phrases to me like *ching chong* and *go back home to where you came from*. I thought about what I would've done about it besides splashing a carton of skim milk in one of their racist faces, then quickly disappear into the hallway. I was one of the very few Asian kids in that school. Retrospectively, I would've placed my used Samsung Galaxy, passed down by my uncle, into my shirt disguised as a pocket protector. Then turn on the phone's video camera, go back up to those kids, let them know I didn't hear them and to repeat what they said.

Then I would let them know I video recorded every stupid thing they said and if they ever said it again I would post this clip to my YouTube account of like 500 subscribers, mostly family and other Southeast Asian peeps so "you all, would be targeted to get a beatdown." Like if I pressed this button right now, this video would be uploaded for everyone to see. Then later that night I would post up the video anyways 'cause well, I wouldn't be conscious of consequences yet and someone has to be an example.

Our Hmong people have a history of stories that have been passed down from one generation to the next. These days with most highlights of our lives being caught on video and uploaded that moment, there is not much room for imagination or lies.

No exaggerated details in storytelling.

So when I tell stories about the playground when other kids would say racist stuff to us, I can't just tell everybody, "yeah we straight beat him up." Because when the Vine video comes out, it shows that I threw sand in their eyes and pushed them down the slide and it looks like I was the bad guy, and a dirty fighter. Well, I was.

I was thinking about status updates I would have posted as an angry and emotional teenager and all the shitty poetry I wrote during that time. Then when I realized it could affect my adult life, I would've had to deactivate my account, change my Facebook name and start a new page. But back then...

I wouldn't have had private messages from family I never knew in Fresno and Thailand to keep up with each other's lives and get connected world-wide.

I would've clicked "like" on the Flux Capacitor's fan page.

I would've followed Blackstar, Mountain Brothers and Aaliyah on twitter.

I could've blocked the gang members that wanted to recruit me back then.

But, oh yeah, we did have our own social media back then, Asian Avenue and MySpace, but I don't remember anything I ever posted or did except promote Delicious Venom hip-hop songs and meet people from other states with outdated photos on their profile page. But I can't find any of that stuff anymore on the internet and maybe I'd rather just tell you my stories from those days from my own perspective.

Looking back, I realized that I grew up around a good amount of violence, whether it be racist bullies or gang members, that I never expected and my parents survived war for us to be here as refugees. I felt sorry for myself and what I had to go through because I was a silent, gentle child that had to fight, run, and overcome. This is what really influenced me to become what I am today.

Now, I fight to give back to my community and help provide the resources that I never had, whether it be afterschool youth programs or visiting schools as a positive speaker. I run to motivate a movement of young people to express themselves and their stories through poetry and hip-hop workshops. I overcome to honor my parents' sacrifice and ancestors' history for me to be here today. I keep striving to pass on our stories from one generation to the next. I fight to survive and write to thrive.

This would be the latest Facebook post that I would type for the world to see.

Writing Exercise: Back in the Day Games

Write a game you played outside back in the day (when you were a child).

> Examples: Freeze Tag, 4 Square, Duck Duck Goose

Write a person you played the game with.

> Examples: my friend Pat, my brother Vong, my cousin Washay

Write a specific location that you played the game at.

> Examples: at Franklin Elementary jungle gym, at my cousin's front yard, Phalen Lake Park

Write at least 3 phrases you shouted during this game.

> Examples: "Whoo hoo," "You can't catch me," "Oh no you didn't!"

Write about the specific weather and what you were wearing during that time.

> Examples: We were playing freeze tag in the snow in our onesie snowsuits. We played 4 Square on a hot summer day with our soccer shorts and no shirts on. I was playing duck, duck, goose in my Transformers shirt and corduroy pants.

Write one moment during the game that you felt an emotion and why.

Examples: I felt joy, I was running freely across the grass. I was angry that I lost but we played again and again. I was anxious I was going to get chosen and had to chase Washay around.

Write about your feeling now, thinking back to that time.

Stories that Must Be Told

Luis Lopez

The first time I wrote a story about the place I grew up, South Texas's Rio Grande Valley (RGV), I had it workshopped by a mostly white class in Minneapolis. Minnesota has a strange relationship with the RGV, as most places in the country have not heard of the quiet area. It is a summer retreat for Minnesotans fleeing the harsh winter months, and because of that that does allow for some point of reference, albeit a very different one from someone who grew up there. My main question was wondering whether I had managed to capture a feel of the place. Had I included enough nuance, enough detail, to summon pieced together fragments from deep within their memories to equal my own of this land? The class told me, "It's so outside of my experience."

"I love that it shows me how a different culture lives." No one could say if the story felt authentic, could speak to its achievement in verisimilitude. They liked that there was some Spanish in it—reminded them of Junot Diaz. They seemed to agree that it was a distinctly "un-white" story, without any white characters either named or alluded to, a look behind the curtain. Could they conceive that people of color felt shut out by the majority of American Literature? Their experiences nonexistent amongst limitless pages? Did they feel that everyone could identify as a dissatisfied white professor looking to step out on his wife? Are white lives so universally applicable in their opinion?

Growing up in the Rio Grande Valley, the most popular book at Bryan Elementary school during my time there was a collection of Southwestern folktales. The book itself *appeared* impressive, a stitched-together tome with a blood-red cover, its pages heavy and wrinkled like long ago papyrus. The school librarian kept the school's only copy behind her desk. Before you could check it out you first added your name to the waiting list. The list was columns deep, the names written with whatever pen was lying around.

Whoever checked out the book, for that week, collected a series of acolytes to follow them and the holy tome around. Most of the stories were not new to us; we had heard them from our parents and older relatives, but there was something special about seeing them in black and white, on a page, an eternal record; names we were familiar with—we existed—and one of us, Juan Sauvageau, had cared enough to write down our histories. There was no book I could find about being without your father while he's in a nursing home recuperating, nothing about killing time after elementary alone at the pizza place while waiting for your mom to get off work at the laundromat, nothing about being angry, nothing about not yet knowing you're brown because everyone else around you is brown. Juan Sauvageau's book, *Stories That Must Not Die,* was not the catalyst that made me decide to become a writer; instead, it served as a testament that the world had made a place for us and especially me.

The story I submitted for workshop didn't feel authentic to me. Sure, there were landmarks, and knowledge of the area, but an atlas can't bleed truth onto a page. Memories aren't fingerprints to be imprinted on empty space. I included in the piece the detail of a woman who had started a local restaurant in her garage. Each night for closing she simply slid down the garage door, a detail that was added to the chain of restaurants after she sold the name, an homage to origins, an attempt to return to some of the authenticity of the original idea. I felt as if I had become the restaurant chain owner.

I would have loved for someone to say, "It doesn't feel right," but there's not a lot of white undergrad students that will say that to *any* piece, much less one written about a culture not of their own by an author of that culture. This is where a non-white workshop lead would be the most helpful. Too often white workshop leaders do not offer the pushback needed to gain verisimilitude in the piece being critiqued. They are too ready to accept whatever reality and conditions are created by a person of that culture believing that the writer's own experiences supersede good writing. Because of that the famous workshop complaint of, "But that's what happened," suddenly gains traction. This creates an atmosphere in which the writers of color involved in the workshop are now responsible for speaking for all races when issues of cultural appropriation and exoticism arise.

Stories That Must Not Die must've enjoyed great success, because around middle school there was a huge number of horror books available in the library and even a few by Latinx authors. A Latinx author visited our school for a reading, I don't remember who he was or what book he wrote. I do remember hating the book. It felt watered down to me, as if he kept asking an editor if it would scare kids and after hearing Yes, he rewrote it again until he received a No. I was becoming jaded of everything, either because I was starting to read the Russians or because I was a teenager.

I was exploring more of the world through books, and as it turned out some did bother to write about poor people, although their version of poverty somehow seemed a lot nicer and cleaner and smoother than my own experiences. They would present poverty as something to be escaped and something that could be escaped with enough effort and will. During my time at middle school there was an incident that I would later fictionalize and convert into the story that I submitted for that first Minneapolis workshop. Besides the school's students, it also followed administrators and teachers as they dealt with the fallout of the incident, but of the characters I created for this world—some with a very close real-world equal—I decided not to include a facsimile of myself because after finally escaping the Valley I did not dare to write myself back in, forever to be trapped there by my own imagination.

In a different workshop, a year earlier, this one being led by a person of color, the workshop leader felt comfortable enough to ask me why in the stories I had submitted to his class were there no Latinxs. Why had I not written about the land and people that I had come from? I couldn't articulate my reasons. At that moment in my life, I was ashamed of my rejection of the land that made me—especially what other people of color would say about this rebuff. I didn't yet understand how much of my histories I would always carry with me. It was this push that had me revisit my past and allowed me to take hesitant steps towards embracing all that I was.

One of the first things I did was buy a water damaged copy of *Stories That Must Not Die* online from somewhere in Ohio or the Midwest. My memories of the stories had them exulting in their South Texas setting. Armadillos, horned toads, names that end in "z," superstitions, dirt, you could tell the man who wrote them held the area and their people in great esteem. So different from my earlier feelings. But I think it's much easier for people to love a place where they end up versus where they began. As an adult I was able to discern the distance that the author wrote with. It felt so much like my own work writing about the Valley. I looked into the author. John Sauvageau (nicknamed Juan) began his life in Quebec. Not South Texas like I imagined as a boy. Incredulity is how I would describe my reaction to this knowledge. Plus, I was pissed. The thought that he wasn't from the Valley, much less not Latinx, had not even crossed my mind. Like seeing an old tombstone and scrubbing away at the headstone until the real name is finally revealed under layers of muck. When I was a kid did I think he was one of us because his name was

Juan or because he recounted the stories so well? Genuineness is
something to be achieved, something to be worked for; it isn't granted
by a name alone, it takes hard work, it takes dedication, it takes truth,
it takes a system of honest feedback—something that is not easy to
achieve in a workshop and is made all the more difficult by issues of
race and poverty, but it must be pursued because the more voices that
are added to the conversation, the more we know there are others that
think and feel like we do—and the closer we get to that kid with the
busted lip hunkered over the Mortal Kombat 3 arcade game.

References

Sauvageau-Pro, J. (1989). *Stories that must not die*. Los Angeles, Calif:
    Pan American Pub. Co.

Writing Exercise

Grab a memorable book from your childhood and reread it enough
to remember the author's voice. Inflict upon a character in the story a
happening from today's newspaper. Start your piece by trying to stay
as true to the author's voice as possible, then slowly incorporate your
own.

How would that character react to this new story? How would this
story affect the character's personality?

Telling Stories That Should Not Be Passed On

Wesley Brown

"I could tell you something," my father said to me, beginning when I was seven or eight. He not only could but he did, especially after he'd had a few drinks. He told me stories from his childhood and youth that at times were harrowing, but never ceased to hold my attention. One could argue that it was inappropriate to be told, at such a young age, that my enslaved great-grand mother's thumb was permanently splayed out by her master using a straight razor to slice it open whenever she did something not to his liking, or my grandmother, who died at the age of 48 of complications from rheumatic fever, asking my mortified father to perform a necessary hygienic task that she was too weak to do for herself. There was nothing I could do but listen to him who, for whatever reasons, chose to unburden himself to me with these unsettling stories from his past.

As the 10th child of 12, my father was nursed through two bouts of pneumonia by his mother, who was not about to lose him after turning over in her sleep and smothering an infant girl named Frankie. My father, Leonard Abraham Brown, was the repository of his family's history. To paraphrase a line at the end of Toni Morrison's novel *Beloved*: These are stories that should not be passed on. This was my mother's view. Cosy Sheila Pitts did not tell me stories of any painful experiences in her past. Her stories to my sister, Evelyn, and me insisted on the importance of education. She was the valedictorian of her high school class in Fountain Inn, South Carolina, and the first in her family to attend college—but had to withdraw during her first year for reasons she never shared with me. It was my father who revealed what my mother did not want known, at least by me: that she'd become pregnant with my sister out of wedlock, which ended her college aspirations; and when my father and mother married, he legally adopted my sister. I was 11 or 12 at the time and the reason my father gave for telling me was that a neighbor who was a heavy drinker had made some remarks to my father, questioning his physical resemblance to my sister. I don't remember having any strong emotions in any direction. By this time, I looked forward to having him take me into his confidence, telling me things that people do that are hidden in plain sight, but without making any judgments. In retrospect, I came to understand that, for my father, it was better for me to hear from him about my mother having a daughter out of wedlock and marrying my father who adopted my sister than learning about it from someone who would turn it into something sordid and shameful.

The opening line of Joan Didion's book *The White Album,* "We tell ourselves stories in order to live," crystallized how important it was for my father to tell those stories and by extension how indispensable it was for me to discover the stories I needed to tell. And I found many of them through trips to the South to visit relatives, as well as images of the burgeoning Civil Rights Movement of the 1950s and early 1960s.

In 1954, my family was shaken by the tragic shooting death of one of my father's older brothers by a drunk, black off-duty cop at a Harlem after-hours joint. I also have a vivid memory of a summer trip that same year with an aunt who took me to Charleston, South Carolina, to visit her relatives, which included an afternoon spent at the site of the old slave auction near the city's harbor. I've never forgotten the photographs in *Jet* magazine of Emmett Till's face, bludgeoned into non-recognition; the compelling television footage of blacks during the Montgomery Bus Boycott; black students braving the vicious taunts by whites as they integrated Central High School in Little Rock, Arkansas; the Freedom Riders risking life and limb on buses traveling through the deep South; the black and white students being assaulted during a sit-in at lunch counters in Raleigh, North Carolina; the assassination of Medgar Evers in Mississippi in June, 1963; and the bombing of the 16th Street Baptist Church three months later in Birmingham, Alabama, which took the lives of four black girls. Although I was not directly involved in these unfolding historical events, I was drawn to them in ways similar to the experience of listening to my father's disturbing stories.

As much as my ears became attuned to the personal tragedies in my own family and in the world more generally, humor and laughter in the face of wrongdoing was always within earshot. Sometimes it was my roguish Uncle Johnny who could make my father bust out laughing, even after treating him badly; or my mother's older sister, Bernice, who talked with women friends in a strange lingo called "Tut" in front of her uncomprehending husband when she'd had enough of his terrible behavior; or being present during the lively barbershop banter about whether God would ultimately smite the wicked since He didn't love ugly, which triggered the comeback that "He ain't that thrilled about pretty neither."

My gradual move toward a more direct encounter with risk and danger arrived in June of 1965. I'd made the decision to go South to work on voter registration after two "Snick" (Student Nonviolent Coordinating Committee) staff workers spoke at the SUNY Oswego campus where I was a student. Their visit occurred during the period of the assassination of Malcolm X and the Selma to Montgomery march. I don't doubt that my parents admired the courage of the young people putting themselves in harm's way. However, they were not prepared for me being one of them. Perhaps my father expected his stories would've been a warning that the world was a frighteningly unpredictable and dangerous place, and that I should not, needlessly, put myself in the way of its wrath. These were among the reasons why my parents left the South. And here I was determined to move closer to the site of the hurt and dangers they had fled.

The months I spent in Mississippi were life changing, forcing me to see myself and world I inhabited in ways I could not have imagined. I was in the heart of the Mississippi Delta, helping to register black people who had been denied the right to vote in a country that was sending young men, many of whom were black, 10,000 miles away to bring democracy to Vietnam's Mekong Delta. Nothing I read or heard in the mainstream media reported this perspective or the entrenched economic, educational, and political institutions that kept rural blacks in a condition of penury not that far removed from their circumstances after the Civil War.

Once I arrived at the view that the narrative emerging from my young life was one that had to involve putting myself into a movement to change the glaring disparities between what America promised and what it practiced, it became clear that I could not, in good conscience, serve in the Armed Forces of the United States. Perhaps, without my knowing it, my Mississippi experiences and my determination to make common cause with others, wanting to create a story of our lives where we had a lot more to say about its direction, were the early indications that writing might be a way for me to find my own way in the world, rather than allow those embodying the diction of the powerful to do it for me.

After leaving Mississippi, applying for and being refused con-scientious objector status, graduating from college, and becoming involved with the Black Panther Party in the late 1960s, I decided to make a serious commitment to write and found two mentors in Sonia Sanchez and John Oliver Killens, whose writing workshops at the

Countee Cullen Library in Harlem and at Columbia University provided me with an invaluably supportive group of young black writers
who challenged and encouraged one another.

Finding my voice as a writer was aided by American writers such as
Mark Twain, Herman Melville, Stephen Crane, Gertrude Stein,
William Faulkner, and Ernest Hemingway, and the discovery in 1970
of William Melvin Kelley and Toni Morrison, whose work cut to the
quick of the injuries the nation has inflicted upon its citizens and those
we have inflicted upon ourselves—which were of a piece with my
father's stories. And reading Zora Neale Hurston, Ralph Ellison,
Flannery O'Connor, Ishmael Reed, and Toni Cade Bambara gave voice
to the hilarity that seasoned all the bad luck and trouble I overheard
from aunts and uncles and in barbershops.

My refusal to report for induction into the army in 1968 was never
far from my mind. And in January 1972, I was sentenced to three years
at a federal penitentiary in Lewisburg, Pennsylvania. Ultimately,
neither my father's grim cautionary tales nor my mother's silence about
personal catastrophes in favor of upward mobility narratives were able
to protect me from the consequences of the story I was writing into my
own life. I was incarcerated for 18 months, most of which were spent
in a minimum security farm, just outside the walls of the maximum
security prison. If I'd served my entire sentence inside the wall, I'd have
been sized up, immediately, as someone who'd never been in prison
and would've been subjected to persistent threats of violence.

In *Notes from the House of the Dead,* Dostoyevsky wrote that if
you want to grasp the nature of any so-called civilized society, you
need only to look at its prisons. Even from the relative safety of my
minimum security facility, I found nothing to dispute Dostoyevsky's
assessment. All of the hierarchies, the ethnic and racial group
hostilities, and the reliance on violence as the instrument of social
control were present in a more extreme form.

I worked on a novel while incarcerated that had nothing to do with
my experience in prison. After my release in 1973, a writer friend
chastised me for not incorporating my time in prison into my autobiographical coming of age story of a young black man. Initially, I was
reluctant to consider this, thinking it was still too raw in my mind to
do justice to the experiences. However, after more thought, I had to
acknowledge I really didn't want to enter the emotional minefield I
knew was waiting for me. I asked myself why my father had passed on
to me all those terrible stories. Remembering something Toni Morrison

once said provided a possible answer: Coming to terms with a deep hurt often requires not keeping our distance but moving closer to it. So with more than a little trepidation, I wrote my way through emotions I hadn't allowed myself to feel while in prison, and my first novel was all the better for it. In every story or novel I've written since then, I've tried to remember my father's need to repeat his stories to me. That has given me the courage to write stories I'm reluctant to tell, making it not as likely that I'll be at the mercy of the historical and personal hurt that claims us all.

References

Didion, J. (1997). *The white album*. New York: Noonday Press.

Dostoyevsky, F. (1950). *Notes from a dead house*. Moscow: Foreign Languages Pub. House.

Nation Horrified by Murder of Kidnaped Chicago Youth. (1955, September 15). *Jet*, 4-9.

Writing Exercise

Whether it's death, illness, betrayal or failure, we all live in fear of something. And the writers who speak to us most profoundly are often those who expose fears we would prefer to keep hidden. Think of an aspect of your own life that is the source of great trepidation and dramatize it in a short story.

Rejection Not an Option

Fear of an Apocalypse: Racial Marginalization on the Act of Writing

Hei Kyong Kim

> I have a reoccurring dream of fast spinning tornadoes plunging down upon earth. I dream that the world goes black and there is nothing but the sensation of my heart ravaging the inside of my chest, threatening to rise up and spill over because... game over.

Sometimes I get caught up in thinking that I'm not a writer. Even though I have been writing since I was a kid, I get sucked into the thoughts of how I'm unable to "make it" and instead became a listener of stories (psychologist). As irrational and self-defeating as that sounds, there is an explanation for this type of thinking. There is a history that goes back to my birth and my fate of loss and displacement. It goes back to a crib where a neglected newborn lay in a foster home across the sea, where a people—my own people—refused to accept me because of the shame I stirred in their collective blood. It arises from a response of growing up in a state that is mainly white; a city that has some diversity, but not to the extent I needed; a family that tried to embrace race, but in the end could not fully grasp that colorblindness and "just loving the child" was not enough. It arises from the feeling that I've never really belonged anywhere.

> Marginalization is a beast that rages and tells you, you are nothing. It warps the mirror you search for answers in, until you stop looking for answers and reflections of who you are and how the world sees you.

My favorite place is my bedroom. No matter where I live, my bedroom has been a place where I read and write and dream; a place that is safe and cozy and accepting; a place where I laugh and cry, sometimes all at once; a place I create and birth and nurture; a place that does not judge me and is strong enough to hold any emotion I've had without worrying about collapse or destruction. My bedroom offers an unedited space for me to be as wildly creative and expressive as I want. As a child, before I was able to write, I'd play make-believe for hours, acting out dramatic or violent stories that would make *good* television or movies. As I grew older and quieter, transforming my play to paper, psychology interpreted my pretend as re-enactment of grief and trauma. But psychology also told me that I was more nonverbal than verbal—learning disabled—and was puzzled by why I loved to write so much. According to its tests, visual art should have been my medium. But maybe psychology had it wrong. Its tests were administered before my grief and trauma had been worked on, at a time of distress and captivity (I was hospitalized briefly for depression and reality testing). Psychology at that time did not understand the profound impact of preverbal trauma, marginalized identity, and color-blindness in transracial adoptive homes. Psychology had a need to put people in neat little boxes full of numbers and data and generalizations in order to understand people on their terms. But it left out so much; it stripped voices and the richness of the psyche, simplified the true complexities of humanness.

Writing has provided me an outlet for self-expression, an opportunity to create my ideal world, to right the wrongs, and to be given the chance to exist in this universe. It has provided me with a voice when I feel silenced or unimportant. It gives me depth, it gives me drive, it gives me life. I once had a friend tell me that if she hadn't read my writing, she wouldn't have guessed that I had such deep thoughts in my head. Although that was kind of a backwards compliment, it makes me wonder if I hadn't found writing, would I now be so dissociated that I'd be like the millions of other zombies walking the earth.

My People

In the 1990s I finally put myself out into the world. The Twin Cities' Asian American and other literary arts communities showed interest in my writing, and people wanted to hear what I had to say. I received grants, publications, mentorships, and opportunities to work with writers I adored. There was nothing better than workshopping stories, poems, plays, and novels. I was in awe of the community and this was probably one of the only periods of time where I did not feel silenced or oppressed, and I blossomed into who I was as an Asian American woman. It was a time I integrated my experience with race, gender, culture, and social activism into my work. By then, I was a mother of two and working towards my BA in English with an emphasis in creative writing. I was participating in readings and social events and potlucks. I loved it. I loved getting to know people and their art. I was meeting other Adopted Koreans through my writing as well.

I loved who I was and all the people in the community of that renaissance era. I loved myself.

So I wrote a young adult book about a rebellious Korean adoptee, one that I had always wished was around for me when I was growing up. The book was picked up by a literary agent and I got swept up in the excitement and the hope. But I forgot about how rejection impacts me. Nobody likes rejection, but because I'm adopted, I am even more sensitive to rejection and it becomes solely about my core personhood. But the biggest problem I had was that the publishing industry did not understand two things about my book: diverse Asian American voices, and adoption. I understood the feedback about craft and style, but what truly struck a nerve was the character assassination—the comments about the protagonist being "too angry," "unsympathetic," and "unrealistic." I am one who always values and gives merit to critiques, but the reality of the mainstream industry—white, stereotypical, and racist—seemed to blindside me.

I forgot myself and wrote the book without considering a white or non-adopted audience. Some of the feedback from the mainstream publishers spouted comments about realism and perceptions that could not be imagined from their out-group perspectives. Their imagination of adoption and orphan rage could not reach beyond mainstream societal understandings of telling the character that she should be grateful. The editors' discomfort with rage and identifying with the adoptive parents only perpetuated the stigmatization of people who are traumatized and haunted by mental health issues, leading to narcissistic and compassionless understandings of adoption trauma, judging how traumatized people should or should not behave. It is hard to listen to intense anger—to validate, to find compassion and nurturance, to give room for voice. However, that's where the healing lies for most people, adopted and non-adopted alike, because beneath is great pain and suffering. And that compassion and empathy were what I felt was missing from the publisher's perspective of my novel's character.

The mainstream industry also could not comprehend other representations of Asian Americans being angry because we are seen as model minorities; they could not feel comfortable with an Asian adoptee hating being raised by white parents and hating how Asian-raised people treated her; they could not imagine her being external in her behavior because Asians are submissive and quiet and internal, because they are wise and philosophical and indirect. My character did not fit their template and so they rejected her. The publishing industry wanted me to conform and to give a more socially acceptable ending than the one I had given—the teen protagonist who found peace and calmed her rage by having a baby and marrying into a "real Asian family." They could not have that because it did not fit their template. They could not see the depth and the reality within the adoption community (only years later would I be inspired to write an essay for *Parenting as Adoptees* to address this personal line of thinking). So yes, I took it personally and shelved the book and told myself that my then husband was correct—writing should remain a hobby, and I should find a love for something that could support our rapidly growing family.

I meant to... I really, really meant to...

But there was always laundry to wash and fold, food to cook, a house to keep clean, traditional culture to observe, family events to go to, birth to give, babies to raise, years of graduate school in psychology to complete. I was preoccupied with being a good mother to six young children and a perfect *nyab* (the Hmong word for "wife"). I was really just searching for who I was and what I was worth. I was too tired to write, but when I did write, it stirred things.

I played make-believe again—this time in a journal—where I indulged in pure fantasy out of sadness, need for salvation, loneliness, misunderstanding of depression. Fantasy was mistaken for reality and I woke up to rubble and psychological violence and sleepless terror and an oppression I've never experienced before, all because my fiction was believed as truth. I realized how powerful words are (real or not, mine and his) and how they wounded everyone in my family. I was embarrassed.

> A beast arose
> My marriage ended
> My children cried
> My colon erupted
> A death occurred within me

I stopped writing for many years.

But then I had a dream where I was in a brownstone building as zombies started to roam out of their hiding places and into the streets. I could not go up the stairs because somehow they were also attacking from the roof and the basement. In total despair, I melted to the floor and decided I had to kill my children and then myself. I sat with a feeling of horror for a long time before noticing a co-worker—a psychologist—in the kitchen fighting a zombie. He was a white man, also with children to protect, and he was as passionate as me in helping people on a day-to-day basis. So why was I frozen? Was it the differences in privilege, lives lived, nervous systems? If he could fight why couldn't I? I never figured it out but the thoughts were enough to lift me from my hell and surge my adrenaline so I could stand up, grab a broken broom, and whack the crap out of the monster so we would not perish.

I am not a known name, and I am okay with that. I remind myself that I write for me. I write for the Asian American and Korean Adopted community. I am a selfish writer... I write for release, for expression, for authenticity. I no longer seek validation or approval. I write to express the social injustices and marginalization that occurs in the world and the impact it has on my children. I write to expose marginalized experiences in hope that there will be less someday.

Once I realized this, I wrote *The Translation of Han* and published it through a small grass roots press. Despite some people frowning on how it was distributed through a corporation and some people considering it to be more like self-publishing, I chose this avenue for myself. Publication elitism is oppressive and silencing and has caused a huge block to my writing, warped my self-esteem and identity, told me I was not a writer when I am.

As Toni Morrison so eloquently said, "If there's a book that you want to read, but it hasn't been written yet, then you must write it." And so I did.

References

Kim, H.K. (2008). Birth cycles. In A. Chau & K. Ost-Vollmers (Eds.), *Parenting as adoptees* (pp.170-185). Minneapolis, MN: CQT Media & Publishing.

Kim, H. K. (2014) *The translation of han.* Minneapolis: CQT Media & Publishing.

Writing Exercise

Since I am both a writer and a psychologist, I will suggest an integrated freewrite exercise. Mind-body is essential in staying connected with ourselves. When I start to notice disconnect, it impacts my creativity, my concentration, my writing, and my mood. I become distracted and cannot focus on writing or listening to the stories I hear. This is what I consider "writer's block." Take time to ground yourself by settling in a quiet space and close your eyes, take in a few slow deep breaths, feel the ground/floor with your hands or feet, track the sensations and the energy in your body. Listen to any voices that arise, or images that pop up. Once you feel settled, just start writing for 15-20 minutes.

Picking a Goot' Indin (*a play selection from* No Res Rezpect)

William S. Yellow Robe, Jr.

I was asked to be on an artistic committee to help a white theater company up north select an Indian play for the very first time in their 30th season. The Great Rocky Mountain and Plain Theater wanted to do something to reflect the Indin communities in a celebration of diversity. Sounded like they were going to be applying for a major grant, or they had been awarded grant money.

Sitting there as quiet as I could be, not being "stoic," but being quiet because I never really was familiar with drama, or screenplay writing. No, play writing. I knew a lot of Indin poets and novelists, but not many play writers. I heard stories that a young woman from the western part of the rez went to school and is writing plays. I wondered if they are considering one of her plays. I can get behind that—one of our own.

On the committee was me; one "Passes as the People" Indin, Duane Red Rainbow Soaring Eagle; one Indin-ologist, a professor from the community college who brags about teaching the younger generation of "how to be more Indin," Walt Bush; one cultural Mythologist, Laurie Camus; and a "Shame-men" from the local tribe of Rainbow people, Benny Love Child, he just said "Aho" when he agreed with anyone, but now he just drummed on the arm of the chair chanting "ahem" quietly to himself.

Pat Osborn the artistic director sat in his chair with a huge pile of plays in front of him. We had talked about 10 different plays. Only one written by a Native Tribal person and the cutting is getting thin right now. He knew what he wanted and was going to do but he wasn't telling us.

The last play we were looking at was from Kelly McWright. I never knew Kelly wanted to write a play. It was a good story. Based on her older sister and Kelly's life. I don't know how this group would take it. It isn't a *Dances with Wolves*, or an episode of *Dr. Quinn, Medicine Woman*. She had a hard younger life and there it is on those pages. I don't think these folks can take it.

"I am simply charmed by Keith Sager's *My Path*," said Laurie. She started to wave her arms in the air. Thankful she uses a lot of patchouli oil. "This play is the essential Native expression in post-colonial

America. It is a celebration of Pan-Indian-ism." She softly tugged at a few hairs on her chin and glared into our eyes.

"But he's not Native," I said, "Aren't you supposed to be looking for a play by a Native person."

"Well, let's be quite frank, we all are a little bit of Indian descent here at this table," said Walt. "I'm of Indian ancestry."

"Ahem!" said Benny. "It is so, it is so." He nodded his head and looked like he was ready to pass out. I'm not sure. If he starts to slobber then I know he's gone. He did that once at a social and we had to call the paramedics. He got really mad at us because he told us he had been astro-traveling. That slobber must be some of the residue from the launch.

"Brother and sisters," said Duane. "We are at a place that is made from the white heart of our white brothers. But we must decide with strong Native red hearts as to what the best gathering of words will represent us."

"What?" I looked around.

"Indeed brother," said Laurie. "We have to find the best play with the best heart. Ms. McWright's play may not be suitable because it's so, how should I say it, dark rez."

"Dark rez?" I looked at Laurie, who locked a glare into my eyes.

"Ahem," said Benny.

"Her words are very hard and may not present the best view of our people to our white brothers and sisters," said Duane.

"She is Indin and wrote a strong play," I said. "She is taking a big chance in doing this and I know folks from the communities will be touched by it. They need to hear and see this."

"Well, see! It's too reservation. We want a play that will reach out beyond the reservation borders and into the global community," said Laurie.

"Yes, I've read similar literature like this and this type of fare only finds life within those who are trapped. Never reaching beyond that," said Walt.

"Ahem," said Benny.

"Take a cough drop or something Benny!" I said. I didn't want to get mad but they were making me mad and what made this situation worse is that I had no footing on this ground. I was hoping I wouldn't do something wrong and spoil it for Kelly.

"We've done O'Neill," said Pat. Everybody looked at him. His pale hands nearly lost in the pile of scripts. His thin mustache highlighted his smile. "Ms. McWright's play isn't too dark. We've done some very dark and horrific plays in the past. Like Lear and the Bacchae set in Wal-Mart." He chuckled.

"She's the only real Indin person in this group," I said.

"You don't know that," Laurie snapped. "How would you know? Did you ask them for their enrollment card like a good Indian Nazi?" Duane, Benny, and Walt smiled at this comment. She played the enrollment card. Ironic she did this because she doesn't have one nor did the other three.

"No, I didn't ask them for their enrollment card. I did something worse. I asked the communities if they knew them. I asked who their relatives are, who they grew up with, if anybody went to ceremony with them, who prayed with them, or when they lost a member of their family were any of these people there to comfort the loss of that family. No one knows these other playwrights, but they know Kelly. One woman said she had always been afraid for her girl Kelly growing up because she wasn't sure she would make it. When I told her Kelly went to school and was writing stories she cried and hugged me and told me to give Kelly a hug for her and to say hello. My girls remember dancing with Kelly in the grand entry at our last social. They always admired her shawl and could recognize her at any celebrations because of the shawl she carries. The communities know her as their own," I said.

"Well," said Pat, "Her work is strong but there is this playwright, Mac Prive, who is an up and coming playwright we would love to work with and see a great future with him."

"And he's not Indin, is he?" I sat in my chair. I looked down at the reflection of a huge blurry light from the fake particle board conference table.

"I wouldn't know," said Pat. "We in theater aren't involved in that problem of identity that seems to weigh down the Indian communities."

"Oh-aho!" said Laurie.

"Ahem," said Benny.

"Good, we have strong hearts here," said Duane.

"I can agree with that," said Walt.

"At least, we know who we are and those who are a part of us," I said. I got up and walked out of the room. I felt so twisted inside. I was angry, sad, and raging that I might have messed this up for Kelly and even worse, made it more difficult for other Indins to get into this field.

I might have closed off the road into the fort. Or maybe I started a new path?

Writing Exercise

Please find the following words in a dictionary:
- Savage
- Heathen
- Renegade
- Red Man
- Red Skin

These words are often used to describe the Native American Indians of the North and South American continents. The contrast is that most Native American Indian Tribes and Nations are called "people" or have the word 'people' in their names.

What words would you use to describe a person you've never met before and who is completely unlike you? Would you ask a person what they would like to be referred to as?

Perfectly Untraditional

Sweta Srivastava Vikram

I spent part of my formative years in North Africa: the politically unstable country of Libya. My father, a metallurgical engineer, worked for a company that was hired to build a steel plant in the city of Misurata. I became a storyteller and writer as a byproduct of my displacement.

As the daughter of an expat, I was shielded from the hardships of the daily struggles of the locals because they, the Libyans, choose to keep foreigners at bay. As long as we behaved and kept our distance, we were welcome in the country. My Dad's Libyan colleagues never brought over their wives or children to our home. And, on rare occasions when we visited them, my Mom and I were ushered into women-only living rooms. My Dad and brother drank coffee with the men in a separate space. My Mom and I didn't speak a word of Arabic or enjoy the sugary coffee. But we found a way, often comprising awkward gestures and smiles, to communicate with the women.

I remember while my Mom wore a sari and sat up in front with my dad in the car; the local Libyan women clad in chador walked a few steps behind their husbands. Oftentimes, I noticed that Libyan men had four wives. It wasn't a unique sight to see a man drive up with his sheep in the front seat. The wives sat in the back of the pickup truck. I was told that sheep were considered a lot more indispensable than women.

When I tried discussing these issues, I was asked to "watch out." But stories have a mind of their own. At the age of 7 or 8, I started to both consciously and subconsciously collect stories and notice gender complexity. Strong women, they were around me. But that didn't mean they were empowered. I had grown up around good, liberal men but the society was full of men who made rules for women without regarding their desires.

As a writer and poet, I noticed that from an early age, my stories had strong female characters or voices. It wasn't a deliberate effort; strong female voice came most naturally to me. Maybe my partial upbringing in Libya had something to do with it.

Fast forward a few decades, I wrote my first novel *Perfectly Untraditional*. I was beyond excited. Here is what happened: I had submitted a novella to a competition because I felt connected to the story. A female agent contacted me after reading it and suggested I write a novel. Up until then, I had thought of myself as a poet, who sometimes wrote personal essays. Fiction was a whole different ball game.

I was nervous and excited. But, mostly, grateful. The agent saw something in my writing that I hadn't seen. I diligently commenced work on the book. At the time, I was in graduate school and working full-time. I would wake up at 3 a.m., every day, to write for three hours before I left for work and then school. I wrote in the subway. I wrote on weekend mornings. The story poured out of me.

Those days, amongst the South Asian American writers, Jhumpa Lahiri and Chitra Banerjee Divakaruni were the ones I revered. I didn't always connect with the characters in their novels or their stories; but that didn't matter. I was a fan of their flawless writing. And the fact that they had paved a way for the rest of us aspiring South Asian American women writers.

Once my novel was ready, I started to shop it around. Since New York City is home and haven to the world of publishing, I started to query agents in the Big Apple first. One of the big name agents, based out of New York City (let's call him John), took an interest in my writing. I was head over heels. If a New York-born and raised Caucasian man with no connection to South Asia could see merit in my work, the entire world could. Or so I believed.

I sent him sample chapters; he asked for the entire book. We met in person. But it turned out to be a not-so-happy story after all. He said, "I like your writing. But America isn't ready for a happy immigrant story." He went on to say that he liked my writing and the storyline, but he needed me to change my protagonist. If I did what he said, he would represent me.

I was stumped. And conflicted. I was an aspiring novelist and John was an experienced agent who wanted to represent me. Who was I to say no? And ruin my chances of getting published?

Perfectly Untraditional has a strong female protagonist who finds out the truth about herself after she moves to the United States from India. Distance gives her perspective and insight. It allows her the freedom to think as an individual about her professional and personal life and choices. She is not some sappy, emotionally torn wreck. She is a woman with a strong mind.

No, this book isn't an autobiographical novel. But it echoes the sentiments of a lot of first-generation Indian women from my generation. We had the privilege of growing up in a global world where immigration didn't translate into "terrible circumstances back at home" or "permanent displacement." It meant "searching for better opportunities," wherever we might have found them. I felt tremendously grateful for moving to the United States in the late 1990s—a time when visiting India once a year, buying Indian groceries, or making a call to India were all doable. I felt appreciative that I could embrace a new culture and country with open arms without the fear of losing where I came from.

That's part of the sentiment I wanted to convey in the book. I wanted to tell the story about first generation immigrants who moved to the United States, from India, in the mid to late 90s while still in their early 20s. Women who were well-educated, held jobs, managed homes, wore skirts and stilettos with as much ease as they wore a sari, sipped wine, and were on a quest to find their identity. The women I knew.

I said to John that not every South Asian/Indian woman would have the same stories or experiences to share. We aren't all alike. We can't be stereotyped. Jhumpa Lahiri, a second-generation immigrant, writes the stories about her parents' immigrant experiences (earlier books especially). I am of a different generation and so are my stories.

John gritted his teeth.

Paraphrasing, he said: America is just getting used to stories about South Asian immigrants. But, America isn't ready, he emphasized, for books about strong immigrant women. Americans won't read immigrant stories that have a female protagonist who is happy.

Meeting with John made me realize that the image we have of a culture or race, is so often conjured by media. Or a sum total of the few books we read. How can anyone ever believe that a country with 29 states and seven union territories would have only one story? Many Americans I have met have said that I was nothing like the Indian women they knew. But I am like so many others I know. With over 1.2 billion people, India is the most populous democracy in the world. There are different strata, classes, cultures, cuisines, experiences, and stories that shape up India. I was writing about one such segment: a generation of South Asian women, like me, whose stories had yet been told.

Talking to John was like reliving my Libya experience all over again: men telling women what to do without paying attention to what she has to say or offer. I wasn't going to be treated like one of those women in the back of a pickup truck in Misurata. I couldn't let a man, who had no idea about South Asian culture, dictate who my female character should be.

It took me less than week to realize that John would represent me, a South Asian writer, if I agreed to tell a story about a submissive female protagonist torn between her homeland and motherland. Demure, sari-wearing, God-fearing, broken English-speaking female character, who bought fresh groceries during the week and waited to call India over the weekends. A stereotypical and predictable story.

It wasn't an easy decision. But I had to tell John NO. I refused to compromise on the integrity of my book. Of course I was scared that no one would buy my manuscript. And my efforts on the novel would go to waste. But, soon, I started to believe that if I didn't believe in a story, I couldn't expect my readers to believe in it either.

My experience with John made me acutely aware of the different kinds of people existing in the publishing world. But it made me more determined in my resolve. I didn't want to allow one negative experience to turn me into a hater.

I focused my energy on making the book better and looking for other homes for *Perfectly Untraditional* instead of resenting John. As creative types, we have a certain quota of creative juice in us. How we use it is up to us.

In a few months, a leading literary agent in India signed me up and Niyogi Books published my book. *Perfectly Untraditional*, despite being controversial, was well received. The book launch and book tour were gratifying and my family, friends, and cousins were able to attend.

When I look back, I feel grateful that John and I didn't work together. Because had the book come out in the United States, my parents wouldn't have been a part of the book launch. My Mom passed away suddenly two years ago. And, one of the best gifts I have given her is that she could attend the New Delhi launch of *Perfectly Untraditional*.

Writing Exercise: To Heal

On five individual 3x5 index cards, share a way in which you or someone close to you has been stereotyped.
- Shuffle the cards.

- Select one card.
- Write a response to that card/stereotype in a poem form.

Healing the Heart

Our Silence Won't Save Us: Recovering the Medicine in Our Stories

Anaïs Deal-Márquez

I was cursing the blistering February wind after missing the 21 line on my way to work, when I got a call from my mother. Her voice was always so caffeinated in the morning.

"I need you to come with me," she told me.

"Where?" I asked her.

"So, I had a dream last night."

"Ma what are you talking about?"

"Just listen, que I'm trying to tell you," she responded.

It was that tone I'd learned early on was an indicator to shut up.

"You've never known where I grew up," she went on.

"You know about your father, but it's time," she said.

I could hear the mix of sadness and urgency in her voice.

When my parents and I left Mexico for a first-ring suburb of Milwaukee, we found ourselves surrounded by mainly upper class white folks that prided themselves in a liberalness rooted in voting blue. I remember holding Mami's hand on the first day of third grade. She looked down at me and gave me a tight squeeze before I ran into my classroom; and, she was waiting for me at 3:15 sharp outside the school building.

It would be a few years before I heard her tales of running away from army brats that made the daily existence of a Mexican border child in the Southwest a living hell.

"You're going to El Paso?" I asked her.

The approaching bus splashed my pants with muddy slush and once again I found myself cursing this winter vastness.

"Que dijiste?" she said.

As my fingers started to numb I tried to focus on her voice.

"No te preocupes," I told her.

I was reminded of all the times we had spoken of this trip.

"So you're finally going, mami?"

"No no, *we're* going." I started hearing her excitement building up.

"It's not going to be easy," she went on.

"But I'm working on my spiritual medicine. I'll be prepared."

As she spoke of her medicine, I thought back to the circle of matriarchs in Mexico I was raised in, or *las brujas* as my mother would lovingly say. Women who were unapologetic about taking their space from the men in their lives, relearned traditional medicines to ground their daughters, showed up to each other's children's birthdays with food to share and a good tequila for their sisters, and held each other through the different stages of heartbreak. As I heard my mother speak of her spiritual medicine, I thought back on the women that were helping her hold this moment. My tears caught me off guard.

As an adult I go back to these memories that come in waves, of women's laughter surrounded by screaming children and charred tortillas as a reminder of what holding space has looked like for my family and for our ancestors.

"Ok, let's do this," I told her.

* * *

Before Mama and Abuelita made the journey across the border to Texas in the 70s, my great grandmother made that same journey in the 1910s. The story goes that Stellita Perez was sent to Texas as a child when her mother married a man who wanted nothing to do with her children. She arrived at a time it was common practice to lynch Mexicans at the border and as far north as Wyoming. Only a handful of the thousands of cases would be documented.

On January 28, 1918, Texas Rangers and ranchers showed up in the village of Porvenir in Presidio County, Texas, where they rounded up nearly 25 Mexican men, took 15 of them to a rock bluff nearby and executed them (Carrigan, 2015). My Great-Grandmother would arrive one year later. I wonder if she could pinpoint when the desert spit her back out and sent her back to Mexico.

All these women live in my chest. There are some stories I know and others I am still trying to uncover. As I think of the responsibility of storytelling, I have to hold the complexity and strength of all they have been. I think of all these mujeres and of our shared migrations, of the stories of how they've searched for laughter, how they've survived, and how they've fought back, because that will always define the places from which I write. Telling our stories rooted in the complexity of our lives, that weave pain with joy, that hold our memories, is a radical act of writing ourselves into a world determined to bury us.

* * *

When my family immigrated from Veracruz in 1998, I found myself surrounded by teachers that thought if they hammered me enough with

Midwestern anecdotes on the American Dream I would forget my language. That maybe I would forget the feeling of belonging, of music that made sense to my bones. Mine is a story of what happens to little brown girls that are told their brilliance is not golden enough, harmless enough. That are told their brains are not made for algebraic equations, because their education started off wrong.

I came to writing out of necessity, because everything around me felt like it was falling apart, like my body was being cut up into pieces at a rate I could not prevent. Depression in fifth grade had me trying to press rewind on endless panic attacks that had me questioning my own existence. Reading became my escape. The same year I was transported to the fantastical world of *Harry Potter*—I began writing—transforming these ticking time bombs onto the page. I started writing down memories, to package the ones I still had. I learned to make myself promises to never forget what we left behind: the waterfalls, loud laughter against the ocean, champurrados at the plaza during Christmas, family parties that ended with children being serenaded by the revolutionary lyrics of nuevo canto and Mexican rancheras. My writing was born of cultural traditions of storytelling and music-making embedded in my family. As I get older, I become more obsessed with opening spaces for speaking to the trauma of our displacement and survival and the healing properties of how we create. I write to give language to those stories of how we have loved, cooked, laughed, cried and survived.

* * *

Early on in my own journey, when I first started claiming the title of poet, I found myself in a classroom surrounded by mainly white writers, and I remember thinking, one day we will refer to each other as colleagues, perhaps once we've been published and have shared enough podiums at readings. This classroom resembled most of the spaces I crossed into as a college student, trying to negotiate my lived experience into theories made on the page, but this time it wasn't school.

It was your standard writing workshop, and when it got to be my turn, I began sharing words about a cold grandfather, mostly absent and violent when he was present; sharing words about brown women hurting, bodies breaking, and children's rage of having to grow up too fast. The first comment cut through the silence. "It's interesting you choose to write about identity, but don't you find that to be limiting?" A white woman needed to know. If you're a writer of color that writes of stories centering your culture, your brownness, your blackness, you have heard this question. In that moment you are an exotic artifact in a museum, an object to be studied. Questions like that serve as a potent symbol for what it feels like to be a writer of color in a white literary world that most of us have become all too used to hearing.

As a young Mexicana writer I prioritize building spaces for other writers of color at different stages of their journey to learn and grow with and from each other. I think of accountability and how we model pushing back against a white literary culture of co-opting our stories and our bodies but disregarding our lives. What are the questions I'm willing to engage? What knowledge is not open for the taking? The questioning of what my boundaries around white writers has had to be, and still is, a part of my journey. The truth is that we don't have one single guide for what it means to honor ourselves as we write our stories. We make it up as we go and each of us has to create processes that feel true to what we need. In my case, I'm unapologetic about playing with language, disrupting whiteness and the privilege it brings with it. My writing is not about making others feel comfortable. I write because our stories and our bodies have been made to be silent for too long, yet we're still here.

Writing matters to me because it is a witnessing act that requires courage and pushes me to test my limits, and that lives in the discomfort and the unmasking. At its core, it is a sacred act for myself, my mother, my grandmothers, and our future generations. Those of us who write to speak to these lives in our bloodline always have to remember that we are the keepers of the stories others cannot or have not been able to tell, and that through our writing we uncover lost medicine. There is healing power in our courage to write about the things we are afraid of forgetting, and writing past fear in general. I find myself writing about the things that weigh heavy, which is to say the stories we are raised on. The stories that go untold, the ones we are told not to bring up. This also means writing that disturbs whiteness and complacency. I write about women correcting each other's recipes in the kitchen, fighting to survive intimate violence, fighting to survive colonialism, always finding humor in the most painful of heartbreaks. I write about migrations and what loss of language feels like when you're trying to remember noises and smells across the border. I'm interested in contradictions and the complexity of writing humor into narratives of displacement, and nostalgia into humor.

* * *

Existing as a queer, Mexican, woman of color writer in a literary world that centers whiteness means you have to find your solid roots, you have to be clear on why you are here and why you are writing. The most significant challenge of this reality is that there are going to be people that try to tell you what is valid and what is not. People who have not lived your life or that of your ancestors and will try to erase, exotify, and exaggerate certain parts of your stories to meet their own expectations. We have to have the courage to write from our places of truth, to strip away what is toxic and claim life-giving spaces where we are able make room for the medicine in our words.

References

Carrigan, W., & Webb, C. (2015) "When Americans lynched Mexicans." *The New York Times*. 20 Feb. 2015.

Writing Exercise

- Write your own definition of *survival*. What does it mean to you?

- Make a list of 5 ways women in your family/community have resisted.

- Think about an important story or moment in your cultural/family history that has been made invisible?

- Tell this story by highlighting each of the 5 attributes of resistance you've identified.

Writing: Healing from the Things I Cannot Change

Lori Young-Williams

I come from multiple places. I have many stories. I am a mixed-race, middle class woman. I write poems, prose, and personal stories as a way to heal from the racism and sexism that I've encountered in my life. Being a mixed-race girl who grew up in the white suburbs of St. Paul, Minnesota, during the late 70s and 80s, it was a challenge to find a group to belong to, and friends who would accept me as I am— black.

Writing kept me from going crazy. I was able to dream, and dream big. Dreams were poems and stories. They asked questions. They searched for my Self.

I didn't believe I was a writer until my early 20s. I wasn't prolific like Maya Angelou or Toni Morrison, nor did I write well-constructed poems like Alice Walker or Rita Dove. But I kept writing because writing helped with my moods. Writing helped me work through my grief, sadness, or anger. It helped me acknowledge that I wanted to belong. Writing helped me to heal.

* * *

What am I healing from? From being the one who lived. I am healing from being the one who did not die. The one who continues to live, the one who continues to remember. I have lived most of my life in the shadow of the one who died.

One of my biggest life challenges has been the illness and subsequent death of my sister Kim when I was 14 and she was 15. I needed an outlet for all of my emotions. Writing is how I dealt with illness and death at a young age.

* * *

I am healing from wanting to be anyone but myself. I am healing from low self esteem.

Why couldn't I accept myself as is? Why did I want to be someone else? I felt others' lives were easier than mine.

I believed my white friends had it easier than me because they did not have to navigate life through the lens of race. Having moved from the city where I saw many black, brown and white people, I made the assumption that I did not have what others had because of the color of my skin. I know that may be hard to believe a child making that leap in thought, but it's what I heard at home. My parents talked often about the inequalities of blacks and whites. I was afraid of not fitting in and fearful that I would not have friends. I wanted to belong and fit in so whatever I was not was what I wanted.

I didn't have examples of self aware black women, brown women, women who loved their bodies and the skin they were in. My closest representation was my sister Kim. She may not have liked that the boys teased her because she was heavier, and mom worried that she would not have as many friends as our older, thinner sister Debra. But Kim loved who she was, thick and lighter in skin tone then me and my siblings, she conformed, but not like I did. There was a distance she emitted about belonging. She was not afraid to go against the grain. She was quiet about it, but she followed her own beat.

Kim chose to die after two and half years of living with leukemia. She said enough is enough. When she died, I lost my best friend and my beacon to follow the beat of my true self.

How did I survive Kim's death? How did my family? Did being a mixed-race family have anything to do with our strength?

I turned to writing.

* * *

I grew up knowing my mom's side of our family—German and Norwegian, farmers and mechanics from Menomonie, Wisconsin. Mom said friends from the town were sad they couldn't find a nice White boy for her to marry. Grandpa Lem said he wished she wasn't marrying my dad, but he would not disown her. My cousin Jeannie said there was talk about my dad being part of their family. Her father, my uncle walked my mom down the aisle at their wedding. I don't know if anything came of the talk. All I saw growing up was acceptance of my dad when we went to visit. I knew little about my dad's side of our family—a black family from Philadelphia.

> Taunts and laughs like a fiery sun
> cover my body as school children
> make fun of my coarse, wild hair.
>
> Yet the sultry moon coaxes me to dream
> my sister standing in the snow,
> arms at her sides, smiling.
> I am fine.

Encircled by the love of white mother & black father.
Encircled by the love of farmers and salt mine workers,
alcoholics and the A.M.E church.
Encircled by the troubles of brown becoming black,
brown becoming cream, brown becoming me.

I suckled from my mother's breast
white on white. Never knew anything
but the nourishment of her love.
Never knew as a baby born to her
I would grow a third eye.

My third eye guides me.
The questions I ask, how I ask,
how I answer, and what I say.
To each group, Caucasian and Negroid
my third eye filters my feelings
so I offend no one.

Yet the sultry moon coaxes me to dream
of my sister standing in the snow
arms out stretched, smiling.
You are just fine.

My dad would tell me I looked like his mother, Grandma Lizzie. I
have one memory of her.

There she is.
My angel.
Resting on a dark brown four-poster bed.
All in white, her gown, the sheets,
her face a golden brown, hair pulled back,
black with wisps of silver.
I walk towards her, looking at her hands, her face.
She smiles at me.

I wish blue walls would fall away
and turn into blue sky.
We would fly off somewhere magical
in that four-poster bed,

with the sheets flapping behind us,
leaving her sickness in our wake.

Just me and my angel.

Grandma Lizzie became my muse and the women from her family
started to come forth, her daughters, my Aunt Alma, Aunt Lottie, Aunt
Rose, and Great Aunts Lottie, Nettie, Gertie and Vernice. Black
women from my father's family sought visibility through my writing.
They became the focus of my Master's in Liberal Studies (MLS) final
project.

*   *   *

Hurricane Katrina hit in 2005 and black folks were migrating again,
not that we ever stopped. I wanted to know what the Great Migration
was like for black women moving from the South to the North.
Specifically what was it like for my Grandma? What was her story?
What were her sisters' stories? History is told from the male
perspective and can be sexist in its telling. I crafted my master's thesis
and project around the voice of my Grandma. How could her voice
help me to heal? My final project, a public performance (a reading with
photos projected on a large screen) showcased what I learned through
oral storytelling, interviews, journaling, and conjuring[1] what I call my
emotional truth.

I could have done a master's in fine arts, but an MFA might not
have given me the opportunity to get to know my father's family in
depth. It may not have given me the chance to study the migration of
black folk from South to North, including my family's story of
migration. I was more concerned with learning the history and finding
the story, at the time, than with writing it.

My Grandpa Isadore migrated first, leaving his wife and
two children in Allendale, SC. When Grandma Lizzie and her
children (my dad's older siblings) left for Philadelphia,
Grandma encouraged her sisters to follow suit, and they did.
Grandma and her siblings lived close to each other and helped
each other out. They continued the various ways of life from
the South in the North, from the Old World to the New World.

Both Grandma Lizzie and Grandpa Isadore had gardens, a
way to make ends meet when there wasn't enough money to
buy food. She and her sisters continued to go to church and

raise their families in the church. They were even able to convince their brother Bubba Willie to move from Pittsburgh to Philadelphia so they could all be together.

Migration was about opportunity and having a better life for your children as well as yourself. The stories of my father's family migration helped me heal. Knowing one's history is healing. I was now able to point to women who looked like me and not only listened to the beat of their own drum, but also reached out for what life could give them regardless of their skin color.

* * *

My dad and I became close after Kim died. He became the beacon that went missing after Kim's death. He and I thought and believed in the same things: that there should be fair and level playing fields for all that want access to the middle class, that you do unto others as you want done unto you, and that my mood would not dictate his mood which meant someone else's mood should not dictate my mood. He lived his own life.

When he came to me in a dream months after he died, he told me I have to live my life and no one else's. I knew then I had to heal and be Me. Healing takes place on the page as well as in my mind, heart, and body. Writing is a healing component to my health because it allows me to release in a healthy manner what weighs me down, unlike binge eating and drinking.

I still get in a jam, blocked or stuck, trying to tell my story, my truth, trying to be honest with myself on the page. Sometimes I shy away from the page because I am afraid truth will hurt, but I know what I've written has been healing.

* * *

I know my history. I know who I am. I don't need to be anyone else.

Notes

1. Frank X Walker taught conjuring in a Split Rock Arts class "In Search for Authentic Voices: A Mixed Genre Writing Workshop," July 23-28, 2006.

Writing Exercise

How did you get here?

How did you get here, today? What are the details of your journey to the pages of this book, to this page, this exercise? Start the day you were born, or start at any focal point in your life that got you to seek out writing, needing to write. Whom did you meet on your journey?

Has writing been a healing process for you?

If so, what are you healing from? Journeys are a process, sometimes requiring movement, sometimes staying in one place; sometimes moving forward, sometimes back. Weave your story on paper. Write freely. Write for at least 15 minutes.

Stories from the Heart of Dark-Eyed Woman— Sikadiyaki

Olive Lefferson

A Native kid trying to figure out my place in the world, I wanted more than anything to be a writer. I wasn't sure which was louder, the criticism of others or my own critical inner voice. Through writing classes and reading Native authors, I came not only to love the craft of writing but also to value the oral traditions of my family and culture. I found purpose and meaning by providing a space for other Natives, some of whom struggle with addiction and homelessness, to use writing as a way to heal themselves. In the process I have found my own place as a writer and a Native in a white world.

I didn't grow up traditional. I didn't have regalia. I didn't dance. I didn't speak Blackfeet. But I grew up with an oral tradition. My grandmother told us Napi stories at bedtime. My mother told stories of her childhood, the early days of the reservation, of her uncle Mountain Chief pitching his tepee outside their house on Birch Creek and eating supper on a tablecloth on the floor because he wasn't used to sitting in chairs. She talked about her time in a mission school run by nuns, about the hard work she did as the oldest of five girls with a widowed mother, and of the fun they had going to dances in a wagon filled with cousins. All that I learned of our family history, I learned from my mother. I have stories to tell as well.

I was born in the Indian Health Service hospital in Browning, Montana, on the Blackfeet Reservation, in 1951. We lived in Browning when I was a child. After we moved to Seattle when I was in eighth grade, I wasn't around Indians other than my family; my dad was white, my mom Blackfeet. My identity was, frankly, a difficult one for me. When we lived on the rez I was too white—and when we moved to Seattle, I was too... other, too non-white. I felt like I didn't fit in anywhere.

In Browning, even as a kid, I recognized that I was one of the lucky ones. I had both parents, I never went hungry, our house was warm and there was always enough firewood. My mom always had a job and my dad had one most of the time. Mom kept a fastidious house, but the one we lived in in Browning was far from fancy. It had been my grandmother's house in the 1930s and 1940s. We didn't have running water or inside plumbing. We had a hole in the ceiling where it sagged and we'd tried to push it up with a broom handle. In Seattle, everyone seemed rich. And white.

Not long after we moved to Seattle, I decided I wanted to be a writer. I threw my heart and soul into writing a story. It was inspired by a book my sister Judi and I both read called *Forever Amber*, a racy novel by Kathleen Windsor. I filled several pages with all the romance I could muster. My cousin Snuffy, a year older and 6 inches shorter than I was, found my notebook and read it. Literary genius that he was, he ripped it to shreds. Make no mistake, it was pretty bad, but no one should get that kind of harsh judgment at age 13—or any age, for that matter. I was always a silent child—not just quiet, but silent. I was silenced by sexual abuse and the alcoholism and violence that I witnessed. Snuffy's mocking scorn crushed me, the criticism silenced me and I didn't try to write for over two decades.

I started college in 1986 when I was in my mid-30s. Life being what it is, between three kids and caring for elderly parents and other life events, I finally graduated in 2008 at the age of 57 with a degree in English. In the beginning, the thought of anyone reading the papers I'd written, much less critiquing them in a group, panicked me. I asked my boyfriend to read my first paper, which I was actually quite proud of, and give me some pointers. He was a lawyer and had written many opening statements, briefs, and speeches so I thought he could give me some tips. He rewrote it until it was more his writing than mine. I was devastated. I wanted to quit school. Instead, I decided I would never again let him have that power over my writing.

I absolutely loved school. I got good grades, excellent grades really. I was always good at the mechanics of writing: punctuation, grammar, and spelling, and I loved writing but it was hard! I wanted to be the kind of writer that was spontaneous, that could whip out something worth reading while sitting in a cafe drinking strong coffee and looking intellectual. I now believe that type of writer is as rare as unicorns. Anyway, it certainly never worked that way for me. Even now, it takes me forever to complete a writing project. I strain over every word, forever editing myself, correcting, tweaking, deleting a comma here and adding a semi-colon there. Still, telling a story, shaping the characters, and filling them with life, became a joy to me, like a puzzle. I could take quirks I'd seen in one person and traits from another, mold all the pieces together and make characters that come alive and become people I want as friends or want to stay away from because of the evil they're capable of.

In college, as in junior high and high school, I was almost always the only Native in class. The readings were never by Native authors. It was as if they didn't exist. But I knew that they did exist. I had read Louise Erdrich's *Love Medicine* and *Beet Queen* and *The Bingo Palace*. I read James Welch's *Indian Lawyer, Fools Crow*—one of my all time favorite books—and *Winter in the Blood*. In a poetry class I had an assignment to write a review of a book of poetry so I chose *The Business of Fancy Dancing* by Sherman Alexie. I realized that my classmates and even most of my professors had no idea what incredible literature they were missing out on. I recognized that the Native authors that I read back then and the ones I've discovered over the years are amazing storytellers.

College classes and other writing classes I've taken over the years gave me the opportunity to tell stories. In fact, they forced me to tell stories. I got excellent feedback to make me a better writer from friends, professors, and fellow classmates, even the negative comments, like the one from a young woman who told me that a little Native boy in one of my short stories wouldn't have a Sponge Bob backpack, that that was not realistic, like Native kids don't know about Sponge Bob?

At a Fourth of July party in 2002, I met a woman named Luanne. We spent the whole evening talking about writing. I was excited and fascinated to talk to someone who wrote screenplays and was in the process of writing a novel. We became dear friends and she has been an invaluable mentor and supporter of my writing over the years. When I said that I wasn't really a writer since I had never been published, she said, "All you have to do to be a writer is to say 'I'm a writer' and then write." It still took me at least five years to say I'm a writer out loud. I used to wonder who would like my work and how I would ever get published but I've realized that what is most important to me is that I write because I love it. If I can craft a story or an essay or a journal entry to my liking, then I'm happy.

For several years I ran an art program at a day center for urban Natives in Seattle. Within the art program we had a writing group which was at first facilitated by a volunteer who was a poet. After she left, I ran the group myself. I would give a prompt, we would write about it and then read aloud what we'd written. The stories people wrote were most often about the trauma they'd suffered throughout their lives, the anguish of abuse, addiction, families torn apart, homelessness. No matter how lighthearted I thought my prompts were, they still wrote about sadness. We cried. We laughed. We ate. It became more of a support group, a safe place for them to share all the sorrow that is a part of their past and their present. Their writing was amazing and even though I gave them the choice, they almost always chose to read their work aloud, to have witnesses to their grief, to share similar experiences, to have others say I feel your pain, you shouldn't have had to suffer like that.

When my dear friend Heather joined the writing group she put together some zines with their writing and we sold them to raise money for our writing group. They were so proud that their work was "published." Since I left the day center, she and I have continued the writing group. We write letters of forgiveness, we write journal entries, we share the rose and the thorn of our week. We are the Writing Warriors, determined to stay together to tell our stories. I've learned so many lessons from them, about their different tribal traditions, about resilience and how to laugh through our grief.

I belong to another writing group as well. This is my "fancy lady" writing group. Ellen has had her memoir published and is set to perform a one woman show she's been working on. Emily has an MFA in poetry and has written a young adult novel which she has turned into a screenplay. Paula has an extraordinary gift for writing humorous and insightful vignettes about her Italian family. Because they haven't had a lot of contact with Natives or Native writers, they look at my stories with a fresh perspective, giving me invaluable feedback, asking questions about things I take for granted that everyone knows. I've learned, though, that most people really don't know very much at all about Natives or Native culture or Native writers. These women are a strong support and urge me to share my stories for that very reason.

Nowadays I work as a case manager for a nonprofit in Seattle that serves chronically homeless men and women who are mentally ill, chemically dependent, and/or medically compromised. My clients and I spend a lot of time waiting at appointments which gives us an opportunity to get acquainted. I never fail to ask them if they like to read, what kind of books they like, and if they like to write. I've hit pay dirt a couple of times. One client was a journalist before the onset of his symptoms so we talk about writing every time I see him. He likes to write poetry and I encourage him to submit it for publication and enter poetry contests. Another client was very quiet until I asked what he likes to read. He said, *"Harry Potter,"* and lit up like a Christmas tree when I said I love *Harry Potter*, too. It thrills me to have these conversations and a few have seemed interested when I have encouraged them to write.

The older I get, the more I see lessons all around me. A lesson that too many people never learn is the art of criticism. There was a time, a long time ago, that I let Snuffy's cruel words cut me to the quick. I used them as a reason to feel sorry for myself and used them as an excuse to not write. Now, I think to myself, what if I hadn't listened to him? Or better yet, what if he had been more evolved and instead said to me, "Way to go, cuz! Keep at it and someday you'll be a great writer." Or what if my boyfriend had said, "It looks good to me. You've got this." What if, instead of letting him rewrite my paper, I had told him I have no place in my life for someone who is so critical? What if I put aside my own insecurities and just wrote?

I spent years questioning my identity as an indigenous person and thinking I had to fit into a category of someone else's making. I could usually pass for White—lost my rez accent and everything—but was I Indian enough for Indians? I finally realized that it doesn't matter if other Natives think I'm too white or that I'm just the "white woman in the art room." There are no blood quantum police and no one can tell me I'm not Native enough.

The same goes for my writing. I spent years second guessing myself and wasted a lot of good writing time thinking I had to be published to be a real writer. I let criticism keep me down. I let other people's harsh words make me feel bad. I don't have time for that anymore. I have stories to tell and I will be a writer on my own terms. If writing letters to our incarcerated relatives with my writing group is the extent of my writing, then so be it.

Like Natalie Goldberg says in *Writing Down the Bones*, "If you want to write, you have to just shut up, pick up a pen, and do it. I'm sorry there are no true excuses. This is our life. Step forward. Maybe it's only for ten minutes. That's okay. To write feels better than all the excuses" (2005, p. 183).

I write from the part of me that is Native, the girl roaming the prairies finding arrowheads, the victimized woman silenced by abusive men, the strong woman I have become, out of necessity, out of experiences, good and bad, that have shaped me over the course of my life.

References

Alexie, S. (1992). *The business of fancy dancing*. Brooklyn, NY: Hanging Loose Press.

Goldberg, N. (2005) *Writing down the bones*. Boston, MA: Shambhala.

Welch, J. (1981). *Winter in the blood*. New York: Penguin Putnam.

Writing Exercise

Criticism has been defined as: (a) the act of passing judgment as to the merits of anything; (b) the act of passing severe judgment; censure; faultfinding; (c) the act or art of analyzing and evaluating or judging the quality of a literary or artistic work, musical performance, art exhibit, dramatic production, etc. (see www.dictionary.com/browse/criticism)

We have all been subjected to criticism regarding the quality of our work. Unfortunately, too often it is of the "severe judgment; censure; faultfinding" variety, which can be crippling and can silence our creativity. Re-imagine a conversation with those who have silenced you. How would you respond to their criticism? What have you learned in terms of offering criticism to others? What advice might you give to a budding writer/artist to deal with harsh criticism of their work?

A Fundamental Human Yearning

Michael Kleber-Diggs

Once a week, I teach poetry in prisons. I do this a few months a year. I sit in a 14 x 14 room with men who have committed significant crimes, and we talk about poetry. We write a bit. We share feedback on pieces we're working on. We read works by women, people of color, famous former inmates, and poets my students admire. I never ask the men why they're in prison, and I never look it up even though an easy Google search would allow me to know. I know my students are in a maximum security facility facing very long sentences or life in prison and that they are, or at one time were, able to do something quite serious or terrible or both.

When I agreed to teach the writing class, I made myself a number of promises. One of them was that I would offer my students uncon-ditional positive regard. It's a concept I learned in my psychology class my freshman year at college. It means accepting and respecting others as they are, without judgment or evaluation. Counselors use it as part of therapeutic practice, and while I don't see my students as patients and certainly don't see myself as their counselor, I consider our time together advanced by a single-minded devotion to our positive growth as writers—all of us. This is the main gift I have to share. Anyone can offer ideas about writing; I want to encourage my students towards their voices.

I resolved to do just that. But at first I didn't get it right at all.

The first time I walked into the classroom to meet my students, I had been in a prison exactly four times. Once in college as part of a class I took called *Violence, Aggression and Terrorism in the United States*; once in law school as part of a class I took on sentencing theory; once about a month before my poetry workshop began, to attend a writing forum; and once when I was at that same facility taking a training class required for frequent visitors to correctional facilities. Through my last two visits I gained an initial sense for the building and some understanding of what my students were like.

The prison was immaculate in every open space and every corner, inside and out. It operated with the accuracy of an atomic clock. Let me state here that head-in-the-clouds poets and military precision make an odd couple. In the prisons I've visited, process and consistency are worshiped like gods; they have to be. Deviation is despised, and exceptions are never made. I resolved to meet the place on its terms. I made plans to show up early every week, ready to teach. I didn't have difficulty respecting the rules—I was a guest, all too eager to conduct myself in a way that would allow me to be invited back.

The night of my first class, after clearing security, I made my way through the facility and into the classroom, where, one by one, my students were patted down and entered the classroom to size me up. I was scared, but only that I wouldn't do well as a teacher. The organization through which I teach attracts a number of phenomenal writers and educators. People with MFAs and experience teaching creative writing—two things I did not hold. I worried I would not be good enough.

Eventually, 10 students arrived: white, black, Asian, Latino, and Native American. They were young and old, mild mannered and intimidating, taciturn and jocular. Some were nervous initially and others were completely at ease at all times. For the first class I planned to walk through the syllabus and classroom rules, then ask my students, "What is poetry?" During the remaining weeks, I planned to talk about different elements of poetry: sound, meter, metaphor, image, etc.; I planned to reserve time to study poems written by others, to host a guest lecturer, and to offer feedback on the poems shared by my students.

When I planned my class, I started with an ambitious and maybe even aggressive syllabus. Among many other things, I wanted to delve into consideration of voice and line breaks, and I had a thoughtful lecture planned on what I consider the four general types of poetry: dramatic, lyrical, narrative, and abstract. I thought by lecturing on these topics and providing examples from representative works, I'd offer the men an outstanding introduction to the art. Midway through my second class, just as I was working toward a groundbreaking insight on the narrative form, I turned to face the stark realization that I'd lost the class. Not a single student was with me. What's more, I'm pretty sure they thought I was an asshole.

It was not that the topic was too advanced or too deep. In my experience, many students who take classes in correctional facilities want the material to be challenging and insightful. As I gathered experience as a teacher, I grew fond of telling friends and family, "I'm pretty sure I'm the most educated man in the room, but I know for a fact I'm far from the smartest." My students could get the gist of what I was saying, they just didn't care to hear it.

As I left that night and walked toward my car, two mature does pranced in an adjacent field. I would later notice a tendency for wonders to greet me at the end of my shift: a double rainbow, a spectacular purple sunset, a rainstorm that swept toward me across a rural expanse and waited to reach me until just after I shut my car door, those two deer. That night, the does in the field did little to lift my spirits. I was not connecting with my students. I was failing as a teacher just as I had feared I would. I was, I thought, not good at this.

* * *

Karen is twisting the tassels at the end of a chenille throw. Karen is my wife now, but at the time she was my fiancée. Her work with the tassels is the work of sadness. We have just found out her pregnancy will not go to term. She calls me at work to tell me the news, and I leave immediately. My co-workers look at me the way people looked at me when I was 7—the way they looked at me at my father's funeral. This time, I know I have lost something significant before other faces tell me.

We are in bed next to each other, processing this. At the time this happens, I have just come into my fourth decade, and my wife is about to leave hers—I am 32, and she is 39. In addition to the deep sadness of this loss, we're also tasked with confronting the fear of the unknown. We both want to be parents, but we are not young. We realize now it may not work out for us. This miscarriage is also the first tragedy we face together. It comes a few days before our first grand celebration. Our wedding is planned for a week later. I feel I know something of marriage already. I feel I understand that the two of us will share tragedies and celebrations together.

We lie next to each other and hold each other. A chain of involuntary reactions begins. First, I cry. We both do. I'm sad for the loss of the baby, but I'm also saddened by Karen's sadness. I'm also afraid. I wonder if I'm up to all that will be asked of me in my life with her. I wonder if I have what it takes to be a husband and suddenly doubt I have what it takes to be a father. Second, holding her next to me, feeling her hips and stomach with my hands, rubbing her hair and her back, causes me to get an erection. I curse my body. I curse its candor and how it betrays me sometimes. I pull my hips back so as not to offend my beloved, but I've already offended myself. Third, as I watch her twist the tassels, as I contemplate her sadness, I spin away from the scene. I find myself wanting to write about it. I have a central image; I have my way in. I can build a poem around the chenille throw.

I recoil in disgust with myself, at my weakness, my distractibility.

Now, I'm more forgiving. I think about that Natasha Trethewey poem "Elegy." The one at the beginning of her sublime collection, *Thrall*. The one where she confesses that while she was fishing with her father and imagining his death, she was also gathering images toward a poem about both.

I know there are other definitions and other meanings, but to me this is what it means to be a writer. I see helplessness in the title; I see involuntary reactions that betray us sometimes. I see detachment. I see—to use of form of the word Trethewey used—a measure of cruelty.

I wish I could tell you I always wanted to be a writer or it was always easy for me to wear the label. I want to write you a fairy-tale story about a boy who grew up in southern Kansas dreaming of being the next Langston Hughes. I want to say the boy endured, at all times steadfast to his craft, at all times loyal. I want to tell you how he persevered and negotiated several difficult trials that we learned later shaped him into the artist he needed to be. I want the story to end with the boy receiving some prestigious prize, with his words echoing for generations.

But my story as a writer isn't written yet, and most of that isn't true for me.

I grew up black in the 70s and 80s. My father was a dentist, and he was murdered just before my twin brother's and my eighth birthday. My mother has a master's degree in psychiatric nursing, and spent most of her career teaching at a university and working as a licensed clinical therapist. I studied political science. I went to law school. I practiced law for a while, but I wasn't suited to it. I worked in a corporate setting and thrived in it. I started a business, and after three years it failed. I returned to the corporate world. I'm now part of the legal team at a logistics company. That's one version of my story.

In another, the pen has always been with me. I made a newspaper for my school when I was in fourth grade. It was called the *Isely Informer*. It got shut down. It was too real, too truthful; the administration had to smash it. I wrote poems in high school (I know a lot of people say this about their high-school poems, but mine were truly awful. This is how bad they were—I was kind of obsessed with acrostic poems). I wrote short stories through high school and college and law school and after. I sent them to friends and shared them with lovers. I keep many of them in a pile of chaos inside an old wooden box near my writing desk in my study. I talk about organizing them all the time.

Still, I didn't think of myself as a writer until September of 2000, when I saw Karen twisting tassels on the chenille throw, when I realized that I couldn't help myself.

And I didn't call myself a writer or a poet or accept it when anyone referred to me as a writer or poet until 2015. Prior to that point, I rarely referred to myself as a poet or writer, and when I did, I didn't really believe it. When anyone introduced me as a writer or poet, I suppressed the urge to debate the point.

In the summer of 2015, I sent a letter to a dear friend, and in it I referred to myself as a poet with some line like "one of the things I like about being a poet is ..." I didn't realize I'd referred to myself in that way until well after I'd sent the note. Somewhere in my subconscious I'd finally accepted my identity.

What took me so long? I think I have an answer.

For most of my upbringing, I was taught to think of myself as part of the Talented Tenth. For the uninitiated, Talented Tenth refers to an essay by the black educator W.E.B. DuBois. In it, DuBois makes the case for higher education for blacks. When I grew up, it had taken on a different meaning, at least as I understood it. It meant that you were the child of college-educated parents, and that you were likely to be educated yourself. It meant that you were special. It often meant that you were in Jack and Jill of America, Inc., an organization founded by middle and upper-middle class black women as a way to provide cultural, social, and educational opportunities that black children might not have otherwise. Maybe it meant that one or both of your parents had joined a profession or were in a black fraternity or sorority. It certainly meant that you were expected to go to college and to do well there and thereafter. At my house, it also meant that while you were at college, you should gravitate toward the professions: medicine, law, education, engineering, accounting, business, or finance. If you were a wild child and you liked to draw or whatever, maybe you could go into something like architecture. Of what I considered my available options, I chose law.

Here, let me clarify two points. First, this is not some essay where I blame my mother for keeping me from being a writer for 20 years; quite the contrary. I first thought of being a lawyer in eighth grade, when an attorney came to our school on Career Day to talk about what her day-to-day work was like. I remember that she was attractive, and I remember that she mentioned three words that really piqued my interest—*library* and *research* and *writing*. I loved law school, and there were many aspects of being a lawyer that I loved—research, writing, logic, rhetoric, argumentation, negotiation. While I don't consider myself well-suited to the law as a profession—I'm oriented toward "yes" in pretty much all things, and I'm terrible at client management—as the great poet Maya Angelou once said, I "wouldn't take nothing for my journey now." Most of my writing is sourced by ideas. Most of my ideas are shaped by my thinking, and much of what I value in my thought process I refined in law school.

Second, by the time I got to college I knew a wider range of options was available to me. I could have gotten any degree and gone on toward a PhD, satisfying any whims and honoring any perceived parental dictates at the same time. My twin brother followed his bliss, film studies, and I might have taken his example. While it's true that I loved studying Hobbes and Locke and Sovietology and urban politics and administration, it's also true that I don't remember the names of many of my college professors. It's also true that my favorite college class was creative writing. It's also true that as long as I live I will never forget the name of the T.A. who taught that class, Chester Sullivan, or a short story of his that he read to us. It was about a man with a wrench working on a public fountain at an apartment complex.

In other words, it's also true that like Walt Whitman I am vast; I contain multitudes.

And this is also true: For many years, I didn't pursue writing actively and publicly because I didn't really believe that anyone cared what I had to say. This is the pernicious and subtle work of bias. This is result of moving through the world with the opposite of unconditional positive regard.

In spite of countless examples to the contrary—Baldwin, Hughes, Ellison, Morrison, Walker, Angelou, James (and who could hope to fill such lofty shoes?)—I didn't think my voice would be valued in the world. In many ways I still don't. To the extent that I go forward anyway, I do so as a result of that helplessness I described earlier. It's not that I feel the world hungers for my stories. It's not that I think most of what I want to write about is as valued in mainstream publishing as other stories are. It's more that I'm resolved to sing my songs anyway, and I'm content to sing them to those in the world who want to hear them.

* * *

After that first night at the prison, I drove west, toward home. The sun was in retreat and low in the sky, more red than orange. I thought about the men in my class. Not for the first time, it occurred to me that there but for the grace of God go I. I was blessed to grow up in a healthy home, with a mother who bettered herself so her family could have better. I grew up never doubting that I was loved, a flower on the land of an earnest gardener. I lived in a well-groomed middle-class neighborhood and attended vibrant schools. I played the cello and had private music lessons and played sports and enjoyed extracurricular activities. I grew up knowing I would go to college and knowing I would have support there—my mother's money and example and guidance to sustain me. There are better launching pads than mine, but none more perfect.

By contrast, to a person, the students in my class had it rough growing up. Their childhoods were often wildly dysfunctional and sometimes shockingly cruel. Most of my students grew up poor, attended under-funded schools, and lacked loving guidance from healthy role models. Where I was often told about the options that were available to me, my students were usually defined and constrained, limited by perceptions and bias and the anger that accumulates under such circumstances (their anger and the anger of those around them). I thought about this as I drove home, and I thought about it again the next day. Eventually, I reduced what distinguishes us to an accident of birth.

But in many ways my students and I are the same. We have had our lives disrupted by violence. We know how it feels to be seen as "other." Many of us have had to define for ourselves what it means to be a father. We're all grieving profound losses. We're writing our way out, and writing is our way of thinking. Writing helps us come to terms with the things that confound us. We call ourselves poets. It took us a while to get there. We still seem surprised by it.

At some point I learned that a woman who works in the prison brings scraps from her garden to the nearby field. She leaves them there so the deer will come.

It's possible I'm wrong about accidents. I grab my notebook and uncap my pen.

In the process of writing this down, I realized there was a third option. My students are the same as all of us. When we are together in the small classroom, working on the same writing exercise, we are seekers searching for the same kind of freedom. We are all writers. Dwelling in that idea, the answers came to me, both of them. How to teach my class, and what my students wanted from me. I resolved to listen more than lecture and to teach image and sound and meter using examples from their work.

I did not arrive at this conclusion by thinking about how to make the class better. I arrived at it by understanding how alike we all are. Some of us are called to work with ink and paper and words. Some of us are involuntarily enchanted by images and ideas. Writers are unique in that we feel compelled to write things down; we like to play with syllables and sounds. But all of us need a way to make sense of mysterious things. We all want to know the loving gaze of positive regard. All of us are creators. No matter the source, we want wonders to greet us at the end of a difficult shift. All of us want to tend and be tended. We surrender to the same fundamental yearning; the same desire courses through every human body: we all hope our stories will be valued in the world. We just want someone to listen to us, because all of us need to feel heard.

References

Angelou, M. (1997). *Wouldn't take nothing for my journey now*. New York: Bantam Books.

Du Bois, W. E. B. (1903). *The talented tenth*. New York, NY: James Pott and Company, 1903.

Trethewey, N. D. (2012). *Thrall: Poems*. Boston, Mass: Houghton Mifflin Harcourt.

Whitman, W. (1881). *Leaves of grass with sands at seventy and a backward glance o'er travel'd roads*. Philadelphia: Impr. Ferguson Bros. and Co.

Writing Exercise

Journey to a Destination. Write about a journey of becoming. Start by selecting what you became when you arrived at your particular destination. For example, you might write about your journey to becoming an artist or a writer (or any career, maybe you're a plumber or a dentist). You might also chronicle your journey to becoming an adult, a parent, a widow(er), an honest person, or something not literally true like a flower or granite. You could write about becoming an abstract noun like bravery or kindness or even an adjective like resilient or vulnerable.

Start by picking the thing you became or identifying your destination. Set a timer for 5 or 10 minutes. Write down all the things you associate with your journey and your destination. What did you see? How did you/do you feel? How did you change along the way or after you arrived? Be uninhibited in this initial writing. Abandon concern for style or word choice or penmanship, and don't limit yourself to things that make sense for this exercise, just write as much as you can as freely as you can for 5 or 10 minutes. When this is done, go back to what you've written and circle the ideas or passages that really captivate you or that you consider to be the essence of your journey/destination. Focusing on the things you've circled, draft an essay, a poem, or a short story about your journey/destination.

Creating Literary Spaces

Writing Through Homelessness

Beatrice M. Hogg

When the director of the women's shelter in Sacramento asked me to teach a writing class, I knew that it was an impossible task. First, a class needs students, bodies that will attend on a regular basis for a specific time. In a chaotic temporary women's shelter, there were new faces, new stories, and new challenges every day. But with my newly minted MFA in creative nonfiction, I couldn't wait to talk to other women about writing. As the Benefits Coordinator at the shelter, I met with every new resident and noted how I might be able to assist them with becoming self-sufficient. It would be interesting to hear what they had to say about their own lives.

I thought about my own life. After I moved to Northern California from Western Pennsylvania in 1988 to become a writer, I found that I spent a lot of my time explaining my background. No one in San Francisco, San Mateo or Sacramento understood what it meant to be an Affrilachian adopted coal miner's daughter who was left-handed, the only Catholic of color in her hometown and orphaned at eighteen. In my MFA program, I declined the opportunity to attend school for another six months to take pedagogy classes. Unlike most of the writers in my program, I never wanted to be a teacher. In my low residency MFA program, I had to contradict a white male student in one of my critique groups when he stated that I grew up "poor in a coal mining town." I told him neither *Matewan* or *Coal Miner's Daughter* defined my life. I was an only child in an eight-room house with a father who only drove Cadillacs. I knew that the women at the shelter were also stereotyped. None of them came from the same background. "Homelessness" was not a single narrative that defined all people who were unhoused. Everyone had their own story. My workshop would give them a place to share their truths.

A 90-minute weekly writing workshop would be something that all women could attend if they were interested. I considered it a workshop because it had to have a limited structure, but the shelter still called it a "class." Each week, I would select a topic for the ladies to write about in class. Then, the ladies could read their stories and get feedback from me and the rest of the group. I would read some of my essays to get discussions started. New participants could start at any time. I would take notes during the workshop to provide management with verification of what went on in the class. Case managers would offer the class to women at their weekly meetings. I would turn in a weekly roster of workshop attendees so women would get credit for attending. The workshop would be called "Exploring Writing with Beatrice," but quickly got shortened to "Writing with Beatrice."

I couldn't wait to get started. On that first Thursday afternoon, May 5, 2005, I wondered if anyone would be there. For my first class, there were nine ladies present. Most of them were women of color, as were at least half of the shelter residents. I had brought in a box of books from my personal collection and asked them to pick a book. I gave them about 30 minutes to skim the books and asked what they thought of them. Most women picked poetry or biographies, indicating that they enjoyed reading short pieces that they could relate to their own lives. After a short discussion, I gave each one a notebook and asked them to write something about themselves. Some women read their pieces out loud to the class. We spent a few minutes talking about universal truth in writing. I talked about some of the things that I had learned in my MFA program. The hour and a half passed quickly. I wrote in my notes, "I hope that I will be able to hold the interest of the students for the next five weeks and be able to give them some information that will assist them in any future writing endeavors." I copied the roster and put it in the class binder. I was committed now. The next week, five women returned.

Would the class last? "Exploring Writing with Beatrice" lasted four years. When I started a full-time government job in February 2006, I moved the class from Thursday afternoons in the lunchroom to Saturday mornings in one of the unused classrooms. Being able to shut the door to the outside world made a difference in group intimacy and class participation. Even though I never got that pedagogy certification, I learned a lot more from the women who attended my workshop over the years.

Within the first six weeks, one of the things I discovered was many of the women wanted to participate, but not everyone was comfortable with writing. Some had dyslexia and others had poor spelling skills or learning disabilities. Even though the class was called "Exploring Writing," I opened it up to participants who preferred storytelling to writing. I learned to be flexible. I used a book from my MFA program, *Fruitflesh* by Gayle Brandeis, to think of topics to explore with the group. Reading some of my own essays helped me to bond with the group. If I was willing to share my story, they felt comfortable sharing theirs too. But I had to set some rules. I didn't allow the women to use our time together to complain about shelter restrictions and policies. Instead, I tried to get them to use their feelings as a catalyst for the class exercise. If a topic or story was too triggering for a student, I would give them the option of leaving and getting credit for attending or stepping outside during the sharing.

The workshop was a safe place. I didn't want anyone to feel that they were being censored. When I mentioned in passing once that I had written erotica, several women wanted to write erotic stories for their boyfriends or husbands, most of whom were incarcerated. I had to remind them that the shelter name was the same as the local church that founded it and discussing erotica would not be appropriate. But I offered to loan my books on writing erotica to students or offer critiques via e-mail. Not censoring also meant realizing that a topic that might have seemed harmless to me could be a trigger to others.

One week, I gave the class an assignment to write about their mothers. Since I had lost my mother when I was thirteen, I had an idealized version of motherhood. One of the women wrote about how her mother traded her innocence for drugs when she was twelve. I never again celebrated "mothers," but instead asked women to write about "positive female role models." Almost everyone had known someone in their life—a friend, relative or teacher—that inspired them, encouraged them, or was there for them during hard times.

Near Father's Day, I asked students to describe a positive male role model. I shared several stories about my father and our sometimes difficult relationship. Writing a long essay about my illiterate, strict father from an adult point of view had been one of the most insightful pieces that I had ever written. Previously, I had never thought of him as a person. Taking away some of my teenage pain and replacing it with the viewpoint of an adult who was unprepared to become the parent of a teenager, gave me a new respect and love for him. Some women chose to write about their fathers, some wrote about godfathers, brothers, or spiritual leaders.

Families and loss came up a lot in the workshop. Many of the women had their children with them in the shelter and parenting while experiencing homelessness was difficult. I encouraged women to write stories to share with their children someday, to let them know about their homeless journey. I read an essay about meeting with my birth mother, but never learning how she came to her decision to give me up for adoption. Sometimes it was hard to talk about loss, as most of the women had suffered many losses in their lives.

For some classes, I used props and books to inspire class writing exercises. Years ago, when I lived in my family home in Pennsylvania, I found a trove of vintage photos in my basement. The photos were pictures of Black people taken in the 1940s and earlier. In *Fruitflesh,* Brandeis talked about using photos as a writing prompt. It would be interesting to share the photos with the class and see what stories they inspired. The ladies loved the photos and eagerly selected one to write or talk about. They held them gingerly, aware that they were holding someone's family history. One student wrote a piece called "Big Mama/Home Cooking," because the woman in the photo reminded her of a neighbor from her childhood in Georgia. A photo of a couple and three little girls wearing matching dresses touched another student. She could see the pride in the mother's eyes as she posed with her children. She imagined them on a Sunday outing just before posing for a photo. Other students imagined the personalities of the daughters by their body language. The vintage photos were a way to get students to reflect on their own lives. I remembered sitting with my mother as a little girl, looking at family photos and hearing her stories about growing up in North Carolina.

Tim O'Brien's book *The Things They Carried* was the inspiration for another exercise. In the book, O'Brien listed the things that soldiers carried on their backs. I asked the women to list the things in their purses or backpacks that meant a lot to them. One woman carried her expired real estate license. Some carried medicines for themselves and their children. Others carried batteries for their children's toys. One student carried keychains to use when she got keys to her next home. I carried a vintage photo of my mother sitting on the back porch of our family home.

Home was a topic I used many times over the years. Despite what the media says about people experiencing homelessness, every woman wanted a home. In my class notes I wrote, "I wondered about giving this assignment to women in a homeless shelter, but then I realized that 'home' is not necessarily a place. It can be a feeling, a sensation, and a remembrance." The women agreed that home was a place where they felt comfortable. Some women identified home by heirlooms that were passed down through the generations. Another student stated that certain types of trees reminded her of home. "Home" was always a topic that engaged almost every woman in the room.

My favorite workshop was the first time I asked the group, "If you could do anything in your life without any boundaries or limitations, where would you be in twenty years?" It was a variation of a writing prompt from *Room to Write* by Bonni Goldberg. I told the women to enter an invisible time machine and take all of us along with them by giving sensory details. Women smiled as they wrote about their new lives.

Three members of the class shared their stories. An older student, who would be in her seventies in twenty years, wanted to travel. She wanted to visit Hawaii again and spend a month relaxing by the ocean. She planned to visit relatives in Madrid, Spain, preferably in the spring so she could see the flowers bloom. She also wanted to visit relatives in Barcelona and Paris. Eventually, she wanted to own a villa in Puerta Vallarta and have a boutique that catered to wealthy tourists. When she described the sand in Puerta Vallarta as white like snow with tiny flakes, everyone in the class could imagine themselves on the beach. Another student, who would be in her forties, wanted to be known as a wise woman. She wanted to go to Belize to find out more about her heritage. Her mother had left the country at a young age, but never told her much about it. She also wanted a career in a creative field, a successful businessman husband, and a son and daughter.

One young lady wanted to be a CPA in a high-level field, with the income to afford her dream house in Seattle. She described her seven-bedroom house with dark wood furniture and plush carpeting. The back yard would have a garden, a swing, and a honeysuckle tree. When I reviewed the exercise the following week, several new students wanted a chance to participate. One new student wanted to be a special education teacher in San Francisco. She would live in a three-bedroom apartment in a Victorian building. She described each room in the apartment, from her stainless steel kitchen appliances to the sheets on her queen-sized bed.

Another woman wanted to live in a big house in the South with a country-style kitchen and cherry hardwood floors. Rural Oregon was the dream location for another student. She wanted to live on a 20-acre farm near Bend, Oregon. Besides growing vegetables and developing new tomato varieties, she wanted to be a horse trainer and dog breeder. After the classes, I typed up the stories and gave each student a copy of her personal story the following week. I advised them that now it was their turn to make it happen.

In some classes, students wanted information on how to construct essays and novels and how to begin journaling. The women enjoyed doing poetry rounds, where a piece of paper went around the room and each participant could only see what the person before them had written. The lines of the poem usually had an invisible connection and the women took pride in creating something together. Over the years, we talked about topics as diverse as cars, pets, birthdays, weather, aging and regrets. Sometimes I had eleven women in the class. Other times I only had one or two. But each week, I looked forward to hearing a new story and sharing one of mine.

Over time, the shelter management changed. The caring, friendly manager who took the time to listen to every resident was replaced by a new manager who saw the shelter as a public relations opportunity. The shelter changed from being a respite for homeless women in need to a results-oriented program that only accepted those willing to follow a specific plan for maximum PR effect. In the summer of 2009, the workshop was phased out.

During the early days of the class, one woman gave me the best compliment ever. She said, "When we are in this class, we aren't here anymore." I hoped that the workshop enabled a lot of women to transcend their situation for ninety minutes. Even today, I often wonder if any of the women got the chance to realize their dreams. I hope that the workshop inspired some of them to continue to write and be creative after they left the shelter. At the end of one class, a student asked, "What makes you think that anyone cares about your life?" I countered with, "What makes you think that they don't?" Everyone has a story. I started writing because I knew that if I didn't, the lives of my parents would be lost forever. Every time that I shared a story about them, their memory lived on.

Two years after the end of the workshop, I experienced homelessness. Two days after my fifty-fifth birthday, I was at Venice Beach, where I waited in the dark of a cold January evening for a bus that would take me to an emergency homeless shelter for the night. Journaling my experiences helped to keep me sane and gave me an outlet for my feelings of hopelessness and helplessness. It was hard to remember that I had once been a government employee and a workshop facilitator. I became an anonymous middle-aged African American woman wandering the streets of Santa Monica with nowhere to go.

I remembered some of the lessons I'd given to the ladies in my class and used pen and paper to chronicle my experiences. I thought about what I had learned from the women I had encountered in the four years of the workshop. They were strong, intelligent women who did not let homelessness define who they were and who they would become. I was determined to survive, too. During three years of long-term unemployment and staying in the bedroom of a friend in a mostly white neighborhood after my return to Sacramento, I continued to write about the world I was attempting to navigate. Instead of reacting to the covert racism I perceived in my temporary environment, I wrote out my anger and frustration on the page. After finding a job and my own apartment, I put my essays together in a book. Maybe one day, one of my former students will pick it up and think fondly of "Exploring Writing with Beatrice." The power of writing has always given me strength and I hope that it inspired strength for them too.

References

Gayle Brandeis, *Fruitflesh* (2002). New York: HarperCollins Publishers.

Tim O'Brien, *The Things They Carried* (1990). Boston, MA: Houghton Mifflin Company.

Bonni Goldberg, *Room to Write* (1996). New York: TarcherPerigee

Writing Exercise

In my workshop, I did several exercises about things of sentimental value and sacred objects. What is your Artifact of Power? Is there one thing that you possess that gives you power? I have my father's United Mine Workers of America ring. When I think of what he had to go through as an illiterate African-American coal miner, it gives me strength and reminds me of my own resiliency. Write about your Artifact of Power. What does it mean to you? Share it on the page. Put what you wrote in a place where you can see it frequently. Even if your Artifact of Power isn't always accessible, you can draw from its power whenever you need to by reading your words.

Teaching Creative Writing in an Alternative Setting: Come Clean, Be Real

Carolyn Holbrook

> Words are to be taken seriously. I try to take seriously acts of language. Words set things in motion. I've seen them doing it. Words set up atmospheres, electrical fields, charges. I've felt them doing it. Words conjure.
> —Toni Cade Bambara

On one of the many days when I stood at the front desk in the Minneapolis South High School office signing in my tardy daughter, the assistant principal asked me to come into her office. I braced myself, expecting to be warned of possible consequences for Ebony's habitual lateness. But instead, Ms. Rudel said she had been observing my relationship with my daughter, which she characterized as close, loving, and beautiful. She said there were many other African American girls at South who could benefit from having a mother figure like me in their lives, then asked if I would consider taking one or two of them under my wing.

Relieved and surprised, I was pleased that the way I relate to my children had caught Ms. Rudel's scrutinizing eye. However, she was unaware of certain things in our circumstances. Ebony was just beginning to recover from a struggle that had begun two years earlier when Tania, my middle daughter and her closest sibling, left home for college. In some ways Tania had been the mother figure to Ebony that Ms. Rudel hoped I could be to one of the young women she had in mind.

She didn't know that when Ebony was in middle school and Tania was in her junior year of high school, I had accepted a full-time position working outside of our home. This was new for Ebony, because until then I had been working at home her entire life.

Tania and Ebony were the last of my five children still at home, and they spent a good two years together after school doing homework and watching *After School Specials* on television until I got home from work every day. But Tania was accepted to an Ivy League college in her senior year. While our family was proud of her and very excited, Tania's good fortune was devastating for Ebony. All of her older siblings had left home, I was no longer working at home, and now the sister she was closest to was a thousand miles away. For the first time in her life, she was home alone after school every day. She was feeling lost and abandoned, and I felt like I needed to keep her close, to protect her. I didn't want to disrupt her life any further by bringing a strange girl into our lives, but I wanted very much to find a way to honor Ms. Rudel's request. There were plenty of options for ways to get involved at South High. It is still known for its diversity of educational opportunities—from its exemplary academic, fine arts, and world languages programs to its resources to help troubled teens finish school.

After some thought, I decided to volunteer to teach a creative writing class in the Mother Infant Care Education program (MICE), the school's program for teen parents. Ms. Rudel and the director of the program agreed, and with the help of my friend Julie Landsman, who had recently published a memoir about teaching in an alternative school, I developed a ten-week course I was pretty proud of.

When I entered the classroom on the first day, I was surprised and pleased to see that, countering stereotypes, the students were not all Black, and were not all girls. There were several responsible, caring young fathers who were in the program with their babies' mothers.

The first two weeks were tougher than I anticipated. Those kids' daily lives were full of chaos. Some were in foster homes with their babies; some still lived at home, and whether or not they felt supported by their parents, they were responsible for the care of their child or children. Some were emancipated and were trying to work, pay rent, and go to school. Some of the girls were in unhealthy relationships and couldn't imagine a different way to live. The teacher told me in advance that she never knew from one day to the next who would show up.

Creative writing was the furthest thing from those students' minds. Nevertheless, I tried to connect with them. I used prompts Julie suggested that had been successful for her. I also used prompts I had designed based on things I heard the students say to each other and to Sue, their teacher. I also came up with prompts based on items I saw in the classroom: colorful posters of famous people, or nature scenes with inspirational quotes scrawled across the bottom in large, decorative fonts; pictures of celebrated elders or smiling babies; and items strewn randomly around the room. But nothing worked. I was not able to interest them.

One day, one of the girls cleared her throat and gave her glasses a gentle nudge to keep them from sliding down her nose. "Um, Ms. Holbrook," she said. "You're nice, but this is boring! No disrespect, but you don't know nothin' about us. Why you think you can come in here and help us by trying to make us write about things that don't mean nothin' to us?" Around the table, heads nodded in agreement, and I suddenly realized that in my effort to be professional and to avoid disappointing Ms. Rudel, I had denied those young women and men the very thing they needed from any adult who worked with them—to just be my authentic self, to just be real. I made a split-second decision to drop the lesson plan I had so carefully put together and to come clean, show them that I knew more about them than they thought—that the reason I wanted to work with them was because I was one of them. I had my first child when I was seventeen.

I closed the page on the book of poems I had planned to use for the day's prompt and looked from one student to another: the light-skinned black girl who was unable to see her own beauty and her partner, Corey, who adored her and their baby; the blonde girl whose seven-month fetus bore down on her bladder causing her to get up every few minutes to use the restroom, thankfully located in the classroom; and then to the teacher, who nodded slightly, wondering how I would handle the situation.

"I wasn't one of the popular girls in school," I told them and went on to say that I didn't wear pretty dresses or go to school dances, like the Central High Prom or the swanky debutante ball like my sister Joanne. Nor was I surrounded by adoring boys like Joanne and her friends always were. Secretly, I wanted to be like my sister, but it simply wasn't in the cards for me. My personality wasn't the type that attracted popularity. Instead, my friends and I got into fights and talked back to our parents and teachers. And the boys in our south side neighborhood pretty much ignored us.

My mother and stepfather were strict, but one thing my siblings and I were allowed to do without supervision was to take the bus downtown for Saturday afternoon matinees. My friends and I looked forward to those weekly excursions because a group of boys from the north side projects also went to those movies. It was 1961, and they reminded us of the gangs in *West Side Story*; the rough, sexy white boys we saw on reruns of James Dean movies; and of Sidney Poitier, the gorgeous actor from the Bahamas who played Greg in *Blackboard Jungle*. And, unlike the south side boys, they liked us.

Before the 1960s, when I became a teenager, the north side was like a family. Everyone looked out for each other. It didn't matter if you lived in the projects or in one of the middle-class homes near the projects. But by the time we were in our teens, the projects had become more isolated, with poor Black, Native, and Mexican families making up the majority of its residents. We were forbidden to go over north, which made the boys from the projects all the more intriguing. We often lied to our parents, telling them we were going to the movies, and spent Saturday afternoons with the project boys instead. It wasn't long before I fell in love with a boy named Lonnie. He embodied the bad boys we often saw in the movies, and I found him utterly intoxicating—the way he shaped his words in a rough, raspy voice that seeped out of the left side of his mouth, his upper lip turned up in a permanent grimace. And the crackling energy he exuded when he moved with a badass swagger was irresistible. He was so full of life and so daring—so different from the sons of the Black bourgeoisie whom my sister attracted and our parents expected us to date and eventually marry.

Even though I wasn't a model teenager, I wanted my parents' approval. I was sure they would like Lonnie if only they would meet him. Boy, was I wrong! They made it unmistakably clear that they didn't want him coming around, did not want me to see him under any circumstances. But like teenagers since the beginning of time whose parents tried to keep them apart, we found ways to be together. Lonnie had a car and he would pick me up after school several days a week. We made out in his car and made plans for later in the night before he dropped me off a block away from home. "Meet me in the alley," he would say before speeding off, promising to call from the pay phone near my home when he arrived later, after my family was asleep.

Joanne and I had a pink Princess phone that sat on a nightstand between our beds. Luckily, she always fell asleep first. So, on the nights Lonnie was going to call, I was able to slip under the covers with my clothes on and hide the phone under my pillow with no worry that she would hear it ring. Like clockwork, his call always came right before midnight. "Ready, baby?" he rasped and then whispering as though he feared that Joanne would hear him, "I'll be there in five minutes."

My bed rested against the wall by our bedroom window, which made my next steps easy. I quietly placed the phone back in its cradle and returned it to the nightstand, glancing over to make sure Joanne was still sleeping. Then I slowly opened the window and crawled out onto the slanted roof and closed the window, leaving it open just a crack to ensure that I would be able to get back in. I'd jump down from the roof and creep out to the alley where Lonnie was waiting.

We never stayed out longer than an hour or two. I wanted to be sure I was back in bed in my pajamas before my family or our neighbors woke up. But one night, Lonnie said he had been watching a small gas station that was open late. The guy who worked there seemed bored and weary, so Lonnie assumed he would be easy prey. He said was going to teach me to drive his old two-tone Buick. I knew he meant that I would drive the getaway car. Something inside of me trembled in fear at that thought—but only for a moment. The biggest part of me was excited, knowing I was about to become a bad guy's girl like Maria and Anita in *West Side Story*.

We drove around an empty lot until Lonnie felt confident that I could handle the Buick. Then he drove to the gas station and parked a few houses away. He got out, leaving the engine idling, then kissed me. "You know what to do." I slid over to the driver's seat, heart pounding, shoulders tense. With sweaty palms gripping the steering wheel, I began to question what I was getting myself into. Sure, it was thrilling, but what if we got caught? Was jail as romantic as the movies made it seem? Was this boy worth the possible consequences?

I didn't have much time to wonder. Soon, a noise that sounded like popcorn popping came from the gas station and Lonnie ran out holding a pistol. He jumped into the passenger seat and I took off. We didn't get very far before we heard sirens blaring and saw red and blue lights flashing in the rearview mirror.

The young parents stared in amazement when I told them how that night resulted in my being sentenced to the Minnesota Home School for Girls in Sauk Centre, about a hundred miles northwest of Minneapolis. The doctor there soon discovered that I was three months pregnant and, because of the heart murmur I was born with, sent me back to Minneapolis to spend the remaining six months of my pregnancy incarcerated on the maternity ward at the University of Minnesota Hospital in a bland room with white walls, a cold linoleum floor, and four beds. A steady stream of women came in with labor pains and left within a few days with their newborns. There were also long-term patients, juvies like myself, and women who were there because of difficult medical problems.

I will always remember Dorothy, a woman I became close to who stayed for three or four weeks before her baby was due. She had a weak heart and explained that the doctors wanted to ensure that she would be strong enough when it was time for her to give birth. She went into labor one morning the week before my baby was due. When her husband arrived, I watched him take her hand as she was rolled out of the room. He turned and offered me a smile that contained a mixture of excitement and fear. Sometimes I am still haunted by the helpless look on his face when he returned alone later to pick up her things, his shoulders slumped, his face a flood of tears. Despite reassurances by doctors, nurses, and my social worker that my heart murmur wasn't nearly as serious as Dorothy's condition, I wasn't able to sleep until my son, Stevie, was born on April 23, 1962, and he and I were pronounced healthy.

Tongues clucked and grunts gurgled from the students' throats when I told them that my mother and stepfather wouldn't let me bring my baby home. I had no choice but to put him in foster care or give him up for adoption. I chose foster care. However, I was only allowed to see him once a week, on Saturday afternoons, one hour at a time, for the first fourteen months of his life. Before my mother passed away, I asked her why. "We were afraid of Lonnie," she explained, saying that they didn't think they would be safe if little Stevie and I were in the home and he had ready access to us.

I was awarded custody of Stevie on my eighteenth birthday, but I didn't have a clue how to be a parent. Back then, teen parents didn't have programs like MICE to help us learn parenting skills. I had already dropped out of school and, with less than a high school education, struggled to keep a roof over our heads, cleaning with a motel housekeeping service to supplement my monthly welfare check and selling high-end cosmetics to wealthy white women in Minneapolis suburbs. Trying to manage my frustration was hard. There was so much I didn't understand about babies, and all I knew about being a mother was the example I was raised with. Keep the child clean and fed, but when he needed emotional nourishment, spank him first. It was all the more difficult because Stevie didn't have a clue who I was, this stranger who until now he had only seen on those brief weekly visits.

When Stevie was three years old, I packed up our few belongings and with only eighteen dollars in my pocket took a Greyhound bus to Springfield, Massachusetts, to live with my father and his second family for a while. In many ways, it was a good move. Dad and my stepmother had two daughters. They were gentle people, and for the first time in my life I saw children being treated with love and kindness. I was grateful to see that there was a different way to treat children from the way I had been raised. This is not meant to be a criticism of my mother and stepfather: I truly believe people raise children the way they understand. My mother's childhood was difficult. She had lost both of her parents by the time she was in her early teens and spent the remainder of her childhood separated from her siblings, forced to live with unloving relatives. I can only imagine the extent of what she suffered.

The students listened in silence as I told them the next part of my story, the part where I moved to Boston once I was on my feet to find work, and to follow my dream of getting involved in the arts. When Stevie was seven, I married a man I met in an arts program. My child and I experienced unbelievable violence at his hands. If you have read Ntozake Shange's choreopoem *For Colored Girls Who Have Considered Suicide When the Rainbow Is Enuf,* or if you saw Tyler Perry's film adaptation, you no doubt cringed and maybe gasped, cried, or screamed when the Lady in Red's boyfriend, Beau Willie, hung her two children by their ankles from the living room window in their high-rise apartment in the projects, then dropped them, killing them. But as horrifying as it was, you probably thought it couldn't be real, that it was just an overly dramatic scene in a play. I'm here to tell you that such scenes are very real. It's very likely that they occur more often than anyone knows. The man I was married to hung my son from a sixth-floor window by his ankles to strengthen a point he wanted to make after having beaten me bloody. And that was just one incident.

Clearly, the brief time of peace I had experienced in my father's home wasn't enough to instill a new sense of positive self-worth in me. It took me ten years to find my way out of that marriage. We moved from Boston to New York City and then to his hometown in North Carolina. The beatings continued, and over time I gave birth to three more of my children, feeling more trapped with each birth.

A surprising turn of events eventually showed me the way out. One Sunday morning our small church's pianist was sick and couldn't make it to the service. Remembering my childhood piano lessons at Phyllis Wheatley Settlement House in North Minneapolis, I made a feeble attempt to try playing the songs. Afterward, some of the elderly women in the congregation encouraged me to practice, and before long I was able to relieve the pianist from time to time. After a while, I decided to go back to school and earn a GED, which boosted my confidence even more. And finally, scary as it was, I made a decision to strike out on my own, to return to Minneapolis, now a single mother with a new struggle—to raise four kids on my own and a fifth child, Ebony, who would arrive a year later, the result of a failed attempt to reinvigorate a relationship with an old boyfriend.

I definitely had the young parents' attention now. Questions flowed one after the other, most centering on why I had stayed in an abusive relationship for so long, how I dug myself out of poverty, and how I got where I am now, in this classroom with them.

I answered all of their questions candidly and was especially thrilled to tell them about Miss Johnson, my eighth-grade English teacher. She played a major role in my eventual return to education. Miss Johnson had somehow made me feel like she saw more in me than just a girl who so often gave teachers good reasons to send her to the principal's office, or to simply ignore me, making me feel invisible. She always had a smile for me when I entered her classroom, and she enjoyed the poems I wrote in her class. And even though there are a lot of well-educated people in my family, she was the first person to make me feel like I might someday be college material myself. Her belief in me stayed in the back of my mind throughout my years of struggle. She is the reason why today I look for the light in the students I work with at the private college and the community college where I have taught. Because of Miss Johnson, I know how important it is to focus on that light, even though it may only be shining dimly when students first enter my classroom. I know firsthand that a spark I light may someday catch fire. I also know that, like Miss Johnson, I may not be the one to witness the flames I may have ignited.

After that day, the mood in the classroom perked up. The students began responding energetically to my prompts, producing lots of interesting work. And our conversations about our lives continued.

One of the young fathers in the class was a quiet, rather surly young man named Andy, who never wrote or participated in our discussions. He also never missed a class. Andy seemed more sullen than usual the day after then Speaker of the House Newt Gingrich announced the Republican right wing's so-called Contract with America, which among other things suggested that the nation could reduce the welfare rolls by placing the children of welfare mothers in orphanages. The idea was to prohibit states from paying welfare benefits to children whose paternity was not established and also to the children who were born out of wedlock to women under eighteen years of age. The savings, according to this proposal, would be used to establish and operate orphanages and group homes for unwed mothers.

The morning Andy read about the Gingrich proposal, he sat planted in his seat, legs crossed, arms folded tightly across his chest, his thick blonde eyebrows furled in a deep frown and his lips glued together in a scowl, all making him look much older than his seventeen years. Then, in the middle of a writing exercise in which, as usual, he had not participated, he suddenly blurted out, "I'm tired of the way people like Newt Gingrich and doctors and social workers treat us. I wanna write a letter to the editor!"

A brief silence came over the classroom, followed by agreement from the other students—all whom had experienced offensive treatment by doctors and social workers and even some of their teachers. Sue, the MICE teacher, joined in, confirming that she could tell by a student's demeanor if they had come to class from an appointment or a class that hadn't gone well. And now, Newt Gingrich and his "Moral Majority" were insulting them again by promoting a plan that would exacerbate the nearly unbearable restrictions teen parents were already living under. For instance, for the few hundred dollars they received every month in a check and an electric benefit card to cover only the bare necessities, they had to spend inordinate amounts of time doing paperwork to continue proving month after month that they were qualified—time that ate into the hours they could be caring for their children and completing their homework so they could prepare for self-sufficiency.

Moved by their passion, I once again tossed out my lesson plan. I didn't have a clue how to teach anyone how to write a letter to the editor, but I knew someone who did. The previous summer I had served as interim editor of the *Whittier Globe,* my neighborhood's newspaper, and had put together a series of community journalism workshops taught by seasoned feature writers, sports writers, food critics, and others. One of the journalists was Eric Ringham, then commentary editor at the *Minneapolis Star Tribune.* I called Ringham and was happily surprised by his response. I had hoped he would give me a few pointers, but instead he offered to visit the class the following week, saying that what the kids really needed was instruction on how to write commentary and an effective opinion piece.

When Mr. Ringham came to visit, he went much further. He gave the students a deadline and promised to publish all of the commentaries that were completed by then, and to pay each student whose work he published $100. I would work with them in the weeks after his visit to help them revise their work and prepare the commentaries for publication.

While he explained his work at the *Star Tribune* and his expectations for their commentaries, and even during a writing exercise he gave them, he couldn't help noticing a young woman who kept laying her head on her desk. He called her out on her behavior, letting her know that he thought she must have been bored or just plain rude. She replied that neither was true: she was tired. The journalist in him took over and he became curious, wanted to hear her story.

"Why are you so tired?" he asked.

"I overslept and missed my bus so I walked to school," she replied with a yawn.

No big deal, I'm guessing he thought to himself. But he asked the next question anyway.

"How far do you live from school?"

"Twenty blocks."

Now Ringham was even more curious. "Why didn't you catch the city bus or just stay home?"

"I didn't have any money and I need to get my education."

A dumbfounded look came over his face. He stared at the girl for a moment and then asked when her baby was due.

"Next month," she replied and placed her head back on her desk.

Later, Ringham told me that those kids, especially that young mom who wanted her education so badly that she had walked twenty blocks to school in the eighth month of her pregnancy, changed his view of teen parents. Until then he, like so many others, had bought into the myth that teenagers like them are lazy and promiscuous, uninterested in educating themselves or their children. The intelligence and determination he witnessed that day caught him by surprise.

The students eagerly spent the next few weeks revising their essays. Andy, thrilled that he had been taken seriously, fully participated, taking ownership of the project by sharing valuable feedback on his classmates' work and prodding them through the revision process while he also wrote his own commentary.

The article, "Kids with Kids: Teenage Parents Find Power in the Pen," was published in the *Minneapolis Star Tribune* on Sunday, September 17, 1995, and a few days later we celebrated. Sue brought treats and the kids showed up with their $100 checks in hand, along with a few choice words about negative letters to the editor that had followed the publication. Most of the letters were positive, but I guess it was unrealistic to expect that some readers wouldn't slam the paper for encouraging those awful little slackers by giving them (gasp) money to buy expensive sneakers. Sue and I drew the kids' attention to the letters that praised their determination and those that showed that some readers were inspired and enlightened by their words.

And I learned that by coming clean myself, I had inspired students to find their own voices.

* * *

Previous versions of this essay were published in *Tell Me Your Names and I will Testify*, U of M Press 2020, and *The Poverty & Education Reader*, Stylus Press 2013.

References

Ringham, E. (1995, September 17). Kids with Kids: Teenage Parents Find Power in the Pen. *Minneapolis Star Tribune*.

Shange, N. (2002). *For colored girls who have considered suicide/ when the rainbow is enuf. spell #7. The love space demands*. London: Methuen.

Writing Exercises

During the class that is the subject of this essay, I decided to change my lesson plan several times. Try one of the following exercises:

1. Write about a decision or choice you made that you wish you had not made:
   - Describe who you were at the time.
   - Describe the reason you made the decision or choice.
   - Describe the impact of making this decision or choice. Did you gain or lose anything?
   - How did this decision change you or your circumstances?
   - Who are you now?
2. Write about a decision or choice you made that you are glad you made.
   - Describe who you were at the time.

- Describe the reason you made the decision and its impact. Did you have to give anything up?
- How did you or your circumstances change because of this choice?

3. Describe a time you stood up for yourself or someone else.
   - What motivated you?
   - Describe how it changed you.

Demystifying Diversity: embracing my biracial identity

Daralyse Lyons

"Which race are you?" the facilitator asked. It was clear from her question that it was meant to be an either/or proposition. I was eight years old and we were at an Interracial Parents and Children's group and she wanted to know if I and the other children self-identified as Black *or* White. Around the room, the inquiry went, my fellow caramel-complected peers all identifying as Black, and only Black. When it was my turn, I said, "I'm Biracial. I'm half-Black and half-White."

The facilitator didn't seem to know what to do with that. "But how do you identify?" she asked, as if I hadn't just told her.

"I'm Biracial," I repeated. "I'm half-Black, half-White."

"Yeah, but which ONE?"

I wasn't and have never been just one. I am two things, at the same time, in the same person. I am an integrated individual who has always known herself to be Black and White and claiming all of me has been an important part of my authenticity. I knew that even as a child. I know it more, now.

Even though I grew up embracing my multiethnic, Biracial heritage, I also grew up feeling sad for others who weren't given the space or the opportunity to claim both sides of themselves. I remember being confused when my friends with White biological mothers who tucked them in at night and read them bedtime stories and loved them as much as my White mother loved me claimed to be Black and nothing else. I remember going to book fairs and buying books with Brown-skinned characters. Because these characters looked like me, I felt as if I was seeing myself represented and I relished the stories, yet any of the books my mother or I found that explicitly addressed race invariably presented it as a binary category. A character was either Black or White.

Looking back, I don't believe I felt a void by not having expansive literary racial representation, but that's only because, at home, I was encouraged to embrace the full spectrum of myself. It's only as I got older that I wanted others to have what I did—permission to define themselves based on who they knew themselves to be, rather than on who society told them they were.

As a child, I didn't have language for the one-drop rule, a societal convention that holds that anyone who has even "one-drop of Black blood" will be considered all Black. The origins of this rule date back to segregation and arose as part of an effort to subjugate and ostracize People of Color. Since then, the one-drop rule has been embraced by many BIPOC people and, while this can be empowering for some, it is also divisive and erases the nuanced nature of race.

My eight-year-old self didn't know any of that though. I did, however, know that society's definitions of race were polarized and led people to hide aspects of themselves, and I knew I never wanted to change myself to fit society. Instead, I wanted to be part of shaping a society that made it safe for everyone to be all of who they were.

So, I read. I read about White people and Black people, but no one Biracial, like me. Even though I didn't see people who identified as I do, I fell in love with characters based not on our shared identities but on our shared emotions.

When I was eight and my favorite aunt died of cancer, it was *The Bridge to Terabithia* that saw me through. In that book, I learned about grief and loss and loving people who pass on, honoring their memories. It was *I Know Why the Caged Bird Sings* that helped me heal from sexual abuse, or at least acknowledge its impact.

Reading rescued me, but beyond that, I loved to write. Since I was five years old, I've been scribbling in journals and manufacturing stories out of the ethers of imagination. I'd put pen to paper and words would come pouring out of me in an unstoppable deluge. In the beginning, I wrote about myself, for myself, but in time, I began to view writing as a bridge-builder. After publishing several novels with White protagonists, I realized that I owed it to the world to be more authentic in my storytelling and to amplify perspectives that are often silenced in service of the status-quo.

I began with a poem, written in celebration of my Black/White Biracial identity. The simple rhyming story was intended for children like the child I had been once upon a time. When I was eight and the facilitator told me I had to choose a single racial identity, I refused. By that time, I had acquired an unshakeable sense of myself. But as an adult, I'd learned enough to know that my upbringing was rare. The vast majority of Biracial children weren't being raised to believe that they had the option to see race as a spectrum. By writing about a Biracial girl who doesn't want to claim one race or another and, rather, celebrates all of who she is, I hoped to offer others the same acceptance

I'd felt when I was a child (except, of course, when interacting with that one group facilitator). The text for the book was completed in 2008 or thereabouts, and I was excited to pitch it to publishers because, at that time, there was nothing like it on the market, but there was a definite need.

I sent the manuscript to a handful of publishers and a dozen agents. Then, I waited for their inevitable approval. It didn't come. From those who responded (and most didn't), I heard things like "Mixed isn't a legitimate category," "this book lacks market appeal," and "this content really isn't relevant."

Far from being crushed, I was equal parts disgusted and grateful. I thought literary gatekeepers should be ashamed of themselves and I knew there were young readers out there who were hungry for books that presented race as a beautiful identity spectrum rather than as two oppositional binaries. Nevertheless, I put the manuscript on a shelf and it remained there, mostly forgotten, until close to a dozen years later when, on a whim, I re-pitched it to a single publisher.

The response was emphatic and immediate: Dear Daralyse, I loved your book. I think it's important and I would be honored to publish it, assuming you haven't received an offer.

Working with Elizabeth Hasegawa Agresta, a Canadian-born Japanese artist and illustrator who has three multiracial children, was a beautiful process from start to finish. She brought my words and my vision to life, creating a narrative out of images. It was especially meaningful that Elizabeth based her art on pictures of me as a child. Having never seen myself represented in children's books, my story was now its own children's book. I wrote the book under the pseudonym Maggy Williams because, at that point, I'd written extensively for an adult audience and I was advised to keep my books and my brand separate, but I've never hidden my identity, or shied away from the spotlight.

Since its publication, *I'm Mixed!* has won awards and received innumerable positive reviews. I've gone to schools to read the book and lecture on its contents and am always surprised when people thank me for having written it, because, to me, it's the realization of a dream. To be able to claim the fullness of my racial identity and to encourage others to embrace who they are is the most meaningful thing I've ever done, personally or professionally.

On the drive home from the Interracial Parents and Children's Group, I asked my mother "Why did that lady want me to lie?" Mom told me to just keep being honest with myself and others, and assured me that the world would eventually follow. It has. It's taken a long time, but it has.

After the positive reception *I'm Mixed!* received, I wrote many articles and essays about race, spoke to groups large and small, and participated in Diversity Equity and Inclusion (DEI) panels until I reached a point in my professional life when I knew I had to do diversity work that was different than anything I'd seen being done. I wanted to be part of encouraging a more embracing, more integrated, more inclusive society. Once again, I needed to be willing to step outside of the box and to create something unprecedented.

I knew there was a need for diversity work that focused on integrating all aspects of people and on allowing individuals to self-identify rather than allowing our broken society to tell people who they have to be. So, a Biracial friend (AnnaMarie Jones) and I began the Demystifying Diversity Podcast. I was clear at the outset that I wanted the project to be a wide-ranging journalistic initiative that covered many more issues than Biracial identity or experience. I wanted our work to change the world, not only for those who shared our particular racial or ethnic identities, but for everyone.

The two of us craved a way to inspire systemic change and to amplify a variety of voices and perspectives. We wanted to build a better world.

After the first season, AnnaMarie moved on from the podcast to run for and win a local office position as her town Commissioner, and the podcast became mine to continue to nurture along with the help of my wonderful business partner, Zack James.

Over the course of a few years, I've been blessed to interview several hundred people and to listen to stories of struggle and resilience. I've written the book *Demystifying Diversity: Embracing Our Shared Humanity* and its accompanying workbook. I've given a TEDx talk entitled "Black or White? Refusing to Choose & Embracing Biracial Identity." I don't have a vested interest in whether others who share my same racial and/or ethnic composition identify as I do, but I want to be part of building a world where, when one person asks another their identity, their response is met with respect and love, and never negated.

The truth is that Biracial stories still aren't being told enough. Sure, there's some research about Biracial people, but there aren't nearly enough narratives and the data doesn't match the stories being told.

There are studies that suggest that those of mixed-race identity are at risk for greater feelings of alienation and possible risky behavior than our mono-racial counterparts, White or Black. Other studies provide compelling evidence that demonstrates that many Biracial Americans experience increased social capital. In fact, according to one Pew research survey, a mere 4% of Biracial people view their race as a liability while 19% of us report feeling that our Biraciality has been an asset, and 76% say their race has made no difference.

There is no one experience of being Biracial, just as there's no one experience of being any identity. I think it's important for our stories to be told, and I think they should be told unapologetically and without attempting to force Biracial narratives to fit into existing categories. After all, not fitting in so often encapsulates what it feels like to hold a nonbinary identity in an all too binary world.

That's why, on September 14, 2021, I strode confidently onto the TEDx stage, the sky overcast, a storm brewing, dressed in a navy blue dress, gold earrings, a gold necklace and gold shoes, took the microphone and took a deep breath.

I knew what I was going to say. I'd been saying it since I was a child. This time, though, there was no one to negate my perspective. I looked out at the audience, locked eyes with my mother, who was sitting in the second row, and began my speech.

"Over the course of my 38 years, I've been asked hundreds of times 'What are you?' My answer has always been the same. 'I'm Biracial. I'm half-Black and half-White.'"

I'm happy to say that the world was ready to hear me and to embrace me, exactly as I am and as I've always been.

References

Lyons, D. (2020). *Demystifying Diversity: Embracing Our Shared Humanity*, Modern History Press, Ann Arbor, MI.

Lyons, D. (2021, December 8). *Black or white? refusing to choose & embracing biracial identity | Daralyse Lyons | TEDxLehighRiver*. YouTube. Retrieved July 3, 2022, from https://www.youtube.com/watch?v=Xjm8H3FSGdk

Williams, M., & Agresta, E. (2018). *I'm mixed!*. Loving Healing Press, Ann Arbor, MI

Writing Exercise

This exercise will support you in excavating and embracing core, essential truths about yourself, a necessary precursor to living your empowered truth.

1. Begin on a new page in your journal.

2. At the top of the page, write the question *Who am I?*

3. Answer that question (*Who am I?*) again and again and again, writing every answer that comes to mind, without censoring. Continue writing until you've filled at least two journal pages (if you fill more, great, just keep delving!). Your answers will likely vary in scope and in substance. Some things that come up may be identity markers, in my case *I'm Biracial, I'm a woman, I'm a daughter, I'm a sister, I'm an author.* Some of your answers may have to do with characteristics, values, beliefs etc. *I'm quirky, I'm fun, I'm a human being having a spiritual experience...* You may find yourself repeating the same answer. Just keep writing until you've filled at least two pages, asking *Who am I?* and allowing yourself to discover a plethora of intuitive answers.

4. Once you've filled two or more journal pages, read what you've written and circle the top 3-5 answers that feel most central to your conception of your most authentic, self-expressed version of you.

5. Select the one circled answer that you want to embrace and embody right NOW.

6. Open a new page in your journal, set a timer for 10 minutes, and write about how you can amplify, honor and embrace that aspect of yourself.

7. Go be that person, today and always.

Hmong Origin Stories: foundation to writing, teaching, and mentoring

Pacyinz Lyfoung

My grandfather created one of the first written versions of the Hmong language to use as a secret code during the period after World War II when the Viet-Minh were trying to invade Laos. The Hmong lived on the mountains between Vietnam and Laos. The Hmong could not help but be involved in Vietnamese-Lao conflicts, which back then were Viet-Minh vs. French Protectorate in Laos conflicts. As a prominent young, educated, and trustworthy Hmong leader, my grandfather was always courted by the French as an ally who could mobilize Hmong villagers to help with territory security. As a minority group, the Hmong were often crushed and abused by the Viet-Minh. Aligning with the French was a matter of ethnic survival. My grandfather's use of written Hmong messages helped the French baffle the Viet-Minh and contributed to the French being able to stop the Viet-Minh's expansion into Laos. But mostly, through those alliances, my grandfather saved Hmong villages and Hmong lives, which was always his lifelong overarching goal.

When my almost twenty-two-year-old soon-to-be father chose his firstborn's name, he was studying in Bordeaux, France. He dutifully wrote his parents to ask for their advice. He faithfully gave me the name sent back for a girl child. Other foreign-born parents are concerned about how their children's names can be easily read by others or not mocked. In spelling his children's Hmong names, my father displayed superb respect for his father's version of the Hmong language and superb disregard for what anyone else might think.

I can imagine my dad writing my name on my birth certificate, with the same flourish that he used when he showed me how to sign my name: obviously, he had been practicing my signature for when I would be old enough to need one. His father's "Pac" instead of the now standard Hmong "Paj;" his father's "Yinz" instead of the now standard Hmong "Yeeb." My flower name blossomed on the page from his hand, guided by his father's spelling. Thus, I come from a line of traditional but creative men.

Thanks to my forefathers, everyone who meets me stumbles upon my name and cries for help with how to pronounce it. Introducing myself to people often becomes a mini lecture on the origin of my name. It means sharing the history of the Hmong written language. Some letters only indicate tones and, therefore don't translate into sounds. Once people know that, they can get over the extra letters that appear on the page (or Zoom now) and just hang on to the sounds.

Some wonder if they can use a nickname for me, meaning a shortcut, meaning either of the halves of my name, or something that might rescue them from remembering such a difficult name. A lot of people accommodate or even anticipate such requests with some easy and therefore generic nicknames.

I always recall that there are thousands of Hmong women with the name "Paj" or "Yeeb" and now "Paj Yeeb" is even quite popular. But so far, there has only been one Pacyinz. I am pleased to continue the tradition of respecting what my father and my grandfather chose and created. My name is Pacyinz, there is no shortcut and no nickname for that. My name is a legacy; my forefathers' acts of resistance embedded into the spelling of my name.

These origin stories are foundational to my journey as a writer and my organic evolution as a writing teacher/mentor.

I have been an avid reader all of my life, since I learned how to read as a young child. However, I did not develop into a writer until much later. The passing of my paternal grandmother, the only grandparent I really grew up with, a dramatic professional experience, triggered my emergence as a writer. The knowledge that I did not completely miss knowing her became my primary solace after her passing. I felt thankful I had finally learned to speak some basic Hmong when my parents migrated to the US with the goal of living with the Hmong community in Saint Paul, Minnesota. As my parents had intended, I started to have Hmong friends at school, something that never happened in my birthplace of France. I naturally caught up on the Hmong language. When my grandmother eventually came to the US, I was happy to finally be able to speak with her, in my very broken Hmong. Listening to her answers to the many questions I had never been able to ask before fascinated me. With her being gone from this world, I felt catalyzed to write about her, my family, and my community. I felt compelled to start documenting our stories.

I had never really thought of poetry and did not even read poetry, except for class assignments. However, around the time my grandmother passed, I became active with the Asian American Renaissance as a community activist. I remember picking up a flyer about an upcoming reading with Bao Phi, a local Asian American poet. I had never heard of him. I was just intrigued by Asian American poetry, which I had never been exposed to before. My curiosity and interest in learning new things led me to drive to Macalester College on a winter night. I still remember stepping around puddles of melted snow and carefully skipping around patches of ice. I was late, as I usually am, doing too many things at the same time. I was among the last arrivals. The auditorium was already dark. I had to fumble my way to some seat. The light came up on stage and an Asian guy started reciting. It was magic. It was spoken word, which had a vivid cadence. It had anger, irony, laughter, and tenderness. The words built little vignettes of our lives as Asian Minnesotans. I was sold on poetry in one hour. I also realized I wanted to be an Asian American poet, to tell our stories too.

I was not the only one. I was part of that first cohort of Asian American Renaissance poets and Hmong American poets in Minnesota. Many of us were not formally trained as writers. We were young professionals, oftentimes activists, who flocked to poetry readings and poetry workshops. Poetry was still something we did on the side, both something cool and something akin to community work. I recall my adult life in Minnesota as working, volunteering, going to arts events, and developing as a poet. I belonged to the Asian American and Hmong American arts circles. Every week, I went to other people's readings or events, or I had my own writing workshops to attend, readings to do, or events to plan. The beautiful thing about that time was the popularity of Asian/Hmong American poetry. We were all relatively new, so it was really inclusive. Anyone who wanted to write could write and be published in our local journals. We had not developed a more academic sense of aesthetics or canons yet, and the elitism that comes with them.

And yet, my writing journey did not come easily. Although I enjoyed attending spoken word events and spoken word was the most popular poetic form at the time, I knew it wasn't for me. First of all, as an English as a Second Language speaker who arrived as a late teen in the US, I could never talk that fast and that clearly. Second, being French born and raised, and being classically trained in the French language, my best school subject throughout my educational years, spoken word was just too raw for me. Finally, after attending many spoken word events, I was a little bit taken aback by the limited topics.

It seemed as if most Asian American poetry dealt with racism or sexism. I just did not feel that same anger or passion for those topics.

One day, Li Young Lee was scheduled to read at the University of Minnesota. There was a lot of anticipation and I was not sure why. I asked the one poet in my circles, Ed Bok Lee, who wrote lyrical poetry amidst the flood of spoken words, who seemed to write more like Li Young Lee, why. That conversation introduced me to the issue of quality of poetry. Ed said "Li Young Lee is a poet for poets, his writing may be too complicated for common folks, but people who really know and enjoy poetry love his work." That spurred me to order all of Li Young Lee's poetry books from BOA Editions LTD. Reading all of Li Young Lee's published poems at the time, I did not understand or appreciate all of them. However, some of his poems were unforgettable, and to this day remain one of the poetic aesthetics that I strive for, like other poets of my generation. Coming across Li Young Lee's poetry made me understand that poetry is a craft that one must refine. He has been my inspiration and motivation to take poetry workshops to further develop as a non-MFA poet.

When I left Minnesota, despite some brief stint as a member of the Fresno Hmong writing circle that was warmly welcoming, I became too busy with other endeavors and went on a hiatus as a poet.

After I moved to Washington, D.C. and felt settled enough there to have space again for poetry, I was in a very different place as a poet, and the world of Asian American literature had also evolved. There were more career Asian American poets who had won awards and been published by well-known publishers. Compared to them, I no longer felt that I could so comfortably call myself a poet, without those types of credentials and achievements. Furthermore, the epitome of an Asian American poet appeared to have become going to the Kundiman Retreat and being anointed as a Kundiman Fellow. I applied for a couple of years and got the standard response, "your work is great, but we can only accept the top 5% of the applicants." Those rejections made me ponder whether I was not gifted enough to meet the Kundiman's quality standards and whether those standards favored some styles of poetry over others.

Those questions were further complicated by the pushback from my relatives. One of my motivations to write poetry is to write it for my family. We come from a culture that did not have a written language. We also come from a history that suffered trauma from war, refugee flight, and exile. I have felt a sacred duty to be my family historian through poetry, which captures more of our human experiences than academic history. I always write elegies when our elders pass. I have also written more about my paternal grandfather who disappeared shortly after the end of the Vietnam War, and whose absence, thus lack of closing, remain open wounds.

I send my family all of those poems. They would typically say, "it's beautiful," although we don't really understand what it means. My family's response has provided a different kind of push to write in plainer and simpler ways, which is a counterview to the poetic world's call for innovative styles that earn the acclaim of poetry aficionados, but make poetry more inaccessible to common folks. To be fair, efforts like Kundiman to push the envelope of Asian American poetry and create new canons of excellence do help to break barriers and compete in the mainstream literary world. However, the question then goes back to who are you writing for? Are you writing for your people or are you writing for the white audience, so that the white audience will acknowledge your excellence?

In the end, as a poet, I feel very Asian American in the full sense of Asian America being its own cosmos of the world's Asian heritage and culture, so more Asian Cosmopolitan. I really appreciate having all the mix of various cultures and traditions. Other people say they feel like they don't belong anywhere because they are at intersections. I see intersections as my gateway to belong everywhere. As a writing teacher and mentor, this is my strength.

Washington, D.C. was the perfect sandbox for emerging as an Asian Pacific Islander (API) poetry teacher. I had lived there for a few years and had literally begged local poets to start API writing groups, as well as begged Kundiman to start local writing groups. I was attending every local API-led writing workshop I could find, which could be counted on one hand in six years of being a Washington, D.C. resident. I decided to teach my first API poetry workshop out of sheer frustration because no one else was giving me what I wanted as a developing API poet. I volunteered to lead one of the biweekly Wednesday poetry workshops at Split This Rock in May of 2019, which I wanted to curate as a celebration of API Heritage Month. I selected poems from Li Young Lee and API women poets such as Cynthia Dewi Oka and Anida Yoeu Ali, whom I had discovered at the first Refugee Poetics event in Philadelphia the year before. I was also interested in multi-media approaches, having just seen the work of Mengxi Althea Rao, a Chinese woman artist-in-residence at Halcyon, who did a community installation of her paper lantern sculptures that project words on the walls of my yoga studio. I invited her to collaborate on my workshop, but she was already booked somewhere else for that day. That forced me to think of how I could recreate a bit of her magic with my limited skills and resources. I decided to learn how to make origami lotuses with tissue paper, so that participants in my workshop could write their poems on the paper and put a light inside to make some of the words glow through. My fellow poets loved the workshop and had big smiles when they took home their lotus origami containing their words. That experience gave me an interest in teaching poetry again, which I filed in the back of my mind.

The pandemic was a catalyst in my further development as a poet and a poetry teacher. When I got tired of waiting for Kundiman to accept me, I went to take classes at Voices of Our Nation (VONA), a BIPOC writing program. That path guided me to evolve as a BIPOC writer and find a community with VONA. When the US went into lockdown in March of 2020, Faith Adiele and Serena W. Lin from the VONA circles started the BIPOC Writing Party (BWP). The Monday BWP workshops became sacred times of gathering and creativity. I was one of the faithfuls. Writing weekly and drafting one hundred kernels of poems per year did wonders for my writing. When the Atlanta spa shootings hit, I had the stamina to pummel through writing a poem in three days and reading it at the next available Washington, D.C. online open mic. In the intensity of emotions of that week, I completely forgot to read that it was a competition and found myself pleasantly surprised to win that night and was entered in the city-wide DC Poet Project's annual contest.

This unexpected turn of events gave me the confidence to no longer feel bashful about labeling myself a poet. I was doing everything a poet does: writing, publishing, and winning competitions. The realization that I was now a DC poet as opposed to just a Minnesotan poet also crystallized. I decided that I should try to teach a real poetry workshop and reached out to my first poetry school, The Loft Literary Center in Minneapolis. My proposal was accepted. Around the same time, BWP contacted me about becoming a regular co-host.

Thus, in the summer of 2021, I taught my first six-week poetry workshop and started co-hosting BWP for six months. Doing both at the same time provided a good opportunity for some more holistic poetry teaching experience. On the one hand, I took a deep dive into Southeast Asian (SEA) poetry, finally reading every poem in the three

SEA poetry books I selected, researching three new SEA poets, analyzing their styles and putting together the curriculum for my class. On the other hand, I was also now responsible for curating weekly BIPOC writing workshops, making broad scans of the BIPOC literary landscape to provide programming that would be inclusive and relevant to the BWP very diverse membership.

With the first endeavor, it was amazing to see our mini community coalesce through our shared SEA heritage that encompassed both Pacific SEA and Indochinese SEA. Mostly we were generating new SEA American poetry as we emulated the SEA poets we came across. With the second endeavor, I was continuing and adding my own touch to the BWP system. Working with a co-host reinforced the focus on diversity and collaboration in the process and line-up. I believe my best contribution was to open our hosting by encouraging guest hosts to provide their own feedback to the communal share of generated writing and providing more opportunities for our talented members to co-host. In both instances, my poetry teaching/curating expanded access to writing from margins within Asian American poetry and BIPOC literary circles and encouraged emerging writers to dare to write from non-conventional places in non-conventional voices.

My most recent poetry teaching experiment on March 16, 2022 involved integrating poetry as part of API women's healing and breaking the silence, on the first anniversary of the Atlanta spa shootings that took the lives of six Asian women workers and two customers at API businesses. In the future, I would love to do more community-based poetry events where poetry tools can be used as healing and advocacy tools, again expanding the circle of who may dare write in social justice and community building movements.

Writing Exercise

Think about your grandmother's native language. Did you ever learn it? Why/why not? What is your relationship with your grandmother and her native tongue? What is one story from your grandmother that gives you a tie to your culture? Put all those thoughts into sounds and images to create a poem about the day you learned to speak your grandmother's tongue literally, or figuratively.

Thoughts on a Queer, Indigenous, Multilingual, Multiracial Literary Future

Aruni Kashyap

One of the earliest instances when I realized that my state, my region, and my community have a rocky relationship with the narrative of the Indian nation was during a family trip to my grandmother's house in the burning early nineties to attend an emergency.

Our ancestral village is close to Guwahati, the largest city in Northeast India. Only one or two buses connected the village with the city during those days. The roads were potholed. Rural Assam was swarming with the army in search of armed insurgents. I remember my young uncles and cousins above eighteen used to leave the house to spend the night in the forests, leaving the women alone at home to escape torture. The over-fifty elderly men and the younger teenage boys formed Village Defense Parties, spending nights at the entry point of every village so that they could *help* the army if required. It was also a way of pacification. In other insurgency operations conducted by the army in the villages of Northeast India, unhappy Indian soldiers had set fire to entire villages to smoke out petrified people from their houses. I didn't know how it must have felt to be smoked out of your own house and watch it burn. But once, during a wasp infestation, I had seen how confused, hurt, and angry the poisonous wasps were. It made me think about how the army treated people during counter-insurgency to maintain law and order. Our people didn't want that to happen, hence the Village Defense Parties. The city was no better: mottled with Black Cats and Unified Commando Forces soldiers, they were known for being ruthless. But my father had a weapon that often parted the sea and created a passage for us to walk through—his identity card that proved that he was an employee of the Central Government of India. Since the state's people had wanted to secede from India, an identity card proving that he was a loyal Central Government employee who worked for the Public Broadcasting Service went a long way in allaying the suspicion of the soldiers patrolling the city and the highways who treated every Assamese speaker with contempt and suspicion.

As we had suspected, we were stopped. As usual, my father fished out his identity card. But unlike other days, the soldier guarding the street wasn't satisfied. It was late, and he wanted to know why we couldn't wait till the next day. When we said that there was a family emergency, he said with a sardonic smile: didn't everyone have a family emergency? Inside, my mother, sitting in the middle of the three-seater car seat, held my brother's hands and mine with great force, anticipating trouble.

Growing up in the 80s and 90s in Assam, our lives were very different from the children in the other parts of India. Assam, my home in Northeastern India, was struggling under a counter-insurgency operation carried out by the Indian army during those years of the early nineties. We read about the stifling of democratic voices of protest, assassinated journalists, gun battles, skirmishes, gang rapes of women, and tortured men in the evening news. During those years, my mother developed the habit of staring at my face for a long time before I boarded my school bus every morning. Many years later, she would tell me that she started doing that because she had no idea if she would see me at the end of the day. So uncertain were those days. I would exhume these stories later in the US to write my first novel, *The House with a Thousand Stories* (Penguin 2013), that dared to question the widespread human rights violations orchestrated by the Indian army during the eighties and nineties.

We called the rest of India "Mainland India" because the Northeastern states of India are connected to the main landmass of India through a 22-mile narrow stretch of land called the "Chicken's Neck." Living beyond the Chicken's Neck meant that everything reached us late from Mainland India. We received our national dailies a day late; our couriers were slow, and mobile phones that worked in Mainland India didn't work in Northeast India because of "security reasons." Finally, we were also governed by a different set of laws called AFSPA: the Indian constitution wasn't followed when ruling the unruly tribes of Northeastern India. In Mainland India, you can't arrest someone without a warrant, but in Northeast India, you can. In Mainland India, you can't detain someone for more than a certain number of hours, but in Northeast India, you can detain someone on suspicion of terrorism for an indefinite number of hours. In Mainland India, you can't shoot at sight. You can do that in Northeast India. We were dispensable indigenous tribes who fought contextless wars that the rest of India didn't understand or wanted to.

These tensions and intersections have led to the growth of a massive outpouring of New English language Writing in Northeast India that is uniquely different from what the world consumes as Indian English writing—Literature from Northeast India that voices many of the concerns I have raised is a new and exciting area of scholarly inquiry in postcolonial studies. When I moved to Delhi to study literature, I realized that similar concerns echo in writing emerging from Kashmir and other marginal communities of the country. In a sense, we were all responding to state violence, the failure of the state. The impermanent state and the fragile and erratic presence of democracy formed the crux of our writings.

Writers such as I am enter the tradition of Indian English Writing (and South Asian Anglophone Writing) enriched by authors such as Jhumpa Lahiri, Arundhati Roy, Akhil Sharma, Amitav Ghosh, Salman Rushdie, and Vikram Seth, from a location of exclusion even though I feel immensely indebted to these authors. The work I would produce was bound to stretch the possibilities of Anglophone Indian Writing. We traced our roots to the same country, but we didn't have equal social pasts. We are possibly united by the game of cricket, Bollywood movies, hundreds of recipes for potatoes, the chapatis, and rice preparations, and Rabindranath Tagore. But I inherited and was shaped by a multilingual, indigenous literary tradition compared to many other Indian-origin writers who arrived on the shores of the United States through the complex process of immigration enabled by class and privilege. This changed only in the last twenty years, and people from lower-caste and lower-class sections of India have had the privilege of immigrating to developed countries and choosing a better life. This is bound to enrich Indian American Literature.

But over the years, I have sincerely asked myself: who am I? Am I an Assamese writer? Or an Indian writer? Or a Northeast Indian writer? Or a Bilingual writer because I write in my native tongue, Assamese, too? Or an American writer as the US is my new adopted homeland? On the other hand, in the United States, I am a South Asian writer. Plus, due to the amazing work of queer writers who have shaped me, made me feel seen, I feel part of the long queer radical tradition of writing. The answer is more complex and yet can be answered in just one line: I am all of it, but if I had to choose, I would say that I am an Assamese writer.

I may be contributing to the anglophone tradition, working in the English academy as a professor of creative writing. Yet, my English writing is in constant dialogue with Assamese-language literature. For instance, the ending of the title story "His Father's Disease" is a homage to the ending of one of the most widely read novels in Assam. The first chapter of my Assamese-language novel, *Noikhon Etiya Duroit,* is in the short story collection as "The Love Lives of People Who Look Like Kal Penn." So yes, I am a bilingual writer in that sense, but the truth is I am an Assamese writer. I am not thrilled when someone calls me an Indian English writer because it flattens who I am. When I claim to be an Assamese writer, I am claiming a longer, richer, written tradition that goes back to the fifth century and derives inspiration from the poetry of the anti-Brahminical poet Sankardev, Sufi poet from Azan Faquir, Aai Padmapriya, and our folk songs found in Bihus and Oinitoms. I am an Assamese writer—but in the most literary and cultural sense, not in a narrow jingoistic way.

My Assamese literary heritage is also highly liberating and helps me to operate outside western conventions of reading literature. It enables me to step outside the shallow, and often contentious neoliberal literary discourse shaped by social media these days that asks knee-jerk questions posited with a veneer of morality masked as intelligence. This is why, reading my writing through an American multicultural lens of gender or racial identity may not always work. I am an Assamese writer, influenced and shaped primarily by Assamese literary aesthetics, oral and written. I was brought up in oral and indigenous literary cultures; the ability to imagine from various perspectives is seen as an indispensable talent, a strength, a possibility, a requirement. One is judged on whether they are a good storyteller based on this ability to imaginatively inhabit the experiences of other souls. This is an ability neoliberal literary discourse—at times shaped by sociological and anthropological curiosities that decentres the primacy of literary imagination—is not comfortable celebrating; the conversation is also mired by its US-focussed myopia.

For instance, we have something called Thiyo Naam in Assam, where one storyteller stands and tells stories all night from the epics and mundane daily stories. They usually stand in the middle of a group of people who sit on a large carpet or hay covered with a bedsheet, playing cymbals, flutes, and percussion instruments. These functions are often performed in winters when there is less possibility of rain. The storyteller holds just a shawl or a towel (gamusa) which they use as a prop to "become" various characters. The strength of these stories was not merely in the acting but in the lyrics—the text of the story— that have been passed on through generations. These texts are sheer poetry, and the dialogues are punchy, powerful. The storyteller changes into a woman, a child, a man, a king, a warrior, a peacock, a cobra, a mentally-ill person in an instant because there is no time to wait. My culture taught me that there are no limits to the literary imagination.

I use my writing to generate and sustain conversations about justice—about conversations that will uphold democratic principles. To achieve this, I have often returned to my roots, my home in Assam. I use this location sometimes as a canvas, sometimes as a lens, to comment on the vagaries of the nation-state and all my books try to reach that goal. Assam is one of those marginal locations that enables me to see the nation differently. It is one of those states that waged an armed insurgency against state violence, trying to secede. In my poems and short stories, I try to critique the atrocities of the state by foregrounding the stories of survivors from a nearly forgotten or lesser-known armed insurgency. This exercise is an artistic exploration to see the possibilities of oral stories and an act of bearing witness for me as a tribal writer from northeast India. We must create situations for survivors of any kind of social violence to come out and tell their stories so that we can bring the perpetrators to at least a public trial. I think literary forms of social engagement, such as the testimonio form, or the kind of books by Svetlana Alexievich who archived the voices of survivors, enable such possibilities.

While writing, when I started honoring the voices of the survivors, inhabiting their bodies, and was merely the recorder, the intellectual in me stepped aside and remained silent, their characteristics emerged: they would refuse to die, refuse to eat, refuse to stop speaking. The academic me, the intellectual me, who knows literary theory, who has read books, is a useless entity, a hindrance in this process of imaginative reconstruction: too correct, too guilt-ridden, too woke. When he stepped aside, magic started happening. The voices of the survivors took precedence, delight emerged, and I was able to find a language through their voices. Hence, it is our duty to tell these stories and create a conducive atmosphere for more stories of survivors to come out until they have the necessary atmosphere to tell their stories. This is how democracy is sustained.

The oral and written traditions in Assam has enabled me to do that. African Anglophone writers, African American writers such as Toni Morrison and James Baldwin, and indigenous writers such as Louise Erdrich and Joy Harjo and LeAnne Howe, have shaped what I grew up learning and showed me the possibilities of the English language. That's why I say, I am all of it, and yet, Assamese, simultaneously.

That's why I say America's literary future is queer and indigenous, multi-racial and multilingual. And if it is not, we need to write toward it in daring ways.

That winter evening, when my father's identity card didn't open the passage in the sea, something strange happened. My mother, my radical feminist mother who often remained in the background during such situations because the soldiers were never kind to women in our part of the country, stepped out of the car. My mother, a professor of literature in the state's most prestigious college who had rejected many traditional expectations dumped on her, stepped out of the car with her head covered—something she rarely did. Her head was slight, bowed. She had become a new person I didn't know: a timid, traditional woman by covering her head.

Now I know why she stepped out and talked to the soldier who had covered his neck and face with a black cloth. Black Cats—were they called that? "Sir, any problem?" asked my mother, who used to be addressed with respect by her students. She introduced herself. The soldier instantly became jittery, "Sister, why did you step out? Go in, go in, you guys go ahead," he instructed the driver. He was as if suddenly scared of her presence next to him. He hadn't expected her to step out of the car and address him. He had expected her to stay in with her head covered, not step out.

References

Kashyap, A. (2013). *The house with a thousand stories*. New Delhi: Penguin Books

Kashyap, A. (2021). *His father's disease: Stories*. London: Lubin & Kleyner

Kashyap, A. (2020, June 28). *The Love Lives of People Who Look Like Kal Penn*. Joyland: a literary journal in multiple timezones, Issue No. 7. Retrieved July 10, 2022, from https://joylandmagazine.com/uncategorized/love-lives-people-who-look-kal-penn/

Writing Exercise

This exercise is to inspire you to write something by going out of your comfort zone. Travel to a place that you have never been to before. This could be a country, a city in your state that you have always wanted to visit but never visited, or a rural community or a small town that you have found interesting. Read about the history and culture of this place by visiting the archives of your local library. When you visit this city, make a trip to the local library, and read more about this place. Do they have a local historian? Talk to them if possible but go with prepared questions. You will always find something interesting from the recent past that would intrigue you about this place. Return home and write a short story set in this location. One of the significant responsibilities of a writer is to imagine yourself in unknown, unfamiliar places and distill those experiences into fiction. I hope this exercise will enable you to take that imaginative leap and explore the limitless possibilities of the imagination that our current neoliberal world tries to constrain by establishing false boundaries.

Imagining Home: Creating Literary Spaces of Change and Possibility

Neil Aitken

Growing up in a family where we moved often across national and international borders, home was never a physical location, but rather more of a configuration of people, and the books we loved and carried from place to place. There is a rootlessness I often feel in my core when someone asks me where I call home. No one place pops into mind, but rather a reminder that I am always adrift, always inventing home wherever I find myself.

To be born between cultures, languages, and countries is to be the product of a confluence of histories and silences. Many rivers run together in me. Although I could name them Chinese, Taiwanese, Scottish, and English, these labels are never sufficient, they obscure the complex stories of the individuals who came before me, who, like me, fail to fit neatly into the boxes that others have defined. We overflow our bounds, we disappear into the earth here, reappear elsewhere. There are hidden reservoirs, underground lakes, and unknown caverns that connect us together, that we draw on when we write.

My father often told me that you can't draw water from an empty well, but as a writer, you have to spend time reading and living, letting the water accumulate. When I was an undergraduate student pursuing a degree in computer science while writing on the side, I began buying poetry books as a way to educate myself, to start filling that well. I didn't have an agenda, but would wander shelf to shelf in the used bookstores, pulling down books with interesting titles, leafing through their pages, searching for lines and images that startled me or shook me. I didn't know who they were, judged them only by their lyricism and imagination, the music of their transcribed voices ringing in my head. I bought book after book, assembled them into shelves, and then read them frequently. I bought more and more. When I graduated, I took my fledgling collection with me, moved back to Canada for a short time, then landed a programming job in Los Angeles.

I didn't realize how deeply ingrained the impulse to collect books ran in me. Not so much as a proof of material wealth or a demonstration of intellectualism, but rather as a way to keep pushing the boundaries of the known world, humbling myself in the process by filling my shelves with reminders of how much I did not know, of the myriad ways in which the universe is filled with wonder and surprise, of how beneath and beyond everything else, it is grief and joy and yearning that bind us together as human beings.

When I look back now, I see that quite unintentionally and unconsciously, I was building a personal library as an act of resistance to those voices or societal forces that sought to erase me and others who were pushed to the margins, who did not "fit" within what was deemed mainstream, popular, and canonical. One book at a time, I was building a fortress and a sanctuary. My sister once explained to me that the difference between an apartment and a home is that one is a place where you store things and sleep, the other is a place where you are yourself. My personal library became my home. I left the programming job to pursue an MFA, then later a Ph.D. I crossed back and forth across the border. I completed my studies, failed to find an academic position, and moved to the Portland area where I worked and volunteered in literary and cultural organizations. Whenever and wherever I moved, although I might jettison furniture and clothing, I would always bring my books with me. And during the times when I could not afford my own place, I sorted through the collection, selecting a core hundred books that I felt were essential to my sense of self, and took these, putting the rest in storage. This is how I survived.

My library grew from a few hundred books to over a thousand. Today I have over 1,300 books, most of which are volumes of poetry, but the collection also contains literary essays, texts on poetics, translation, geography, history, religion, psychology, literary theory, architecture, design, and technology, fiction that spans multiple genres, and an extensive selection of books on tabletop role playing games. I've come to see my library not only as an extension of my self and my mind, but also as a space for imagination, a space large enough to shelter other minds and other lives.

Liu Hongbin, a Chinese poet living in exile in the UK, notes that "The poet himself is a China." In other words, even as we are separated from the places that we used to call home, we become those places ourselves, as complex and divided, as expansive and rich. To build a library is to imagine a country in which we are welcome, in which we fit in, regardless of how contradictory we sometimes feel.

In 2017, Dao Strom, a fellow writer and artist living in Portland, approached me about collaborating on an art project that would blur the lines between library, performance, and installation. As we discussed the possible directions we might go, we both noted how rare it was for any writer or reader to step into a space where every book on the shelf was written by a writer of color. The more we discussed this idea, the more it seemed essential to create such an experience, not only for ourselves, but for the other writers and readers in the Portland community, especially those who had never seen themselves reflected in the offerings of bookstores and libraries. We decided to call the project De-Canon (www.de-canon.com), and applied for (and received) a grant from the Portland Institute of Contemporary Art, then set about purchasing and collecting a large number of books by writers of color. Dao's partner, a gifted wood artisan, crafted close to a hundred open-ended wooden boxes of a wide variety of sizes and capacities to serve as our shelves. These could be stacked and arranged in a multitude of ways, destabilizing traditional and conventional approaches to order. Books were shelved together based on their dimensions, rather than adhering to any sort of categorization or taxonomy, leaving those who encountered the installation to wander, browsing and discovering unexpected connections, and defamiliarizing the normal library experience.

With the assistance of a local BIPOC-run gallery, we hosted the installation for an entire month and offered poetry readings, film screenings, panel discussions, and workshops in the space. The construction of a wholly BIPOC-centered space with the deconstructed library as its centerpiece had a profound effect on the local community. I recall standing next to the exhibit on the opening night and talking to one member of the public who suddenly became overwhelmed. He told me, "I've never seen so many books by writers of color in one place. I've never seen so many names like mine on the shelves. I've never felt so seen in my life." In that moment, I understood that what we had built was not a one-time installation or a one-month exhibition, it was the start of something much, much bigger.

We had originally planned to dismantle the collection and give the books to the public, intending that these books would become the seeds of many private libraries. However, we had so many people beg us to keep the collection together that we reconsidered. The following year, we applied for another grant from a different organization and again received funding to expand our collection. Unexpectedly, we found a new partner in a local building that housed a community of artists. They offered to host us for free for several months in a large exhibit area (a former cafe space) that was sitting dormant, and so we ended up setting up the full installation as a public reading library, and running an event space there. During that almost year-long residency, we ran workshops and classes, hosted readings and book signings, and provided many local writers and readers of color with access to books they might not otherwise find. The De-Canon library also could be partially dismantled and travel, so we brought the books into class-rooms, museums, book fairs, and cultural festivals. It became a catalyst for discussions, inspired people to write, to read more widely, and to see themselves as the proud inheritors of many literary legacies. Deter-mined not to recreate the very canon-making practices we were dismantling, we invited people to suggest authors and books, soliciting recommendations from other writers from all over the US and beyond. We let go of the idea of ownership, and encouraged others to think of it as a community project, a collaborative effort to construct a literary home.

Despite our love of this project, it soon became clear that the physical incarnation of the library could not last forever. Neither Dao nor I were prepared to take on long-term duties as event space man-agers, nor was it likely, given the shifting whims of real estate markets, that our installation could stay indefinitely in that space. We knew that beloved as the library was, we had to prepare for life after the library. So even as we as hosted events in the physical space and encouraged recommendations and donations to expand the collection, we also branched out online, setting up a website and blog where we could share the model with others, posting images from the library, and writing content that extended the project into other spaces of inquiry and change.

I found myself writing a variety of articles exploring and examining the spaces and mechanisms through which canon and literature are conceived. When I asked myself why I'd never read an essay on craft by a writer of color in any MFA or Ph.D. class, and more pointedly, why my own shelves did not feature any such texts, I started assembling a list of articles, chapters, essays, lectures, books, and anthologies written by writers of color on craft, the workshop, and the work of writing. It turned out to be a much larger project than I imagined. The list grew longer and longer, supplemented by suggestions from other writers I reached out to. The question seemed to resonate with writers, reminding us again that unless the void is named, we risk never seeing it. When I posted the article, "The Invisible Archive: Writers of Color on Craft," it sparked a much larger conversation among academics and writers, spurring many instructors and professors to change their syllabuses and include some of the texts we'd collected. The conversation inspired others to assemble BIPOC-centered anthologies on craft and pedagogy, propose conference panels, and encourage a more concerted effort to decolonize their workshop and writing spaces. The list continues to grow with new suggestions coming in every few months. I might not own all the books in my personal library, but the existence of the list offers me yet another library (a virtual one) in which I can I find myself.

I wrote on other subjects as well, asking other writers of color what having a personal library meant to them and how a book by another writer of color had impacted them. I surveyed graduate creative writing programs throughout the United States and counted how many writers of color were serving in full-time tenure track positions, a study that revealed how often universities portray themselves as champions of diversity, but only house them as visiting writers or adjunct professors, without authority or a clear path to tenure. I studied writing retreats and residencies for writers of color, wrote about BIPOC-helmed literary journals and presses, and examined other avenues for mentorship. In many respects, the articles I wrote for De-Canon were part of my own efforts to fill the empty spaces in the library, to address the noticeable silence on subjects that highlighted inequity, hypocrisy, and erasure. "The beginning of wisdom is calling things by the right name," says Confucius in *The Analects*. Without the right name, without calling things out, how would we know what we need to change and where we need to grow?

What is a library? My personal library has become increasingly complicated, I often struggle to know where to shelve things. The legacy of De-Canon's physical installation and its challenge to conventional orders and categories leaves me second-guessing where things belong. Now books move, shift between sections, arrive in new places. Sometimes they collect in stacks on a desk. Sometimes they reassemble themselves in new places, not always exactly in alphabetical order or separated by theme. My mind is similarly disrupted, order is more fluid, the interior more dynamic, bodies of language and knowledge collide as if tectonic plates, and new texts emerge in each rupture and collision. I am in conversation with the books I have assembled around me, and they with me. And I believe this is for the best. Not kept pristine and locked away, but active and in use.

When I started working as a writing coach and manuscript editor, I turned back to my books and considered them each in turn. Now as I meet with different writers, I'm always listening to what they say in our conferences, what their poems and prose reveals. I ask them what they've been reading, what inspires them to write. I try to introduce them to new writers, new voices, new texts, and thus, little by little, they expand the country of themselves, the library of beloved writing that constitutes their home. My library is not an island lost in a wide ocean, but part of an archipelago, a vast interconnected array of islands, each of whom is a person who is also a library and is also a home.

Sometimes I think back to my first Kundiman (www.kundiman.org) poetry retreat in 2005. When I arrived, I was convinced that there had been an error– how had they let me in? What use could they have for a Chinese-Scottish-English Canadian poet who rarely wrote about identity, at least not directly? Surely there were writers out there who wrote (as I thought at the time) about more "Asian American" themes and were more deserving of this opportunity? But on the first day as we made our introductions, I very quickly realized how wrong I was, how I had had no idea how many others felt the same. We had all come, convinced we were alone, convinced that our lives and our writing were somehow outside of what was expected and permitted— and in that opening circle in a classroom at the University of Virginia in Charlottesville, we had our eyes opened to the truth that all our stories mattered, that there was a place on the shelf for our writing, that what was happening on the front lines of Asian American literature was much more diverse and vibrant, much more compelling and dynamic, much more inclusive than whatever we had been led to believe from the anthologies we'd read and the classes we'd taken. Even today when I run into a fellow Kundiman person, regardless of whether or not we attended at the same time, I am filled with a tremendous love for them and an enthusiasm to hear their work and discover what they have to offer to the conversation. When I facilitate workshops and lead classes, I remember that feeling and strive to recreate it in the creative spaces I'm in.

In short, I believe there's something truly transformative and liberating about the simple act of choosing what books we surround ourselves with. When you include those voices you long to hear and the writing that you wish to see, the library becomes a sanctuary and a haven. When we write and encourage others to write and bring in their work, it becomes a place where we can truly be ourselves, it becomes a home.

References

Aitken, N. (2021, November 21). *Writers of color discussing craft - an invisible archive - de-canon.* De-Canon. Retrieved July 10, 2022, from https://www.de-canon.com/blog/2017/5/5/writers-of-color-discussing-craft-an-invisible-archive

Writing Exercise: Writing Ourselves In

Consider a phrase, statement, joke, email, letter, or historical document which you find abusive, offensive, or exclusionary. Break that text into shorter phrases and space them out. Transform and reclaim the text, writing in between the phrases and lines, adding new bridges and rebuttals, destabilizing the original text's meaning, and inserting your voice into what previously was silence and refusal. Make it your own. Crowd out their voice with yours. Occupy their language.

About the Contributors

ANYA ACHTENBERG is an award-winning fiction writer and poet whose publications include the novel *Blue Earth*, novella *The Stories of Devil-Girl,* poetry collections *The Stone of Language,* and, *I Know What the Small Girl Knew.* Individual pieces are published in many literary magazines and anthologies, including *Gargoyle Magazine, Tupelo Quarterly, Beltway Poetry Quarterly,* and *Harvard Review.* Awards garnered by her work include prizes from Southern Poetry Review, Another Chicago Magazine, Coppola's Zoetrope: All-Story, New Letters, the Raymond Carver Story Contest, and the Minnesota State Arts Board. As of this writing, her novel *History Artist* is close to completion, with an ensemble cast of characters centered around a young Cambodian woman born at the moment the US invasion began; and a poetry collection, *Matadors at the Crossing.* In her occasional blog *Writing in Upheaval,* and elsewhere, she writes on an organic approach to creative writing craft, expanding creativity, countering historical amnesia, how trauma and narration connect, and how history sits in us. Caught in Europe by the pandemic, she is in Berlin as of this date, where history sits *on* her as well as *in.* In the US and globally, she teaches two series of fiction, memoir, and multi-genre creative writing courses, *Writing for Social Change: Re-Dream a Just World,* and *The Disobedient Writer Workshops,* and consults with writers individually. See https://anya-achtenberg.com/

NEIL AITKEN is an award-winning Chinese-Scottish Canadian author, editor, and translator currently residing in Regina, Saskatchewan. His first book of poetry, *The Lost Country of Sight,* won the Philip Levine Prize and was shortlisted for several others. His second, *Babbage's Dream,* was longlisted for the Anthony Hecht Prize. The founding editor of *Boxcar Poetry Review,* he is also a past Kundiman poetry fellow and presently works as a creative writing coach and manuscript editor. Visit him at www.neil-aitken.com.

NIA ALLERY enjoys adventure. She is exploring what it means to be fully human—a daunting task. She recognizes that what gives meaning to this existence is a shift in consciousness: a profound and heightened awareness of connection that tells us how to stay grounded and aware of the webbed relationships with all things. She often turns to the memories of the indigenous peoples, her ancestors, to recreate the wild improbability of knowing that we have the right to be, we have the right to become, and we have the right to belong. She is writing about this adventure to the "far side," fully confident that it is not so far away after all.

BRENDA BELL BROWN, when she was young, wanted to grow up to be a nun, a mortician, or a psychologist. Once she realized her true intent to be the artist that she had always been since childhood, she embraced her true calling and continues to grow in the craft of Black artistry every single day.

Nurtured from youth by the people of her neighborhood—Walker Homes—in Memphis, Tennessee, Brenda is known for her theatrical, millinery, craft, writing, and movement expression. She went on to develop those skills under the guidance of teachers found in "gown and town" on campuses in the communities of Providence, Rhode Island (Brown University); Washington, D.C. (George Washington University); Hampton (Roads), Virginia (Hampton University); and the Twin Cities—Saint Paul/Minneapolis (Hamline University).

Brenda is currently in pursuit of a doctorate in health literacy, aiming to chronicle and share life-saving teachable doctrines based on Black American folk traditions. Her approach to this academic study is highlighted in her thesis written in partial fulfillment of the requirements for an MFA in Creative Writing bestowed by Hamline University (Saint Paul, Minnesota)—*What We Say: Exploring Well-Versed Messaging in the Tradition of Black Americana.*

WESLEY BROWN is the author of three published novels: *Tragic Magic, Darktown Strutters,* and *Push Comes to Shove*; four produced plays: *Boogie Woogie and Booker T, Life During Wartime, A Prophet Among Them,* and *Dark Meat on a Funny Mind.* He co-edited the multicultural anthologies, *Imagining America* (fiction), *Visions of America* (non-fiction); edited the *Teachers & Writers Guide to Frederick Douglass,* and wrote the narration for a segment of the PBS documentary, *W.E.B. DuBois: A Biography in Four Voices.* His most recent book is a collection of short stories, *Dance of the Infidels,* and a forthcoming novella published by Blank Forms. He is a Professor Emeritus at Rutgers University and a former Visiting Professor in the Arts Division of Bard College at Simon's Rock.

CHING-IN CHEN they are the author of *The Heart's Traffic* (Arktoi Books/Red Hen Press) and *recombinant* (Kelsey Street Press) and co-editor of *The Revolution Starts at Home: Confronting Intimate Violence Within Activist Communities* (South End Press; AK Press) and

Here is a Pen: An Anthology of West Coast Kundiman Poets (Achiote Press). A Kundiman, Lambda, Watering Hole and Callaloo Fellow, they are part of the Macondo and Voices of Our Nations Arts Foundation writing communities. They have also been awarded fellowships from Can Serrat, Millay Colony for the Arts, the Norman Mailer Center, and Imagining America. Their work has appeared in *The Best American Experimental Writing, The&NOW Awards 3: The Best Innovative Writing, and Troubling the Line: Trans and Genderqueer Poetry and Poetics.* A senior editor of *The Conversant,* they are currently an Assistant Professor in Poetry at Sam Houston State University. www.chinginchen.com

TAIYON J COLEMAN is a poet, essayist, and fiction writer. Her writing has appeared in *Bum Rush the Page: A Def Poetry Jam; Riding Shotgun: Women Writing about Their Mothers; The Ringing Ear: Black Poets Lean South,* edited by Nikky Finney; and *Blues Vision.* Her critical essay, "Disparate Impacts: Living Just Enough for the City," appears in the 2016 anthology, *A Good Time for the Truth,* edited by Sun Yung Shin. Taiyon Coleman is Assistant Professor of English with a focus in American Multicultural Literature at St. Catherine University in St. Paul, Minnesota, and she is completing her first novel, *Chicago@Fifteen.* She lives in the Twin Cities area.

ANAÏS DEAL-MÁRQUEZ is a Mexican, Minneapolis-based poet. Her work looks at identity, migration, displacement, and memory. She has been published in *Poetry Magazine, BreakBeat Poets Volume 4: LatiNEXT, Pollen Midwest,* and elsewhere. Anaïs is a past winner of the Loft Literary Center's Mentor Series in Poetry, an Intermedia Arts VERVE recipient, and a Lemon Tree House Residency participant.

KANDACE CREEL FALCÓN, Ph.D. (she/they/them) is an interdisciplinary feminist scholar, writer, and visual artist. Their life's passion grounds the power of narrative for social transformation. Drawn to interdisciplinary inquiry and mixed-media methods of painting, fabric arts, and writing, KCF brings together various mediums to make sense of the world around them. A recovering academic, KCF now spends time learning, writing and creating new pathways for education outside institutional structures. She currently lives and works in rural Erhard, Minnesota. Learn more at www.kjcfalcon.com.

SHERRIE FERNANDEZ-WILLIAMS earned her MFA in Writing from Hamline University. She received an Artist Initiative Award through the Minnesota State Arts Board, a Beyond the Pure

Fellowship, a SASE/Jerome Grant, a Jones' Commission Award through the Playwrights' Center, a Givens Black Writers Collaborative Fellowship, and was a Loft Mentor Series Winner in Creative Nonfiction. She is a 2021-2023 Jerome Hill Artist Fellow and is a 2021 Black Voices in Children's Literature Writing Contest Winner. Author of *Soft: A Memoir*, Fernandez-Williams has published poems and essays in journals including *New Limestone Review, Aquifer: The Florida Review,* and the *minnesota review,* among others. She co-curates the Queer Voices Reading Series with Lisa Marie Brimmer in collaboration with Quatrefoil Library and Hennepin County Library.

ISELA XITLALI GÓMEZ R is an essayist, poet, and foodmaker. She is a past winner of the Loft Literary Center's Mentor Series in Creative Nonfiction and Mirrors & Windows Fellowship, and the Beyond the Pure Fellowship through Intermedia Arts. She is the co-author, with Anaïs Deal-Marquez, of *Your Passport to Mexico*, by Capstone Press. She has taught creative writing workshops for high school students. Isela lives in Minneapolis.

MARLINA GONZALEZ is a non-fiction writer playwright, multi-disciplinary theater and media arts producer, director, curator and writer of Filipina heritage. Marlina strives to bring together the power of vox populi (voice of the people) in all her work.

Marlina is a recipient of 2021-2022 Springboard for the Arts Creative Engagement Fellowship and Twin Cities Media Alliance Fellowship for *Our Space Is Spoken For.* In 2012, she received The Joyce Foundation Award for Theater Artists of Color and wrote/co-directed a commissioned play about language and colonialism entitled *Isla Tuliro* (Island of Confusion) for Pangea World Theater and Teatro Del Pueblo. Other awards include MRAC's Arts Impact for Individuals (2022); Filipinx for Immigrant Rights and Racial Justice in MN Civic Engagement award (2021); and SPARK Leadership award from Coalition for Asian American Leaders (2021). In 2009, Filipina Women's Network (CA) named her one of The 100 Most Influential Filipina Women in the U.S. as a Thought Leader and Innovator.

Marlina holds a BA in Broadcast Communication (University of the Philippines) and MA in Radio, TV Film (University of North Texas).

BEATRICE M. HOGG is a freelance writer and social worker who lives in West Sacramento, California. She has a BA in Social Work from the University of Pittsburgh and an MFA in Creative Writing with an emphasis in Creative Nonfiction from Antioch University, Los

Angeles. A coal miner's daughter, she was raised in Western Pennsylvania and has lived in Northern California since 1988. She has been published in several anthologies, magazines and online journals such as *Astronomy, The Sacramento Bee, BUST, Pittsburgh Post Gazette, Ozy.com,* and was a featured columnist at the billfold.com for several years. She has a blog at www.marvellaland.wordpress.com. Currently, she is looking for a literary home for her collection of essays about long-term unemployment, homelessness, shopping and music.

CAROLYN HOLBROOK is a writer, educator, and an advocate for the healing power of the arts. Her memoir, *Tell Me Your Names and I Will Testify* (Minn. 2020), won the 2021 Minnesota Book Award for Memoir and Creative Nonfiction. She is founder and director of the Twin Cities-based conversation series, More Than a Single Story, and is co-editor with David Mura of the anthology, *We Are Meant to Rise: Voices for Justice from Minneapolis to the World* published by University of MN Press, with More Than a Single Story (Minn. 2021). She is also co-author with Arleta Little of Dr. Josie Johnson's memoir, *Hope In the Struggle* (Minn. 2019). She teaches at the Loft Literary Center and other community venues, and at Hamline University. She is the mother of five, grandmother of eight and great grandmother of two.

ARUNI KASHYAP is a writer and translator. He is the author of *His Father's Disease* and the novel, *The House with a Thousand Stories.* Along with editing a collection of stories called *How to Tell the Story of an Insurgency: Fifteen Tales from Assam,* he has also translated two novels from Assamese to English, published by Zubaan Books and Penguin Random House. Winner of the Arts Lab Faculty Fellowship from the Willson Centre for the Humanities, and the Charles Wallace India Trust Scholarship for Creative Writing to the University of Edinburgh, his poetry collection, *There is No Good Time for Bad News,* was a finalist for the Marsh Hawk Press Poetry Prize and Four Way Books Levis Award in Poetry. His short stories, poems, and essays have appeared in *Catapult, Bitch Media, The Boston Review, Electric Literature, The Oxford Anthology of Writings from Northeast, The Kenyon Review, The New York Times, The Guardian UK,* and others. He is an Assistant Professor of Creative Writing at the University of Georgia, Athens. He also writes in Assamese and is the author of a novel called *Noikhon Etia Duroit,* and three novellas.

HEI KYONG KIM is a poet, essayist, and fiction writer. Her writing can be found in numerous journals and anthologies, including *Parenting as Adoptees, Outsiders Within, Seeds from a Silent Tree, New Truths: Writing in the 21st Century by Korean Adoptees*, and *The World I Leave You: Asian American Poets on Faith and Spirit*. She also has a collection of poetry and prose entitled, *The Translation of Han* (CQT Publishing and Media).

MICHAEL KLEBER-DIGGS (KLEE-burr digs) is a poet, essayist, and literary critic. His debut poetry collection, *Worldly Things*, won the Max Ritvo Poetry Prize (Milkweed Editions, 2021). His essay, "On the Complex Flavors of Black Joy," is included in the anthology *There's a Revolution Outside, My Love: Letters from a Crisis*, edited by Tracy K. Smith and John Freeman. Among other places, Michael's writing has appeared or is forthcoming in *Great River Review, Water~Stone Review, Poem-a-Day, Poetry Daily, Poetry Northwest, Potomac Review, Hunger Mountain, Memorious*, and a few anthologies. Michael is a past Fellow with the Givens Foundation for African American Literature, a past-winner of the Loft Mentor Series in Poetry, and the former Poet Laureate of Anoka County libraries. Since 2016, Michael has been an instructor with the Minnesota Prison Writing Workshop. He also teaches Creative Writing in Augsburg University's low-res MFA program and at Saint Paul Conservatory for Performing Artists. His work has been nominated for a Pushcart Prize and Best of the Net and has been supported by the Minnesota State Arts Board, the Jerome Foundation, and the Metropolitan Regional Arts Council. Michael is married to Karen Kleber-Diggs, a tropical horticulturist and orchid specialist. Karen and Michael have a daughter who is pursuing a BFA in Dance Performance at SUNY Purchase.

TOU SAIKO LEE is a spoken word poet, storyteller, hip hop recording artist and multicultural movement builder from St. Paul, Minnesota. He collaborated with his late grandmother, Youa Chang or Zuag Tsab, who does the traditional art of kwv txhiaj (Hmong poetry chanting) to form the duo "Fresh Traditions." Lee is writing a memoir about their collaboration with his grandma to honor her passing, titled *My Grandma Can Freestyle*. He released his first Hmong language Hip Hop album titled *Ntiaj Teb Koom Tes*, which translates to *Unified Worldwide*. Lee was selected to be a speaker by TEDx Minneapolis in 2021. Lee's talk, titled "Reclaiming cultural identity and language through hip hop" can be found on YouTube.

OLIVE LEFFERSON is an enrolled member of the Blackfeet Nation where she lived as a child. Her family moved to Seattle when she was a young teenager. She worked as a legal assistant and a model, among other things. A mother of three grown children, she has traveled extensively, including a five-year sailing trip from Seattle to Marmaris, Turkey. She received her BA in English with a creative writing emphasis. One of her proudest achievements was to graduate alongside her son, who was 2 years old when she began her education.

LUIS LOPEZ grew up in the Rio Grande Valley of South Texas. He has made his home in the Twin Cities for nearly a decade. He recently graduated with a degree in Creative Writing from Metropolitan State University and is considering pursuing a Master of Fine Arts.

JESSICA LYMAN, Ph.D. is an interdisciplinary performance artist and Xicana feminist scholar. She researches Midwestern Chicana/o/x and Latina/o/x experiences, social movements, and arts engagement. Lopez Lyman is an Assistant Professor in the Department of Chicano and Latino Studies at the University of Minnesota, Twin Cities.

PACYINZ LYFOUNG is a French-born and raised, Minnesotan-grown, Hmong/Asian American woman poet. Her favorite artistic quote comes from a lyric from Michel Berger who wrote that "when Cézanne paints, his gaze crosses the eyes of God." She sees poetry as a sacred duty to record her many communities' (family, Hmong, API, BIPOC and women) experiences and histories, as well as find solidarity at intersections. She also sees poetry as a tool that gives voice to communities to create their own healing, power, and futures.

DARALYSE LYONS is an author, an actor, and an activist who believes that the stories we tell ourselves and others transform the lives we live. She has written more than two dozen full-length books, a handful of short stories, and countless articles, and performed in various plays and improv comedy shows. She is a member of the National Association of Black Journalists (NABJ) and a summa cum laude graduate of NYU, with a double-major in English and Religious Studies and a minor in History. After writing an award-winning children's book (*I'm Mixed!*), under the pseudonym Maggy Williams, about embracing her multiethnic heritage, Daralyse found her passion and her purpose educating others about the need to embrace all aspects of themselves. She then went on to create the *Demystifying Diversity* Podcast, and to write the book *Demystifying Diversity: Embracing Our Shared Humanity* and its accompanying workbook. She regularly speaks about issues of identity and inclusion, and has shared her personal experiences in her TEDx talk "Black or White? Refusing to Choose & Embracing Biracial Identity." She works tirelessly as a full-time Diversity Equity and Inclusion (DEI) expert and inclusivity strategist.

MARCIE RENDON, citizen of the White Earth Nation, was honored with the Doctor of Humane Letters, (Honoris Causa, Adler University, USA), 2020 and was listed in Oprah Magazine's 2020 list of 31 Native American Authors to read. Rendon also received Minnesota's 2020 McKnight Distinguished Artist Award. *Sinister Graves*, the third Cash Blackbear Mystery, SoHo Press, arrives October 2022. *Girl Gone Missing* is Rendon's second Cash Blackbear novel and was nominated for the Son's Sue Grafton Memorial Award, 2020. *Murder on the Red River* received the Pinckley Women's Crime Novel Award 2018. Rendon writes children's books and has four plays published. Out of Hand Theater, Atlanta, GA, will produce her script, *Say Their Names*, in their 2022 Theater in Homes project. *Sweet Revenge* had a staged reading at the Playwright Center, with support from the Guthrie Theater Native Stakeholders group, 2021. The creative mind of Raving Native Theater, she curated Twin Cities Public Television's *Art Is...Creative Native Resilience* 2019. Diego Vazquez and Rendon received the Loft's 2017 Spoken Word Immersion Fellowship for work with incarcerated women.

SAGIRAH SHAHID is a Black American Muslim poet, arts educator, and performing artist from Minneapolis, MN. She is a recipient of awards, fellowships, and residencies from the Loft Literary Center, Minnesota Center for Book Arts, Twin Cities Media Alliance, Shangri La Museum of Islamic Art and Muslim Advocates, Strive Publishing, Wisdom Ways, Nicollet Lanterns, and 826 MSP. In 2021 Sagirah was co-curator of the City of Saint Paul's Sidewalk Poetry project and is a writer-in-residence with the *Write Like Us* program. When she isn't creating art, Sagirah celebrates her life as an auntie, usually working part-time at some job so that she can explore poetry with the student-writers of Unrestricted Interest, a writing program and consultancy dedicated to supporting neurodivergent learners through creative writing. Sagirah's children's activity book, *Get Involved in a Book Club!*, is available at Capstone press.

CHRIS STARK is a Native (Anishinaabe & Cherokee) award-winning writer, researcher, visual artist, and national speaker. Her second novel, *Carnival Lights*, a Minnesota Book Award finalist, is about two Ojibwe teen girls who leave their reservation for Minneapolis in 1969. Her first novel, *Nickels: A Tale of Dissociation,* was a Lambda Literary Finalist. Her essays, poems, academic writing, and creative non-fiction have appeared in numerous publications. Her poem, "Momma's Song," was recorded by Fred Ho and the Afro Asian Music Ensemble as a double manga CD. She is also a co-author of the ground-breaking research "Garden of Truth: The Prostitution and Trafficking of Native Women in Minnesota" and author of "Strategies to Restore Justice for Sex Trafficked Native Women." Her writing has been nominated three times for a Pushcart Prize. In 2012 she was a Loft Series Mentor Finalist. Currently, she is a fellow at Villanova Law School, where she is conducting research on the history of colonization, slavery, and sex trafficking of Indigenous women and girls. She also consults with a variety of local and national organizations. She is a member of the Minnesota Missing and Murdered Indigenous Women Taskforce. Chris teaches writing at Central Lakes College. She has an MFA in Writing and an MSW. For more information: www.christinestark.com

SWETA SRIVASTAVA VIKRAM is an international speaker, best-selling author of 13 books, and Ayurveda and mindset coach who is committed to helping people thrive on their own terms. Her latest book, *A Piece of Peace* (Modern History press) was released in September 2021. As a trusted source on health and wellness, most recently appearing on NBC and Radio Lifeforce and in a documentary with Dr. Deepak Chopra, Sweta has dedicated her career to writing about and teaching a more holistic approach to creativity, productivity, health, and nutrition. Her work has appeared in *The New York Times* and other publications across nine countries on three continents. Sweta is a trained yogi and certified Ayurveda health coach, is on the board of Fly Female Founders, and holds a Master's in Strategic Communications from Columbia University. Voted as "One of the Most Influential Asians of Our Times" and winner of the "Voices of the Year" award, she lives in New York City with her husband and works with clients across the globe. She also teaches yoga, meditation, and mindfulness to survivors of sexual assault and domestic violence, as well as to incarcerated men and women. Find her on: Twitter, Instagram, LinkedIn, and Facebook as @swetavikram.

SAYMOUKDA DUANGPHOUXAY VONGSAY is a Lao writer. CNN's "United Shades of America" host W. Kamau Bell called her work "revolutionary." Governor Mark Dayton recognized her artistic contributions with a "Lao Artists Heritage Month" Proclamation. She is a recipient of a Sally Award for Initiative from the Ordway Center for Performing Arts which "recognizes bold new steps and strategic leadership undertaken by an individual...in creating projects or artistic programs never before seen in Minnesota that will have a significant impact on strengthening Minnesota's artistic/cultural community." She is the author of the children's book *When Everything was Everything* and is best known for her award-winning play *Kung Fu Zombies vs Cannibals*. Her plays have been presented by the Smithsonian Asian Pacific American Center (NY), Theater Mu (MN), Lower Depth Theater (LA), Asian Improv Arts (IL), and elsewhere. She has received 40+ awards and honors, including grants from the John S. and James L. Knight Foundation, Jerome Foundation, Bush Foundation, Andy Warhol Foundation, MAP Fund, Forecast Public Art; and fellowships from the Playwrights' Center, McKnight Foundation, Loft Literary Center, Twin Cities Media Alliance, and Bush Foundation/Aspen Ideas Festival. She is currently an Andrew W. Mellon Foundation Playwright in Residence at Theater Mu and a Jerome Hill Artist Fellow in playwriting; and serves on the City of Saint Paul Cultural START Board. Get to know her at www.refugenius.net and @refugenius.

WILLIAM S. YELLOW ROBE, JR. (February 4, 1960 - July 19, 2021) was an enrolled member of the Assiniboine Tribe from the Fort Peck Sioux and Assiniboine reservation located in northeastern Montana. He was a leading Native Tribal/American Indian playwright in the country. He has published two anthologies of his work: *Grandchildren of the Buffalo Soldiers and Other Untold Stories*, a collection of his full-length plays; and *Where the Pavement Ends: New Native Drama,* a collection of some of his one-act plays. He completed five new one-acts for 2016, and one of the plays, "Making IndiXns," was presented by the New Native Theatre of Minneapolis, Minnesota in May 2016. His one-act play "Sneaky" was presented by the New Native Theatre touring Minnesota in 2016. "Wood Bones," a full-length, was presented by the Thunder Bird theatre of Haskell Indian Jr. College of Lawrence, Kansas, in May 2016 and at the University of Maine in Orono, Maine, directed by William, in November 2016. He was a company member of the Penumbra Theatre Company of St. Paul, Minnesota, and of the Ensemble Studio Theater in New York City. He received the Princess Grace Award for Theatre/ Playwriting, the first recipient of the First Nations Book Award for Drama, a Jerome Fellow from the Minneapolis Playwrights' Center. He was a faculty affiliate in the creative writing department at the University of Montana, Missoula, and a Libra Professor of Multi-Culturalism at the University of Maine.

LORI YOUNG-WILLIAMS is a poet, prose writer, and creative writing teacher. She has taught several workshops at various locations in the Twin Cities and Greater Minnesota. She has a Bachelor of Science in Human Relationships and a Master of Liberal Studies, both from the University of Minnesota. She has been published in various poetry anthologies and has self-published two chapbooks. She is currently working on her memoir about her biracial family and growing up in the suburbs of St. Paul, Minnesota.

About the Editor

Sherry Quan Lee, MFA, University of Minnesota; and Distinguished Alumna, North Hennepin Community College, is the editor of *How Dare We! Write: a multicultural creative writing discourse*. Books also include: *Septuagenarian: love is what happens when I die*; *And You Can Love Me: a story for everyone that loves someone with ASD*; *Love Imagined: a mixed race memoir*, a Minnesota Book Award Finalist; *Chinese Blackbird*, a memoir in verse; and, *How to Write a Suicide Note: serial essays that saved a woman's life*.

Quan Lee was a selected participant for the Loft Literary Center's Asian Inroads Program, and later was the Loft mentor for the same program. Previously, she was the Writer-to-Writer mentor for SASE: The Write Place, at Intermedia Arts. Also, she was the poetry mentor for the 2015-2016 Loft Literary Center's Mentor Series.

She was the Artist and Youth Program Manager for the Asian American Renaissance; and volunteer editor of AAR's journals: *Body of Stories,* and *Spirits, Myths and Dreams: Stories in Transit.*

She taught creative writing at Metropolitan State University, St. Paul, MN, and at St. Catherine University.

Follow her on the site http://blog.sherryquanlee.com.

.

Index

Finalist - 27th annual Minnesota Book Awards (Memoir & Creative Nonfiction)
"Joining the long history of women of color fighting to claim literary space to tell our stories, Sherry Quan Lee shares her truth with fierce courage and strength in *Love Imagined*. ...Quan Lee crafts a riveting tale of Minnesota life set within the backdrop of racial segregation, the Cold War, the sexual revolution while navigating it all through the lens of her multi-layered identities. A true demonstration of the power of an intersectional perspective."

—Kandace Creel Falcón, Ph.D., Director of Women's and Gender Studies, Minnesota State University, Moorhead

"*Love Imagined*: this fascinating, delightful, important book. This imagining love, this longing for love. This poverty of No Love, this persistent racism, sexism, classism, ageism. The pain these evils cause the soul...This is an important document of a mixed-race contemporary woman, a memoir about her family lineages back to slavery, back to China, back to early Minneapolis, and about the struggle of finding herself in all of these."

—Sharon Doubiago, author of *My Father's Love*

"When I read Sherry's story [*Love Imagined*], I recognized feelings and meanings that mirrored mine. I felt a sense of release, an exhale, and I knew I could be understood by her in a way that some of my family and friends are unable to grasp, through no fault of their own. It's the Mixed experience. Sherry Lee's voice, her story, will no doubt touch and heal many who read it."

—Lola Osunkoya, MA Founder of Neither/Both LLC, Mixed-Race Community Building and Counseling

From the Reflections of America Series

Modern History Press

ISBN 978-1-61599-108-2

Learn more about the author at **www.SherryQuanLee.com**

Critical Acclaim for Sherry Quan Lee's *Chinese Blackbird*

"Quan Lee eloquently expresses how painful and confusing it can be to embrace the many complex identities that one body can contain. With evocative imagery and words that cut straight to the heart, Quan Lee details her lifelong struggles with both the vagaries and concreteness of race, class, gender and sexual identity. Her guilt and shame are palpable. But so too are her emotional and intellectual triumphs. Like a favorite sad song when we have been dumped by the love of our lives, this volume will be oddly comforting to anyone who has ever been overcome by that sorrow which seems insurmountable."

—Eden Torres, Assistant Professor Women's Studies, Chicano Studies, University of Minnesota

"It's been a long time since I've been treated to a voice so full of honesty about one's struggle to come to terms with her identity. Through elegant poetry, full of exquisite imagery and detail, Quan Lee takes the reader on her personal, transformative journey in which she explores how race, class, gender and sexual identity inform who she is. Along the way, she encounters rocks and boulders that would have stopped many of us. Instead, she turns them over and examines the creatures hiding in the darkness underneath, leaving no stone on her path unturned. She is one of my sheroes."

—Carolyn Holbrook, Adjunct Assistant Professor, Dept. of English, Founder and past Artistic/Executive Director of SASE: The Write Place

"In *Chinese Blackbird*, Sherry Quan Lee renders stories of her complex cultural heritage with the lyrical touch of a poet coming into self-possession. Through the generative power of language, Lee creates an inspirational and a multifarious self. This self blows breath unto the page and into the reader, who may have felt quiescent or invisible, often feeling forced to choose among various enriching worlds, until she experiences the truth that only good literature can unveil about the joys and struggles of defining oneself on one's terms."

—Pamela R. Fletcher, Associate Professor of English Co-Director of Critical Studies in Race and Ethnicity, College of St. Catherine

Septuagenarian: love is what happens when I die is a memoir in poetic form. It is the author's journey from being a mixed-race girl who passed for white to being a woman in her seventies who understands and accepts her complex intersectional identity; and no longer has to imagine love. It is a follow-up to the author's previous memoir (prose), *Love Imagined: a mixed-race memoir*, A Minnesota Book Award finalist.

Praise for Sherry Quan Lee's *Septuagenarian*

"In *Septuagenarian*, Sherry Quan Lee accepts her own invitation to look at life in retrospect, but with a new lens. Pulling from and expanding upon her previous body of work, she examines the version of herself that was writing at that time. The dignity and fire of her seventy-three-year-old gaze taking in snapshots of those selves... straightens my spine and gives me a vision for myself traveling today into my future septuagenarian."
—Lola Osunkoya, MA, LPCC

"Sherry Quan Lee writes courageously to understand herself and the world. She uses rich language and her skills as a storyteller to focus her sharp lens on what it means to have a complex, sometimes complicated identity: becoming invisible as she ages, a history of passing unseen, love and sex, grieving and celebration. She ruminates on history, which repeats itself in the current moment and widens her lens to look at the bigger, global picture to tell truths in poems that tenderly hold memory, time, rituals, trauma, mothering, fear of death and love in many forms. Her poems offer deeply personal, intimate and perceptive insights and opportunities to reflect on what it means to truly live. It feels like I've taken the journey with her, and I'm wiser for it."
—Shay Youngblood, author of *Soul Kiss* and *Black Girl in Paris*

Learn more at blog.SherryQuanLee.com
From Modern History Press

Lightning Source UK Ltd.
Milton Keynes UK
UKHW022111080223
416681UK00011B/2697